The Circle of Silence

A personal testimony before, during and after Balibó

Shirley Shackleton

PIER 9

Published in Australia in 2010 by Pier 9, an imprint of Murdoch Books Pty Limited

Murdoch Books Australia
Pier 8/9
23 Hickson Road
Millers Point NSW 2000
Phone: +61 (0) 2 8220 2000
Fax: +61 (0) 2 8220 2558
www.murdochbooks.com.au

Murdoch Books UK Limited
Erico House, 6th Floor
93–99 Upper Richmond Road
Putney, London SW15 2TG
Phone: +44 (0) 20 8785 5995
Fax: +44 (0) 20 8785 5985
www.murdochbooks.co.uk

Publisher: Colette Vella
Editor: Joanne Holliman
Designer: Hugh Ford

Text copyright © Shirley Shackleton 2010
The moral right of the author has been asserted.
Cover design copyright © Murdoch Books Pty Limited 2010
Cover photography by AAP Image and Getty
Back cover photography by Oliver Strewe/Shirley Shackleton

All rights reserved. No part of this publication may be reproduced, stored in a retrieval system or transmitted in any form or by any means, electronic, mechanical, photocopying, recording or otherwise, without the prior written permission of the publisher.

Every reasonable effort has been made to trace the owners of copyright materials in this book, but is some instances this has proven impossible. The author(s) and publisher will be glad to receive information leading to more complete acknowledgements in subsequent printings of the book and in the meantime extend their apologies for any omissions.

National Library of Australia Cataloguing-in-Publication Data
Author: Shackleton, Shirley D
Title: The circle of silence : a personal testimony before, during and after Balibo / Shirley Shackleton.
ISBN: 9781741964851(pbk)
Notes: Includes bibliography
Subjects: Shackleton, Shirley D.
                Shackleton, Gregory John, 1946-1975
                Human rights workers--Australia--Biography.
                Journalists--Indonesia--Balibo--Death.
                Journalists--Australia--Death.
Dewey Number: 323.0994

PRINTED IN AUSTRALIA.

The paper this book is printed on is certified by the © 1996 Forest Stewardship Council A.C. (FSC). Griffin Press holds FSC chain of custody SGS-COC-005088. FSC promotes environmentally responsible, socially beneficial and economically viable management of the world's forests.

*This book is dedicated to all who loved,
lost and still yearn for those who died
in the quest for freedom for Timor Leste.*

Life is mostly froth and bubble,
Two things stand like stone,
Kindness in another's trouble,
Courage in your own.

Adam Lindsay Gordon (1833–1870)

Creases

I don't know why I kept it
I hung your best suit behind the door.
When we had to move
I took it down once more

It had became invisible, like you
So had the pain,
but when I held it in my hands
I remembered once again.

Expecting moths,
I gave it quite a shake;
Out flew a shock of memories
I thought my heart would break.

There were three small creases
On the inside of the sleeves
And more on the trousers
At the back of the knees.

Permanent creases,
Not so easily erased
But all that is left of you
Oh God what a waste.

AUTHOR'S NOTE

I differentiate between the Indonesian military and the Indonesian people in the way that Falintil (the resistance army) did and do. They call the former 'Javanese' and the latter 'Indonesians'. This is to show that the Indonesian civilians are not responsible for the horrendous behaviour of the Indonesian Armed Forces. And so the Indonesian Army, ABRI, TNI, Operasi Komodo, Kostrad, Kopassus, Kopasandha, Bakin or any other Indonesian military organisation is covered in this book by the term 'Javanese'.

ACKNOWLEDGMENTS

In 1975 I was overwhelmed by sadness until Michele Turner educated me. This was long before she wrote *Telling*, her pioneering book about the Indonesian occupation of East Timor, a collection of interviews compiled from escaped Timorese. Our friendship grew in proportion to the knowledge she so generously imparted. She was the first of a parade of fine individuals who supported me, some of whom shared frightening adventures – I remember an engineer from Adelaide who was travelling through Indonesia in 1989. She was arrested and threatened with violence. Her crime? She had failed to get permission to stay with a Timorese family she had met on the bus from West Timor who had offered to look after her by giving her a bed in their home. Yasmin did not get my joke about the Intelligence department being an oxymoron. 'But, but they were so frightening,' she replied, thinking I did not understand. Highly intelligent, she had no inkling of the war that had raged for fourteen years only one hour and fifteen minutes by air from Australia.

I thank and admire the redoubtable Carmel Budiardjo, a survivor of Suharto's reign of terror, an English woman married to an Indonesian who, upon her release from an Indonesian prison for being a perceived communist, returned to England and published the human rights magazine, the *Tapol Bulletin*. I venture to suggest without Carmel and Tapol there would be no Timor Leste.

Now, we are lucky to have another invaluable resource: ETAN, an online network run by John Miller. If you want to know everything about Timor Leste as it happens I recommend you join ETAN: John@etan.org.

A special mention must go to friends and colleagues whose support was central to any little success I achieved: Andrew

Shirley Shackleton

Alcock, Carmela Baranowska, Penny and Clive Blazey, David Bowman, Dave Bradbury, Dr Peter Carey, Mike Carey, Noam Chomsky, Bernard Collaery, John Collins, Peter Cronau, Mark Davis, Robert Domm, John and Jo Anne Dietrich, Beth Davies, Dr Clinton Fernandes, Professor Herb Feith, Amy Goodman, Di Gameson, Rob Hudson MP, Tom Hyland, Kathy and Stephen Hondrogiannanous, Mary Ann Keady, Arnold Kohen, H. T. Lee, Stephen Langford, Jefferson Lee, Ian Melrose, Father Bob Maguire, Marnie Myall, Sophie McNeill, Hamish McDonald, Andrew McNaughton, John Pilger, Rebecca Parker, Gil Scrine, John Sinnott, Barbara and Ian Spalding, Kevin Sherlock, Oliver Strewe, Rob Wesley-Smith, Vickie Tchong, Jane Touzeau and Tom Uren. Their generosity of spirit never ceases to amaze me. Jill Jolliffe deserves a special mention for her dedication to the memory of the Balibo Five.

And now to three women who have guided me in the making of this volume: Colette Vella, my publisher and Joanne Holliman, editor, for their indefatigable efforts on my behalf. I once asked Colette, 'Did you ever think when you read this manuscript that I was mad and have made it all up?' I was not surprised when she answered. 'Yes.'

In a strange twist of fate on the very day I began to write this book I received a letter from Margaret Gee. She related a time when she was too late to report a story for the *Age* when she was a cub reporter. A young man, seeing her tears, for she expected to be sacked, gave her his notebook containing the information she needed. He also brought her a cup of tea. 'I never forgot him,' she wrote, 'his name was Greg Shackleton.' Margaret is my agent and I thank her most sincerely for finding me such a wonderful publisher.

I also thank those who from unstinting unselfishness wrote a multitude of books that nurtured our spirits and kept our hopes high in the darkest of times. I have at least forty of their volumes and I expect a lot more in the future, this time written by Timorese and especially by the true heroes and heroines of the catastrophic 'annexation' of their homeland.

I thank my family and especially my son, for his assiduous and selfless support for what must have seemed erratic and 'whacky' behaviour when events swept our otherwise normal life into a maelstrom.

I salute the multitudes who worked for Timor Leste's freedom in Timor and outside – aid workers, activists, academics, diplomats, film makers, journalists, photographers, lawyers, students, unionists, observers, politicians, religious workers, musicians and ordinary citizens. They did not seek credit through all the years of the struggle. I also salute the general public who wrote letters and articles doomed not to be published for fear of serious consequences from men with clean hands who wielded secret power. These citizens saw that justice was not a contest between Indonesians, East Timorese and Australians; it was between those who demanded justice and those who sought impunity for perpetrators of crimes against humanity.

They formed a sacred circle all on their own by reporting, studying, lobbying and giving free representation for those who were arrested: they took risks, wrote letters, articles and gave people like me a bed when we were far from home. We are a disreputable lot, we band of hooligans, we rat bags and losers who refused to take no for an answer. I count myself fortunate to have known this happy breed, for we walk with the pride of lions.

Shirley Shackleton

PROLOGUE

Corrugations in the sand at our feet narrow in the distance to streaks the colour of stone, silt and pumice. There is no horizon. Parallel lines repeat where the sky should have been. From time to time sunlight penetrates the smoky haze with the luminosity of a full moon, creating the illusion of a beach bathed in its light. Memories of swimming at night with my husband, Greg Shackleton, flood my mind. I choke back tears and try to concentrate on the exotic scene before me.

I had been studying in Iran and Mr Mashrouteh, an authority on Persian architecture, art, craft and history, is driving me to a Zoroastrian shrine in the desert way beyond the famous walled city of Yazd. He remarks that one's worries disappear in the vastness of the panorama. Life does seem simpler in this timeless silence, yet the landscape is both threatening and exhilarating. Reminiscent of formations that geologists use to measure time and ancient weather patterns, it also reminds me of the film *Forty Thousand Horsemen*. My host is fascinated to learn that the atmospherics of that day in 1917 were not unlike the scene before us now – visibility was so poor that the Australians were guided by the minarets rising from the mist in Beersheba (now in southern Israel). Though Mr Mashrouteh would technically have been on the other side, he admires their achievement. He wants to know if my relatives had been there.

'It's about the only ratbag stoush they weren't in,' I say, explaining that a 'stoush' is a no-holds-barred fight. In order to forestall questions regarding the term 'ratbag', I borrow Lewis Carroll's brilliant exposé of the bureaucratic mind in *Alice in Wonderland* by inserting 'ratbag' instead of 'mad people':

> 'But I don't want to go among ratbags,' remarked Alice.
> 'Oh you can't help that,' said the Cat, 'we're all ratbags here. I'm a ratbag. You're a ratbag.'
> 'How do you know I'm a ratbag?' said Alice.
> 'You must be,' said the Cat, 'or you wouldn't have come here.'

After a fit of the giggles he urges me to give a full account of the last great cavalry charge by the eight hundred Australian Light Horsemen across 600 metres of open desert. The attack's success changed the course of World War I, the future of the Ottoman Empire and the state of Israel.

While my host muses on the futility of war, my thoughts return to Australia and the past year. I had been dismissed as a ratbag by government officials attempting to quash my enquiries into my husband's murder. 'Being a ratbag is a very good thing in Australia,' I say to Mr Mashrouteh. 'All the best people are ratbags.'

This elicits another amused chuckle from him as we return to the car and drive on in companionable silence, until he casually mentions that if we were to break down there would be nothing we could do to save ourselves. The beauty before me fades – we could be back in 6000 BC, five thousand years before the Trojan War, for that was when the Persian prophet Zartosht, also known as Zarathustra, exulted Ahura Mazdā as the one true God and the Zoroastrian religion was born. I had read something of the religion at the British Institute of Persian Studies in Tehran.

Currents of burning air undulate across the immense Yazdī plain. The metronomic sound of the windscreen wiper is dulled momentarily – a large insect has smashed into the windscreen and in a fraction of a second its life is over. The mechanical device smears the poor creature into a bloody collage inlaid with flashes of crystalline wings. This makes me wonder about the manner of the deaths at Balibó: had the murderers gone about their task with the precision of automatons? The act of murder is an intimate affair: the greater the violence the greater the intimacy. I wonder if the perpetrators have a conscience.

Picturing my eight-year-old son's face calms me. Protecting Evan is my greatest priority. The brakes screech; we skid on sand drifting across the road. When Mr Mashrouteh regains control we smile and keep our thoughts to ourselves. He breaks the quiet by pointing to a large circular building set at the top of a hill and says, 'The Circle of Silence.'

The usual term 'The Towers of Silence' is lost in translation and, anyway, it's misleading: there are no towers in the actual structure. Though I know the interior consists of three concentric circles – one for deceased males, the second for females and a third for children – I am otherwise completely ignorant of the finer points of the ceremonies. The immense walls constructed of mud, stones and straw induce in me a feeling of despair and isolation. I search for signs of life. There are no trails of any kind: no wandering footprints, no shadow lines and no wildlife, not even a bird.

'The view is beautiful when it is truly visible,' Mr Mashrouteh says, frowning, as if the scene was deliberately hiding from us. I observe that the silver-lined clouds, the subtly shaded sand and the rain-shadow are more than acceptable.

He whispers, 'You are welcome to stay with us any time, Mrs Shirley, but I must ask you not write to us. Just arrive.' After certain unexplained experiences following Greg's murder, I understand his anxiety. Though ASIO is clearly not the Iranian Secret Service I understand that letters bearing foreign stamps might bring him unwanted attention.

Upon alighting from the car he raises the bonnet while I try to clean the windows. He disconnects part of the engine. When I ask what's wrong, he is evasive. 'Look,' I exclaim, 'if we have to pretend to have a breakdown in order to explore this place, wouldn't it be better if our alibis concur?'

'Bond,' he says. 'MI5.' I cannot help but laugh as he salutes me with British stiff-upper-lip precision. He gets the most out of every occasion.

I remark that the air smells tainted. I am being polite – it stinks. He points to what we in Australia call the Never-Never. 'The smell of death,' he says. I suppress a shudder because an image of the bloody collage is still etched on my retina and the silence, coupled with the chronic stink, brings visions of the underworld.

This is the largest of five shrines that form a circuit for an arduous ritual pilgrimage called *vaqt-e vaqt*, 'time-of-all-times'. Two towers in the vicinity light the way at night and there are several mud-brick dwellings – some for the living and some for the dead. The site does not just serve Zoroastrians from Yazd: some families take weeks to cross the desert from all over Iran – the *ḥaǧǧ*.

My imagination crawls with maggots as I stare across the plain, dreading the sight of an approaching funeral. How gruelling to cross the desert, ragged with grief and desolation, dry-mouthed and dogged in the company of a rotting cadaver, someone you love? Could this endurance test have been designed to act as an antidote to the grieving process?

A ray of sun breaks through a gap in the clouds to reveal stretches of tangled copper green foliage at the foot of the mountain range – bronze and silver, light and shade. In the sudden dazzle I experience a weird reversal: seen from the perspective of the mountains, I would not even be a dot on the horizon. It is shocking to realise how insignificant I am in the general scheme of things. There is a strange kind of comfort in admitting that my problems do not add up to a grain of sand. I reach down and scoop up a handful and recall Victor Hugo's question in *Les Misérables*: 'How do we know the creation of worlds is not determined by the falling of grains of sand?' I let the gritty grains run slowly through my fingers; the residue in my palm looks like fine ash . . . *ashes to ashes; dust to dust.*

We enter one of the dwellings for the dead where ceremonies were held with flowers, sweet-smelling herbs, incense and baked bread. The stink inside is permeable – I stare at pungent remains of fried *sirog* or bread, composed of flour, sour dough starter, spices, garlic, rue and vinegar, and believed to drive away the forces of evil.

I prepare to trek to the monolith, but Mr Mashrouteh announces that we will not be able to gain entry as the opening had been bricked-up by order of the Shah. In a sweep of emotion I feel the despair the decree must cause Zoroastrians, especially when we go to the English cemetery where they are now forced to bury their dead. Compared with the original shrine, the Zoroastrian section looks unnatural – fabricated and false. It reminds me of a lonely grave in Jakarta, which might be little more than a cruel hoax.

Mr Mashrouteh whispers that he has secretly photographed the interior of the burial site. His habit of whispering would make me nervous if I had not experienced it in relation to East Timor. But where I found it somewhat absurd in Australia, it was so commonplace in Iran that I do not think for a moment he might be paranoid. He produces a thickly wadded envelope. 'Do you believe in an afterlife, Mrs Shirley?'

'Not really,' I reply. 'But I might take my favourite earrings along, just in case.'

He bursts into laughter and hands over the envelope. Shuffling the collection of photographs as if they are playing cards I glance at them. Human bones lie in untidy heaps within the perimeter of the colossal site. Numerous intact skeletons are propped in a sitting position against mud-brick walls, their unhinged jaws giving the ghastly impression that the human beings they represent had died contorted with pain. They are immediately replaced in my mind by six skeletons, those of Gary Cunningham, Tony Stewart, Brian Peters, Malcolm Rennie, Greg Shackleton and Roger East.

I start trembling. Mr Mashrouteh explains that the circular building has no roof and that allowed eagles and vultures to pick the bones clean.

> *He set me down in the middle of a valley;*
> > *it was full of bones*
> *. . . and suddenly there was a noise, a rattling*
> *and the bones came together, bone to its bone.*
>
> *. . . and there were sinews on them,*
> *a flesh had come upon them,*
> *and skin had covered them;*
> *but there was no breath in them*
>
> *And the breath came from the four winds*
> *and they lived and stood on their feet*
> *a vast multitude.*
>
> –*King James Bible*, Ezekiel 37: 1–14.

Blood roars in my ears; my mind fills with stereoscopic sound — screams, the tearing of flesh, of blood spurting and the shattering of bones. I put my head between my legs until the nausea passes. Sand stretching before me is ash dusting Greg's bones. Bludgeoned and scarred, the bodies of the five were burned three times. Roger East has no grave. Where are his remains? Out of sight, out of mind? No, never out of mind. The burning air shifts the balance and I spiral like a stone falling into water.

Mr Mashrouteh's kindly, ascetic face hovers over me; his voice echoes as if it is coming to me through water. I had fainted, of course, and Mr Mashrouteh blames himself. In an attempt to make light of my collapse I say that if I had died he could have heaved me over the wall of the charnel house. 'No one would ever know.' He throws me a startled look while apologising profusely. We retrace our steps, both of us locked in our own thoughts.

As the car pulls away I glance back — the ossuary has re-opened something tangible in me that still has the power to harm. The apocalyptic image of those ominous skeletons is not the cause of my distress. For more than a year I have been locked in a circle of silence; a conspiracy of silence created to protect Prime Minister Gough Whitlam, ambassador to Indonesia Richard Woolcott, and a whole raft of anonymous bureaucrats, as well as the murderers. That is the stuff of nightmare, not the Zoroastrian shrine.

Time shifts as I recall Greg telling me he was destined to die young. This conviction acted as a spur and explains why he celebrated his life with such flair and imagination.

My eyes fill with tears as I recall what happened after I had arranged the publicity for Shirley McKechnie's dance school's performance of Ezekiel 37: 1–14, which was held in a Beaumaris church back on 24 July 1966. I was elated because every newspaper I had invited to cover the event attended and it was subsequently reported on the front page of all the Melbourne newspapers. Theodore Bikel's thrilling recording had thundered through the church.

Greg had been horrified when I described my response to Ezekiel's parable after I returned from the performance. He'd had a nightmare, and was extremely disturbed by it, refusing to divulge details. He asked me not to mention it again and he wanted us to have a baby right away. I rode my bike down to St Kilda and after a good, long think I decided I would stop taking the contraceptive pill.

On the drive back to Yazd I recall Greg's reaction and his absent-minded habit of removing the peel from an orange in one continuous circle and winding it around his wrist like a bracelet – another circle. Another silent circle.

That evening I brood on the scenes of the day as I sip gin fortified with juniper berries surrounded by the aroma of hashish and plant alkaloids emanating from Mr Mashrouteh's hookah, or *ghalyoon*. I retire early and hover in a malodorous world of bones and carnivorous raptors, ancient and modern, animal and human.

Before Balibó, politics had been a duty. After Balibó I am forced into a world where lies are common currency. We are living in very dark times. I am not Osip Mandelstam and ASIO is not the Russian NKVD, but the mere suggestion of complicity among those who think of themselves as Great Men incurs the venom of their writers and advisers – no one dares question *their* perceived priorities. My sin has been to demand a full judicial inquiry into the atrocity at Balibó. Seven weeks later, when Indonesian forces invaded East Timor, I included East Timorese victims and Roger East.

In the morning I stare at my face in my travelling mirror – it is round, a circle of glass set in a circle of wood. I cannot plead ignorance. I have read the works of many prescient writers: they have seen the darkness coming and now it is upon me and mine. Official silence over the Indonesian military's savagery and sadistic brutality suggest that ASIO operatives are suffering from amnesia, or something far more sinister.

Am I to pretend that I have lost the power of reason? Personal insults purporting to have originated in Canberra are in circulation. Perhaps, I think, they will continue to underestimate me. Perhaps this is my one, true strength. Presumably the highest in the land assumes that fear of criticism will make my memory lie fallow. 'We will see about that,' declares the voice in my head.

I have always been good at fighting other people's battles, but how can I protect Evan? He must be safe and he must know joy. It comes down in the end to one salient question: Am I a human being? I have to define what that means.

It does not take long to realise there has never been any choice in the matter. There are many reasons for not giving in to the unequal battle, not the least being the long-term effect it might have on Evan if I just get on with my life. When I think of my family and the way they operate by always doing the decent thing, I realise I will simply follow their example. I have been naïve and unwilling to take up a cause, any cause. Now I just want to recapture my wonderful life, but this is going to be a very difficult task.

The visit to Iran has been a retreat from reality, but my little *ḥaǧǧ* has shown me the way and I could not ignore the evidence – the atrocity at Balibó had set the stage for far greater carnage and wanton violence. The multitudinous skeletons I have seen locked in their circle of silence represent the dead and dying in East Timor.

When I leave Yazd, Mr Mashrouteh is still worrying about me. Hoping to give solace, I ask, 'Can I claim to have had an epiphany in a Muslim country at a Zoroastrian burial site? It's as Irish as Paddy's pigs.' When later describing to a Canberra academic what has become for me the Circle of Silence, I am assured it is precisely the place to have an epiphany and there might have been a sinister motive for the closure – it is the perfect place to dispose of one's political rivals. 'If any skeletons were intact it would indicate they were the result of a recent death.'

Perhaps Mr Mashrouteh's motive for taking those very dangerous photographs was not so different from my determination to get justice for my 'disappeared'.

ONE

I was born lucky. When I think about the millions of sperm racing to impregnate my mother's ovum I won the biggest lottery of all. Being born is the most important thing that can happen to us; without it nothing else matters and nothing will ever matter. But how did I win a race bigger than the Olympics? I'm a dead loss at sports – when my father tossed me and my younger brother into the sea Bruce floated and I sank. I remember how Bruce used to laugh when I played tennis. 'Look at my sister,' he would say, 'such a beautiful style. The only trouble is she never hits the ball.'

The sperm that won the race must have tripped and fallen into my mother's ovum headfirst.

I grew up surrounded by a large, loving family. Great-grandparents and grandparents had emigrated from England in 1883 and 1912 respectively: my father had arrived in Adelaide at the age of seven and my mother was born in Australia. James Patrick Venn married Doreen Nellie Link at the height of the Great Depression and they lived in Adelaide. I was their first-born.

My Great Uncle Gabriel William, who survived Gallipoli and was gassed on the Western Front, reckoned I was such a bonzer little baby he entered me in a baby competition on the day of the Sunny South Regatta, a popular annual event in Glenelg, South Australia. A storm blew up as the doctor examined the contestants and the babies howled with fright when high winds rattled the windows. My mother told me, 'You just sat up like Jacky, taking everything in as usual.'

The fleet was destroyed and many drowned. Oblivious to the tragedy raging outside, I won the competition. 'The doctor took immense care in measuring, weighing and testing the children's reflexes,' my mother told me when I was fourteen years old. 'You only lost one point for the size of your head.'

'What? Was it too big or too small?' I asked. I was reprimanded for asking such a silly question. Great Uncle William Gabriel made no attempt to hide his irritation with me. 'Either way it's an insult,' I complained.

'If you're lucky you'll never know, so get used to it.' I submit this as evidence of my fortuitous education. The criticism was bearable only because it came from someone I admired and adored.

We lived on Marion Road, Plympton – turn left at the Halfway Hotel (now called the Highway Inn) as you travel towards Adelaide up the Anzac Highway. When I was four, we moved 'down the bay' to St Leonards. My life, though fraught with all the usual minor traumas, was filled with wonder, adventure and accomplishment. I maintain that at the tender age of five I exhibited early warnings of a love of art by painting the inside of our outdoor dunny with cocoa.

Although I did not have the education I wanted, I was an avid reader, which is an education in itself. Reading way above my age I was influenced for life by Victor Hugo's *Les Misérables* and John Steinbeck's *The Grapes of Wrath*. If you grow up during a war you will develop an appetite for reality or you will seek the safety of Enid Blyton's Faraway Tree for the rest of your life.

I was particularly lucky with my family, especially in being born to parents for whom my brother Bruce and I were the absolute priority in their lives. All my family members were steady workers. The men were accomplished at their individual trades. They worked so hard I do not think they had time to realise or resent how creative they could have been. Little time was wasted in sentiment, and if one of our clan needed help everyone set-to with a will to overcome.

The women, though frustrated by the mores of the times that frowned on men who allowed their wives to work for wages, were not broken by their lives. They fought back as best they could. I found the contrasts in their behaviour incomprehensible – stoic in the performance of their duties, they also wore silly hats, held asinine conversations and behaved in a hare-brained manner, as if being childlike was cute. They could also be coarse in a way that was screamingly funny. The wife of my Uncle Bill, one of my mother's younger brothers, once said about her husband's love of coconut: 'Gawd love us, he'd eat poop if you sprinkled it with coconut.'

My mother was superstitious. I remember a day when we were on our way to visit my paternal grandparents and she prevented me from walking beneath a ladder. 'It's bad luck,' she said. Even before I opened my mouth to ask for an explanation, my father responded, 'Don't teach her rubbish, Doreen,' and proceeded to enlighten me – ladders were dangerous because they were unsteady and people and objects were likely to fall on an unsuspecting passer-by.

Superstitions aside, 7 December became a pivotal day in my life. On three separate occasions that day turned me around ninety degrees:

7 December 1941 – Japanese bomb Pearl Harbor
7 December 1975 – Indonesia invades East Timor
7 December 1990 – I give a paper at a seminar ever held in the hallowed halls of St Anthony's College, Oxford, on East Timor

It is difficult to imagine that Australia would assist the Indonesian people to throw off Dutch colonialism, and then stand by while the dictatorship that seized power enforced their own cruel colonialism on their own people. But it seems unimaginable that an Australian prime minister would aid and abet an Indonesian dictator's desire for plunder that would come close to destroying a people who had nurtured Australian soldiers in World War II.

Pearl Harbor happened just before my tenth birthday. It may not be possible to understand how frightened we were. It was grim. Thanks to continuous newsreels, I watched the progress of the war. The grown-ups tried not to frighten us, but the Rape of Nanking gave me nightmares. (My mother had explained rape after we watched Norma Shearer in the film *Marie Antoinette*. The queen's ladies-in-waiting were dragged into a courtyard and we did not see what was happening to them. I asked why they were screaming and she told me that the peasants were pulling the ladies' arms out of their sockets – that was rape, evidently.)

One day in January 1942, old Mr Inverarity scuttled past our house looking petrified. The Royal Navy ships *Prince of Wales* and *Repulse* had been sunk near Malaya on 10 December. We had believed in the power of those two battleships to protect us – there were only seven million of us, and teeming billions of them! According to Basil who lived across the street from us, the Japs were 'tearing through the islands like a bad case of diarrhoea and our soldiers [our Desert Rats] were friggin' miles away in the Western Desert and in Crete'.

Compared with the terrible ordeals people suffered in other

lands, we knew we were lucky. But I remember faces and voices expressing intense emotions and I soon learned how anxiety can kill. It seemed I was always reading funeral notices that stated that Mrs So-and-so had been Taken by God. We knew, however, she had died of a heart attack when she received a killed-in-action telegram. Dead and Missing columns covered the front page of the newspapers every day edged with big black borders.

All kinds of changes appeared overnight. The sports oval at St Leonard's Primary School was converted into slit trenches and we had air raid drill every day. When the school bell rang continuously we had to get under our desks because Jap bombers were too close for us to take any other form of cover. I was terrified the first time I got under my desk; it offered no protection at all! Two bells meant there was time to walk in an orderly fashion to the sports oval and take our positions in our allotted places in our trench, where we were instructed in the subtleties of being fired-upon from the air. We learned how to move from one side of the trench to the other, depending upon the direction from which the teacher manning an imaginary machine-gun shot at us.

There was a rush to vaccinate everyone before the Japanese landed and farmers were ordered to shoot their livestock, burn their crops and destroy all buildings and equipment in the event of an invasion. I knew that the scorched earth policy of the Russians was the right thing to do – I had heard about it on the news – but while we starved out the Japanese, what were we going to live on? What had the Russians eaten?

In only four months, the Japanese Dragon conquered Malaya, Singapore, Burma, New Britain, the Philippines and the Dutch East Indies. Port Moresby was bombed; Ambon was attacked; even Darwin and Broome were bombed. Evacuees from Darwin whispered that hundreds had been killed; one very angry lady stood up in our church and said that the newspapers had reported the air raids as if they were Sunday school picnics! She claimed that, thanks to Pig Iron Bob's largesse, hundreds of people were secretly buried in Darwin in holes made by Japanese bombs!

We wore identity discs so the authorities would know who we were if we were killed or were too badly injured to speak. We carried emergency bags in case we were bombed. As well as a pair of thick socks, they contained a peg to bite on during air raids to stop our teeth from shattering and earplugs to prevent our eardrums from bursting. There were also little squares of concentrated food that came from the chemist and a tiny packet of barley sugar for morale if we were forced to flee to the hills. I got into heaps of trouble because I ate my barley sugar on the first day.

One great event in my life was made possible by the war. Since the men were away fighting, the Glenelg St. Peter's church choir was forced to admit females. I had to stand on two bricks because I couldn't see over the stalls. One of my fondest memories occurred every Saturday when we sang for weddings – I would stride in with fellow choristers straight off the Glenelg beach. Inside the church no one knew that under our cassocks and surplices we were wearing bathing suits! I was the soloist and I still love ecclesiastical music.

Growing up during a war, even if you are comparatively safe or perhaps *because* you are once-removed, tends to concentrate the mind on the progress of combat. Under those hothouse conditions, it was exciting. I read a great deal about it: I liked to know how things worked and I was fascinated by the contrasts revealed in human nature, but the fascination was a temporary one. By the time the war was won I no longer found the subject thrilling – my cousin Colin Hemingway and the sons of many neighbours, including Basil, had been killed. Several of my cousins were wounded. I think now that I sensed in some strange way that the day might come when I would need to know what to expect.

TWO

My parents allowed me to leave school at the age of fourteen to take up an apprenticeship with Frank Bryan, Adelaide's premier couturier. In four years he taught me to make every kind of garment. I love solving problems and that is what design is all about. I thank my mother every day of my life for encouraging my talent in this area – I had wanted to be a veterinary surgeon and did not fancy the idea of learning to sew, but my mother told me, 'You will never have to trawl around the city looking for something to wear and paying extortionate amounts for the privilege.' Without her advice, I would never have been able to earn my living lecturing or had my own little television show on Channel 7. In the end, however, the fact that a man could call himself a couturier, while a woman would always be just a 'dressmaker' did not appeal to me. So, with veterinary surgery beyond my means, seven years after leaving school, I graduated as a state registered nurse.

 I lived in Britain for three years, using it as a base for travelling throughout Europe, and I worked for the Australian Trade Publicity Department, eventually promoted to the staff of the high commissioner.

I was very lucky because I was taught the craft of public relations and I loved living in England, particularly in London. I go back whenever I can.

On my return to Australia I held executive positions in Melbourne with John and Esta Handfield Public Relations, Sportscraft, the Elizabethan Theatre Company, the Russell Street Theatre and Gallery A, where I was educated by leading designers, architects and artists. I joined Radio 3AW as the publicity director in the early 1960s.

The Sunday before I started work at the station I went in to arrange furniture and hang some paintings in my three-roomed office. I also engaged the services of an electrician to disconnect the speaker system in my rooms. Muzak was piped into every corner of the station except the control rooms and studios. It was in the corridors, toilets, in every office and the reception area. I knew I would go mad if I had to listen to it all day.

A couple of years later, a newsroom cub reporter started coming into my office because he said he could think more clearly in there. It was so peaceful. All the marriage-market hopefuls who worked at 3AW had been raving about him but the first time I saw Greg I thought, 'Oh no, yuk! He's far too good looking!'

I also thought he was interested in my secretary, Laurel Trist, so I told him he could come and have tea or coffee whenever he liked. But as time passed I began to enjoy his company immensely. Greg was intelligent and had a delightful sense of humour. No one has ever made me laugh the way he did and I enjoyed arguing with him. When Greg told me that a hunter had shot off his own foot I cried, 'Hooray! Now the bastard knows how it feels.'

Greg was appalled. 'If you can't tell the difference between a human being and a duck, I'm sorry for you,' he said.

'Oh, I can tell the difference all right. The duck has never done anything to hurt anyone. The hunter has given up his right to be part of the human race.'

'How do you figure that?'

'He indulges in inhumane acts,' I raged. 'People like him are the worst plague on earth. Great big heroes hunting animals for fun and profit make me sick and, as for killing tigers and rhinos from some idiotic belief that they provide aphrodisiacs, it's utterly grotesque. Even if it was true, it's not worth losing an animal so some useless bloody bastard can have an erection.'

His eyes bulged and his mouth twitched. Even if Greg was prepared to concede that I had a point regarding hunting, aphrodisiacs, in his mind, were a scientific fact.

'Name one,' I challenged him.

'Cannabis.'

'It lowers inhibition and that doesn't necessarily stimulate sexual desire.'

'Spanish fly.'

'They are blister beetles and they can cause permanent damage to the kidneys and genitals. The only aphrodisiac for a man is a woman, and vice versa, but there's one remedy I reckon would work. It's in the Kama Sutra.'

His eyes narrowed suspiciously.

'You place the flaccid member on a brick and hit it with a hammer.'

We burst out laughing. The story was repeated all over 3AW until it reached ridiculous proportions. Some said I was mad; others supported me. While I was definitely warming to him and found him attractive in every way, Greg was a bit of a dag. My male friends were snappy dressers, but not Greg. He wore crumpled shirts and baggy trousers in all weathers and added a shapeless, thick green sweater in winter. He had been doing his own washing and ironing from the age of eight, and when I met him his dinner would be forequarter chops, mashed potato and cabbage steamed in milk, and then he ate the leftovers for breakfast.

Some time after we became friends we discussed a book about Odette, the celebrated secret agent who had parachuted into France in World War II. Greg asked me out to see *Carve Her Name with Pride*. Virginia McKenna played Violette Szabo. I didn't tell him I had already seen the film, and that I had hated McKenna in the role because she was blonde and spoke with an educated English accent. In real life, Violette had dark hair and a Cockney accent. When her husband was killed she volunteered for the British Secret Service – her mother was French so she spoke the language perfectly. She was captured three months before the end of the war and held prisoner at Ravensbrück, along with two fellow secret agents.

They were tortured and beaten for information, starved and forced into hard labour. Mrs Julie Barry, a resident of Nazi-occupied Channel Islands, was forced to become a prison guard at Ravensbrück and she was the last person to speak to Violette. After the war in 1946 she told the *News of the World* that the three British women 'were in rags, their faces black with dirt, and their hair matted. They were starving. Most of the inmates in the camp wanted to die, but Mrs Szabo wanted to live. Even among the thousands of women in the camp these three were outstanding. Nothing could break their spirit.'

Violette's fellow spies were in such poor condition that they had to be carried to their place of execution. Violette, with spirit blazing to the end, managed to walk. Mrs Barry said of the three women, 'On each face was a look of utter contempt for the guards.' Violette was the last to be executed, so she watched her friends being put to death and did not flinch when her time came. She was shot in the back of the head. The three bodies were cremated.

I wondered why out of all the women at Ravensbrück these women were shot so late in the war. They couldn't have been a threat by then. It might have been the type of torture they had endured. Perhaps they were sexually mutilated and the perpetrators couldn't risk leaving evidence like that, so their bodies had to be completely destroyed. Greg said he would prefer to be shot immediately, but he understood Violette's will to live. He added that once she was dead no-one could hurt her. She was beyond their brutality. I could not foresee how important this would become for me.

After working without a holiday for three years, my boss and the managing director of 3AW, Miles Fortunatus Wright, told me to take five months off. We ran a radio club for teenagers and one of the last things I did before I left for my holiday was to arrange for all the young lads working at the station to be included in a contra-deal with Peter Jackson menswear. Many didn't own a suit, including Greg, so I wangled a suit, shirt and tie for them all.

I travelled around Victoria and New South Wales, camping with my parents. My father had a habit of going to sleep at the wheel of our car and the tent was so large it took over an hour to erect. Nevertheless I loved my time with them, despite the constant danger of a head-on collision and their continual arguments. We spent a divine week wending down the Murray River on a paddle-steamer.

Greg's letters to me during this time were very thoughtful and loving. When I returned to Melbourne he met me at Tullamarine holding a bunch of pink carnations (his favourites). He knelt in the airport's arrivals area to propose as I came off the plane. I was dumbstruck as I had never expected to get married. I grew up with so much death around me during the war years and was repeatedly told by a neighbour, Mrs Mummy, that my

The Circle of Silence

prospective husbands were all dead or dying. 'Such a shame,' she would say. 'Gone before you had a chance to meet them.'

'By the time I'm 75 you will be 60. It's not practical,' I said. Add to this that Greg feared he would be dead by the time he was 21 – during his early teens he had accepted that this was his fate. I knew a number of males who suffered from a premonition of an early death and so I did not take it seriously. But Greg did indeed face death every day as he suffered from severe asthma attacks. By the time we met he had learned to survive them by sheer discipline and courage. He did not seek death, but he was driven to get the most out of his life and, in part, this was why I was attracted to him.

But I had been thinking about going to Japan to live for a couple of years. I had a flat at the bottom of Darling Street overlooking the River Yarra, plus a healthy bank balance and a good job. Marriage was risky and even though women marry younger men now, at that time it was unusual. I felt I could love Greg and he seemed to be an ideal candidate, but it would take a pretty major event to make me take the final step. He was self-possessed, but I suspected he might need a lot of care. While I wasn't prepared to say yes, in the end I did agree to accept an invitation to meet his mother.

Olwyn Schoenheimer (which is German for 'beautiful home') was known as Shonny. She had been a great beauty, but Greg told me she was ageing resentfully. She had married several times and was vague about the details. Greg tolerated her partners – just.

'She doesn't want to break them,' he said, 'she wants to bind them to her. She's always looking for someone who won't leave her, but it never works because she's impossible.'

'So you're the one male who has never let her down?'

'Yes,' he said. 'I keep her balanced.'

I wasn't worried about meeting her as I never really believed Greg and I would marry. She came to the door holding a can of gold spray-paint and wearing gold shoes and a gold belt. The interior of her house resembled an Inca temple, gold vases filled with dried plants sprayed with gold stood in every corner, on every table and on every mantelpiece. Some of the gold vases were jam jars.

She was lovely to me and I really liked her. She was funny and lively. She talked about feeling young and powerful, although it was painfully obvious that the opposite was true. She said she would kill herself before she had the chance to grow old and unglamorous.

I was shocked as I could see she was serious. She spoke without a trace of fear and her face remained passive. I was intimidated and ill-prepared, but when I looked into her eyes I saw an intensity that demanded a response.

'Kill yourself?' I said, keeping my voice low so Greg wouldn't hear. 'I'm not saying I wouldn't do it if my life was utterly miserable, but I'd be afraid I'd make a mess of it.'

'There's nothing to be afraid of if you jump.'

'That would hurt!'

'Not if you go high enough,' she said, squeezing the trigger and enveloping her world in a golden mist.

Shonny had left Greg's father when he was four and, up until then, he had been cared for by his grandparents. When Shonny moved to Melbourne it was disastrous for him, as he lost them from his life. Greg couldn't remember his father and didn't want to know about him because, although he sent Christmas and birthday cards on an irregular basis, the messages inside were stern and all about being a good person. Never once did he ask if Greg needed help. And Greg did need help.

Shonny's fortunes fluctuated, depending on the affluence of her partners. She told me until around the time she had trained

The Circle of Silence

as an occupational therapist the profession had been restricted to men. She had had to fight hard to be accepted. I thought she had done pretty well as a single parent and as a woman, particularly for those times and because Greg loved her deeply.

A lot of Greg's early memories concerned Shonny's ability to turn difficult times into fun. They often did a moonlight flit. Greg was ashamed of this, but he was loyal to Shonny – and always made excuses. When they were broke she would cook them her special Surprise Chicken. The surprise was that the chicken was cauliflower dipped in batter and deep-fried, served with roast potatoes and cabbage steamed in milk. She made Greg believe Surprise Chicken tasted better than real chicken.

When he was 8 years old, she told him to get her something practical for Christmas – he gave her a packet of Meds. At 10 he started work on a paper round. It was very hard work. He toiled up hills on a borrowed wreck of a bike. Once he was earning he put a beautiful birdcage on lay-by and on Christmas eve he finally paid it off. At the pet shop he bought a bird the owner said was going cheap, though it sang like an angel. Greg had been so looking forward to giving this bird to Shonny for Christmas and had been to the library to read about how to look after a bird in a cage.

After Shonny went to sleep he crept out and placed the cage in the living room and covered it with a pillowcase. He was too excited to sleep, and at four o'clock he rose and removed the cover from the cage. The bird was lying on the bottom of the cage, dead. When Shonny woke up two hours later he was still crying.

'That was our life, people took advantage of our poverty,' he told me. He believed that the shopkeeper knew the bird was sick – the part about it singing like an angel was an added bit of cruelty.

The difference in our ages melted away when we were together. We shared similar faults: flirtatiousness, irreverence, sarcasm and a wicked sense of humour. We were also a touch too practical and rather too certain of our opinions. Greg was my equal in every way – intellectually and politically astute, his humorous observations were hilarious. (In fact, Phillip Adams wanted him to work with cartoonist Peter Russell-Clarke, as he believed Greg's sense of humour would benefit Peter's satirical drawings.) He was always striving to be a better person than his father and his mother's partners had been; he was extremely critical of his own behaviour.

One day my phone rang and it was Greg asking, 'Has the surprise come yet?' I was afraid it might be an engagement ring. Greg was determined to marry me and he was not above enlisting friends to encourage me to say yes. There was a knock at the door. A deliveryman held out a huge bunch of Christmas lilies with a plain white card and behind him was a sparkling new washing machine. Written on the card was the poem that had been given to Violette by English cryptographer Leo Marks.

The life that I have
Is all that I have
And the life that I have is yours

The love that I have
Of the life that I have
Is yours and yours and yours

A sleep I shall have
A rest I shall have
Yet death will be but a pause

For the peace of my years
In the long green grass
Will be yours and yours and yours

Shonny phoned and she was very excited. 'Oh you just can't keep refusing, Shirley,' she said. 'Greg really loves you; don't throw that away. But if you have children I don't want them to call me Grandma.'

By now we had known each other for more than two years. I knew his innermost thoughts and worries. I think I assumed a motherly interest at first. I thought, if he was right about dying young at least I would have given him the family life he wanted. If he lived, we would have the same chance for a happy marriage as anyone else.

On the day we announced our engagement Miles Wright called me into his office. He had intended to announce his appointment as head of the Broadcasting Control Board that very day, but now no-one cared because the whole station was abuzz with our news. Miles told me he had waited all his life to get that job (his actual words were 'aspiring to that position') and he vowed never to forgive me for having stolen his thunder.

Before we could marry, though, Greg and I had a discussion about his surname. When we met I knew him as Greg Sugar. Each time Shonny had married or lived with a new partner, Greg had changed his name by deed poll. He soon grew tired of doing this and just became known as the new partner's surname without legally changing it. Now he complained that he would have to repeat the bureaucratic business again in order to get married. I suggested he might want to revert to his father's surname, Hogg. He refused emphatically. I had met Quintin Hogg in England; he had been called Lord Hailsham but he told me he dropped his title in order to enter the House of Commons. His title has changed several times since then. Shonny accused Greg's father, Bill Hogg, of boasting that he was related to Lord Hailsham, but Greg said Shonny was being catty and Greg's relatives do not believe that they are related to that branch of the Hogg family.

I was quietly relieved that Greg did not want to change his name back to Hogg and that he didn't want to keep Sugar. I made him choke with laughter when I said, 'Even if we start a sweet shop I would not want to be called Little Shirley Sugar'.

A friend of ours, John Sydney, star of stage and screen, came to dinner one night and suggested we put some names into a hat. I rattled off some of my relative's surnames: Hemingway, Austin, James. Greg cast me a sour look.

'All famous writers,' he said.

'You could always change both names,' John suggested. 'What about Hieronymous Hitler?'

We laughed and made up silly names and then agreed to put two names each into a hat and to go with the one that was pulled out first. It turned out to be Shackleton, which was John's choice.

'Here is the seven o'clock news read to you by Greg Shackleton,' John pronounced. Greg thought it was too grand a name and even though I thought Ernest Shackleton's journey to save his crew was a wonderful feat of endurance, I could not forgive him for taking ponies to Antarctica.

'Shirley Shackleton,' said Greg, 'I like the alliteration.' So that was that. Little did we know this surname would be used in spiteful attempts to betray him in the unknowable future.

We were to marry in Adelaide at St Peter's Church, Glenelg, on 7 May 1966. I sent invitations to Greg's family in Queensland. Greg was ecstatic when his paternal grandmother, Nan Hogg, accepted.

I made my going-away dress in dark green silk cut on the bias, but my mother did not want me to wear green for the occasion. Her outfit had been made of emerald green silk, also cut on the bias. During their honeymoon my father accidentally knocked a cup of hot coffee into my mother's lap, scalding her and ruining the dress. She claimed that she had known from that moment that her marriage was doomed (my parents separated later) and she did not want me to suffer the same fate. Plus green was unlucky according to a superstition at that time.

Greg reacted angrily when I decided to wear something else. I told him I was not at all superstitious but I did not want to worry my mother. Greg began a tirade against women. I had never seen him in such a rage. His behaviour was completely out of character. I told him he was being ridiculous and then a long silence followed. Finally he said, 'I can't stand drama queens. They remind me of my life with Shonny.'

This comment took me aback somewhat. 'How come you haven't told me this before? It's always been good old Shonny this and wonderful Shonny that?'

'I was scared you wouldn't marry me. She's quite mad you know.'

On the morning of the wedding I suggested that we visit Nan Hogg at her hotel. We were met by a sprightly eighty year old. It was clearly evident that she had suffered being separated from Greg all those years. He was in awe of her, and very respectful and grateful to her for coming down to the wedding.

Former choristers waited to greet me at the church as I arrived. I was touched that so many came to see me after all those years. My brother's wife Jill was my maid of honour, my brother Bruce was Greg's best man and my father gave me away. Greg loved every minute of the wedding and the reception, and he was grateful to my parents for their generosity, but he couldn't relax. He wasn't nervous about making a speech; he just didn't trust Shonny. She had gone to some trouble to have the seating rearranged so she could sit next to Nan, and Greg did not trust her.

'Who's being a drama queen now?' I asked him.

'She's always hated Nan. It's a wonder she hasn't got it in for you, because you arranged our meeting this morning.'

Talk about an undertow. I wondered how many skeletons were hidden under the hatches in that particular ghost ship. After watching them surreptitiously, I decided that Greg was right to be suspicious. Shonny was up to something. We decided to walk around and speak to the guests, starting with Shonny. Poor Greg. He was caught between his genuine love for his mother, his deep understanding of her frustrations and motives, and his need to protect his grandmother.

I invited Nan to sit with my parents for a while and told Shonny she could have her turn next. I could tell that she knew that I knew what she was up to. I needn't have worried because Nan was well aware of the situation. As I escorted her to join my parents, she thanked me for rescuing her and assured me that she had poured most of the alcohol with which Shonny had been surreptitiously plying her into the flower arrangements.

When we flew back to Melbourne I wore my dark grey dress. The hostess brought us coffee. Greg knocked the coffee all over me. I was badly scalded. My mother would have been horrified. It was not a propitious start.

THREE

Soon after we returned home Greg placed a sign on our front door proclaiming: THANK HEAVEN WE ARE NOT IN AFRICA. I am very practical, except where animals are concerned. Since I'm a sucker for strays Greg figured if we *had* been in Africa I would have been likely to have a menagerie of big wild animals instead of Daisy, my white rabbit. What happened to incur his exasperation was that on the first night in our apartment Greg read the paper while I cooked dinner. When it was ready he stood up to come to the table and his shoe fell off. Daisy had nibbled right through his shoelace – another inauspicious start to domestic bliss.

Greg was always jealous of my male friends. He was never rude to them, so I didn't take much notice, but one would have expected me to be the jealous one. At parties Greg stayed in one position and waited to be approached, which always happened instantaneously, especially with women. At work I was regularly invited upstairs for drinks at the end of the day with the general manager and his staff. Greg would always wait for me in the foyer and would never go home without me. He didn't complain, but he often looked miserable.

At around this time I began to think about leaving 3AW, but I didn't know what I wanted to do. I had a good reputation in public relations circles so I could pick and choose, but I knew myself too well not to know the drawbacks of high-powered work. When your client calls around 5 p.m. and asks you to meet him for a drink, you have to go. I'm very exacting and honourable about work so our marriage would have had to take second place.

A new managing director, Ron Fowles, was appointed to the station. He was a personable young man from Sydney. Soon he announced that the new sound of 3AW was going to be Beautiful Music. I gaped at him.

'Do you mean classical?' No, it was going to be melodic strings, etc.

'Jazz?'

'Certainly not.'

We had a solid audience for news and current affairs and Ralphe Rickman was a respected exponent of Jazz. But Beautiful Music would now be heard every time anyone switched to 3AW. I resigned the following day.

Once I finished work I had a lovely time furnishing our apartment. When I consulted Greg about his preference for colours and furniture, he gave me a wonderful mandate: 'I trust your judgment, Shirley,' he said. 'Go ahead and do what you want. If you are happy, I'll be happy.'

Greg continued working in the newsroom at 3AW. In 1967, the staff refused to witness the hanging of Ronald Ryan; he had been convicted of murdering a prison officer. Greg volunteered. He thought someone should attend. He was extremely upset by the experience and became an opponent of the death penalty. Years later I heard about a feature film called *The Last Man Hanged*. The screenwriters had created the character of a young journalist traumatised by the event. I took the trouble of telling the producer that he did not need a fictional character – Greg was the real thing. He could not have cared less. I thought the poignancy of Greg's own death would have added to the authenticity of the film . . . silly me.

I had wanted to wait until we had been married for at least two years before we had a baby. Greg was a realist – that's why we got along so well together. He still believed he would die young and I realised if he was right about this premonition then I must give him the gift of continuity a baby would offer. I imagined we would have a little boy with all of Greg's charms and brilliance of mind, and I anticipated the joy he would bring us.

Have you seen a chick struggling to quit the egg?
Oh birth, there is no greater struggle on earth,
no greater mountain to climb,
no gaol harder from which to escape.

Rippling winds three floors up rattled windows
sparkling with the strain of constant battering;
it's a paradox, this battle for life.
We withered in the heat of desperation.

Like a bird crawling out of its pain,
wings too weak to find release;
bones no longer pliable, you flapped,
trapped, like a spent and tattered lark.

I thought you had died in the dark.
Your father thought I was dead.
when they gave you to him, he cried,
Well, he did think that I had died.

Now we are peas in a pod.
Glorious, palpable light
pours in from the sky,
we are bonded you, your father and I.

In this world of light and laughter,
flowers and good wishes herald
high hopes for your good and happy
life. It was worth every strife.

Evan was born at 8 a.m on 6 June 1967. Greg had spent the previous day reporting the Arab–Israeli war knowing I was having a long and unproductive *trial*. The obstetrician had sedated me and I was expected to try again in the morning when I was refreshed. Greg had wanted to stay, but I suggested he should go to see a film to pass the time. In the event he saw *Dr Strangelove*, which was perhaps not the wisest choice.

My contractions woke me around midnight and continued until 4 a.m. when they ceased. By the time the doctor arrived I was convinced the baby was dead. He was a brilliant practitioner but as a public relations man he would have gone broke. I can see him now, standing at the end of my bed, hands flapping in distress, saying, 'You are right, the baby is stuck. You have to have an emergency Caesarean. It will all be over in half an hour.' To say that this was not reassuring is the understatement of the century. I was cast into black despair, because I thought my poor little baby was dead.

They had called Greg and he ran all the way to the hospital from 3AW where he had slept to be closer to the hospital in case of an emergency. He could not get a taxi because Melbourne was enveloped in a thick fog. Greg told me later how his fear had increased in magnitude in the surrealistic setting of thick, swirling mist and he was seriously hampered by his asthma. In the end he did not arrive in time to see me before the operation. As I sank under the anaesthetic I overheard a breathless paediatrician telling the theatre staff that he had abandoned his car and had run to the hospital because a thick fog was causing gridlock. As I blacked out I tried to ask why he had bothered, there was nothing for him to do, the baby was dead, but the words came out as if I had a mouthful of marbles.

The next thing I knew I was being moved along a dark passage and the pain was intolerable. Greg was running alongside, telling me that the baby was big. I was amazed about this information; why hadn't they told me his heart was beating strongly? People who have a Caesarean without a trial tell me they had no pain at all, not me. I thought about the beautiful girl in the bed opposite me who'd had a breech delivery, which I knew was worse than my twenty-four-hour trial.

Greg was at my bedside when I woke. 'You won't die now,' I said. 'Our son will live your life for you.' It was a very tender moment and we had tears in our eyes.

As we chatted, Greg said he regretted not being sufficiently established to own a flashy car that would impress Evan. I told him he would probably have a car by the time he was old enough to appreciate it. 'But,' I added, 'the way to really impress him will be to spend time with him and play with him. Children take cars for granted nowadays, but they crave personal attention.' He was quite chuffed at this and behaved accordingly. Greg was the most attentive of fathers and so very happy to have a son. He agreed to try to bring up Evan to not only accept change but to embrace it.

One of the presents we received at Evan's birth was a pink jump suit so I dressed him in it – after all, pink was the traditional colour for boys in the 1800s. I remember a conversation with an elderly lady with particular fondness.

'What a beautiful little girl!'

'Thank you, actually he's a boy.'
'What is her name?'
'Evan.'
'Evelyn, it suits her.'

A little more than two months after Evan was born, we hosted Greg's twenty-first-birthday party. Shonny came under protest as she didn't want anyone to know she was a grandmother. When he was older, she wanted Evan to call her 'my friend Shonny'.

I had never seen Greg happier. Having lacked a father he gloried in having a son and, to top it all off, Corbett Shaw, the 3AW news editor, had elevated him to an A-grade journalist. Many middle-aged journalists failed to reach that standard.

I remember one day Shonny rang me, hysterical. She said she had been raped. She refused to go to the police, so I told her to take a taxi to our house. I rang Greg. He asked a few questions then said he would be home at the usual time. I was flabbergasted. I rang again and asked if he had heard what I had said, 'Shonny has been raped.'

'I'm busy,' he said. 'I'll be home at the usual time. Don't give her any alcohol.'

I was shocked by his reaction. When Shonny arrived, she described what had happened in graphic detail. I made up the bed in the guest room so she could rest but she did not want to – she asked for tea and cake. Greg returned home at his usual time, walking down the passage and calling a cheery hello to Shonny. He came into the kitchen, kissed me, took me by the hand and led me into the sitting room. He sat opposite Shonny and looked into her eyes.

'Now,' he said, 'what really happened?' She lowered her eyes. Her hands hovered nervously around her face. 'Look at me,' he commanded. She stared at him, gave a sigh, cocked her head to one side like a cute little girl and whispered, 'Oh, I lied.'

I ran into the kitchen. Greg followed me. 'I want you to remember this,' he whispered. 'We will talk later.'

They chatted as if nothing extraordinary had happened. Shonny was all smiles when I brought in the roast dinner I had been cooking. I couldn't swallow a thing. Later she went home in a taxi, waving and smiling as if she was leaving on an overseas cruise. The only thing missing were the streamers.

Greg later told me that if she looked after Evan she was likely to go into one of her fantasies and just wander away. But we saw her rarely, though we frequently invited her to visit. When we were alone she would sigh to me, 'I'm never going to get anywhere. You won't either. You're so busy looking after everyone else, you don't look after yourself, Shirley.' She was desperately lonely and though I worried at first in case she wanted to look after Evan, she never once offered.

After Shonny's father died, she bought two fur coats and took her new boyfriend, Clarke, on a world cruise. We had met him briefly. I liked him but he was very wary of us. I often wondered what she told him about us. A year or so later Shonny announced she was going to marry Clarke at the registry office. While I waited for the bride to arrive some of her friends discussed her former marriages and made dark predictions – this one would not last.

'Oh well,' I said, trying to be cheerful, 'third time lucky.' A heavy silence fell, followed by a spirited discussion as to the number of her marriages. Various husbands' names were mentioned and argued over.

'No, she didn't marry that Sugar bastard; he was just a blow-in.'

'I went to the wedding I tell you.'

'She has been married five times, this is the sixth.'

'No Elsie, you are wrong. This is the fourth.'

'What was that radio announcer's name, the pansy she followed to Melbourne?'

'Him! Don't you remember he left a suicide note? She had a wonderful time playing the deserted bride. Called the police. Oh, what a to-do.'

I was relieved that Greg was not present to hear the gossip. Shonny and Greg arrived together, arm-in-arm.

One day while tidying the storeroom I found Greg's football medals and school prizes for literature, history and English. Shonny told me that when he matriculated he had won a scholarship to read law but she would not support him. I suggested to him that night that he could study part time if he wanted to. He said he wouldn't do law now.

'What would you do?'

'B.A. history and literature.'

'Okay.'

He laughed, 'I'd be 28 before I got my degree.'

'You'll be 28 at precisely the same time; you just won't have a degree.'

Shonny was strangely quiet when Greg enrolled at Melbourne University. He warned me she was jealous because I was helping him where she had failed. I thought it was sad because she had looked after him since he was four with only intermittent support. There was no reason for her to feel she had let him down, and I made sure to tell her this, but I could see she still felt guilty.

When Greg began studying a whole different person emerged. More confidence. More purpose. A metamorphosis. He had always had a strong moral base – I knew if push ever

The Circle of Silence   37

came to shove over a moral dilemma at work he would be likely to resign.

Though Greg could be insensitive like everyone else, including me, he was an accomplished lover. The longer we lived together the better looking he appeared to me, and the easier we found our life together. From previous experience I had learned that good looks fade in direct proportion to one's disappointment in the behaviour of the loved one. Greg was considerate and creative. While I healed after Evan's birth he made love to me in a whole new way. This consisted of satisfying episodes of cuddling; in other words I was cherished, a lovely experience that prevented me from suffering angst over my wounds.

During our Time of the Cuddles he entertained me with accounts of his sexual history. He'd had adventures with women who picked up young chaps like him at parties or pubs and took them home with assurances that the husband was away. He'd had to make his escape so frequently that he suspected they did it deliberately – a narrow escape added spice to the experience for them. Some of these escapades were screamingly funny – some frightening. More than once he had leapt naked from the window having grabbed his clothes and tossed them out, while his erstwhile partner screamed to her husband for help. He'd lost a lot of shoes that way.

He was a master of pantomime and one of his more memorable parodies concerned women who looked fantastic when they picked him up, or when he picked them up. His depictions of his disappointment and occasional horror as they removed their accoutrements were hilarious. I gave him my copy of *Adventures in the Skin Trade* by Dylan Thomas, who claimed that all that the citizens of London wanted was, 'love, beer, and sleep; music, dancing and sex, sex, sex.'

Our wonderful son Evan was no trouble. From the day I brought him home he slept from the 11 p.m. feed until ten minutes to eight the following morning. But when he was four months old he screamed all night. I took him to the local doctor who was unable to make a diagnosis. Evan screamed again that night with the same result from the doctor. When he screamed again the next night I demanded another full examination and I said if the doctor could find nothing, I would not leave his consulting room until he had arranged for a second opinion from a paediatrician. I just stood in his office with my hands on my hips, to his obvious annoyance.

After examining Evan's ears, he saw evidence of an infection. 'This child has been in agony.' Thanks to antibiotics we had no further trouble.

Greg, however, was not so easily cured. Work, lectures and study were causing sleep deprivation. When he worked the night shift at 3AW the slightest sound woke him so I would take Evan out in his pram and walk around all day. This was very hard on me. By the time Greg's night duty stint was over I was a wreck.

Despite being a chronic asthmatic Greg was a heavy smoker. I asked if he would consider not smoking in the house or around Evan. He was very shocked and asked his colleagues what they thought. They said I was a monster. He eventually chose to cease smoking, not only in the house but altogether.

I wanted us to buy a house in Port Melbourne or Albert Park and I thought we would be more likely to find one if we lived locally, so we moved to Middle Park. Two removal men arrived at 8 a.m. One was Polish, and he did not speak English; his companion was Spanish, and he spoke neither English nor Polish. And the Pole did not speak Castellano, but I did not know this until Greg's big wardrobe became stuck when they were halfway down the stairs.

The Circle of Silence

I called their manager for help and the receptionist promised to ask him to call me back when he returned to the office. He never did. Greg could have solved everything because he was whizz at moving furniture but he wasn't there, so I had to intervene. By using sign language we finally arrived at our new house, but not until mid-afternoon. I was not at all surprised that some of the furniture was still in the van and the big wardrobe was stuck halfway up the stairs when they went home. I called Shonny and asked if we could stay the night at her place as I could not get up the stairs to make up our beds.

She welcomed us warmly. Clarke gave us chilled white wine and he was quite taken with Evan. Shonny talked happily as we worked together in the kitchen. I thought if she could only be like this all the time, I would love to see more of her. Greg was particularly happy that night and it was easy to understand his devotion to her – she was lively, funny and delightful company. I wondered if we should have given her more chances to help us.

I was reflecting on the frustrations of that particular day and feeling very thankful that Greg was going to be available to supervise the move in the morning, when Clarke asked to hold Evan. Flushed with pride Greg carried him across the room and handed him over. Shonny watched with evident fascination while Evan was bounced on her husband's lap. Her transition to an asthma attack was rapid and violent. We called her doctor and when he arrived he ordered an ambulance.

Greg and Clarke danced around Shonny, attending to her every need, as she was loaded into the ambulance. Her doctor took me aside and asked if anything unusual had happened. I wasted time describing the lovely time we had shared. He interrupted to ask if I could think of anything that might have upset her. I remembered that the attack had started almost simultaneously when Clarke had played with Evan.

'That's it,' he declared. 'She has to be the centre of attention.' I could not believe this. He took my hand. 'She can bring it on, but she can't control it. That's right. She does it to herself and it's very, very dangerous.' Flanked by Greg and Clarke, Shonny was certainly the centre of attention. I smirked inwardly at her propensity for melodrama, but the depth of dread in her eyes as she fought for breath shocked me into remorse. I glanced at Greg; her terror was mirrored in his eyes. They went off with her, leaving me to clear up and put Evan to bed.

I was almost too frightened to think about it, especially since my grandfather, my father and my brother were asthmatics. I hoped fervently that Evan would escape this terrible disease. Greg's asthma attacks did not exhibit any hint of hypochondria and in a dramatic turning of the screw this was probably due to his early awareness of his mother's histrionics, which he loathed. The realisation that she was still manipulating him through fear worried him and yet even as these thoughts pierced my heart I recalled the imagined rape incident. How long could she expect these dangerous gambits to work in her favour? She might need to be the centre of attention, but her afflictions went much deeper. No wonder Greg felt it necessary to warn me never to leave Evan with her. I ended up feeling guilty, as Greg must have been all the days of his life.

Shonny spent several days in hospital, so the doctor was right about the seriousness of the attack. Everything I subsequently suggested to help end the cycle had already been tried by her husbands, friends and by Greg. He was like a drowning man clutching at flotsam as he warned me against getting involved. 'She likes you, Shirl. She can't lie to me. If you annoy her she will turn against you. I can cope with her if you can cope with me.'

Would he ever escape her voracity?

Not long after Shonny was released from hospital I came down with flu. There was so much to do, but I soldiered on

The Circle of Silence

after Greg left for work late that afternoon. I felt worse the next day and asked Greg to take time off. He refused. That night he took Evan out for dinner and when he returned they told me what fun they had had.

'I'll put Evan to bed,' said Greg quite jauntily. I asked what food he had brought for me. 'Nothing,' he said. 'People who are sick should be put in a room and given only water until they get better.' I was flabbergasted. I could see that he meant what he said and, worse, he was teaching Evan the same callous attitude. Fortunately I was too sick to fly into a rage, but I managed to state my case.

'You are not going to teach my son to be a monster.' I struggled out of bed and pulled on some clothes. 'I'm taking him to a first-class hotel with room service.' Greg looked stunned initially, and then he apologised and said he would go to St Kilda and bring back whatever I wanted. He was very contrite. I told him to heat up a can of tomato soup.

While I sipped the soup he tried to explain his attitude. Shonny had not always gone to the extremes I had witnessed, she mostly got her way by pretending to be seriously ill. He then had to do everything for her, including going out in all weathers to find food to tempt her to eat. He could not stand sick people.

'Fine,' I said, 'but you don't apply your stringent standards to yourself.' He hung his head. 'Don't ever do anything like that again, Greg.' I was actually over it by the time we had this conversation, but I will never forget the way he had encouraged Evan to make fun of me. 'Just remember Shonny is a hypochondriac and I am not,' I said. While I was not as angry as I appeared, I meant what I said. I thought about how marvellous he was to have overcome his dreadful childhood except for an occasional fall from grace.

* * *

One Sunday morning I asked Greg to look after Evan so I could search for a place for us to buy. We had been in Middle Park for six months and Evan was crawling by then. I rode my bike to Port Melbourne and on the way back took a turn that led to an area I had not seen before. I passed a shop and dwelling for sale. The brick building was available for a one thousand–dollar deposit. The back gate was not locked, so I crept into the appalling backyard and looked through a side window at three rooms leading to a fruit and vegetable shop.

According to the plan on the sign there were two main bedrooms plus a small bathroom and two small bedrooms upstairs. Despite the garish colour scheme in shades of sick yellow, fever pink and lovely Mediterranean blue it had distinct possibilities. 'When we remove the rusty corrugated iron outhouses, take the slates from the roof, pull up the floorboards and lay the slate tiles and when we paint the rooms white, the house will do us very well indeed,' I told Greg, when I returned home. He almost collapsed laughing. The idea that we would ever buy a house was outlandish enough; to think we could manage refurbishments was absurd. I disagreed but I did not say so.

We had one major problem to overcome: we had a thousand dollars, but the move and lawyer's fees would cost most of that. I made an appointment the next day with the bank manager. I told him that although we did not have much in the way of savings I was keen to buy a house as a way of enforced saving. We were the kind of people who would end up with a wonderful art collection, furniture, records, books and no house. The vendor's terms were reasonable. We could pay the house off on my earnings alone (I had by now begun working freelance for some of my old clients). When he agreed to inspect the premises I knew it was a winner because men love brick.

The Circle of Silence

As we climbed the stairs, he said he could not lend us a deposit, but he could supply a thousand dollars to buy stock. What a marvellous fellow to think outside the square like that. Our lives were stabilised because of him. Two days later I took Evan across Melbourne on the tram to sign the purchase documents. When Greg came home that night he was amazed to learn that by adding his signature to the papers we would have our own home in sixty days.

Several large huts in the backyard of the house next door to the one we were renting were occupied by alcoholics. Apart from fights they kept to themselves. A week after we signed the papers for our new house I found a number of very large firecrackers in the backyard of our rented abode. I asked Greg to explain to the men that explosives that size could have been fatal to Evan. Two days later I was hanging out the washing. Evan was sitting in the clothes basket playing with pegs. A huge cracker whizzed over the fence and missed him by inches.

I have to say that at this point I knew exactly what I was doing, but I had not thought it through. I was too furious. I picked up the hose, turned the tap on full and directed the stream of water into the hut where I could see the boots of the man who had thrown the cracker dangling from the top bunk. For a few seconds nothing happened. Then the reaction came – boots clanged as men leapt to the floor shouting and swearing revenge. By then I was inside and locking the back door. I put Evan to bed in his room and promised to come back and read him a story, then I locked his door and hid the key.

Greg was committing Shakespeare to memory for an exam. Pacing up and down on the front balcony he recited a passage from Hamlet as I ran onto the balcony . . . 'Though this be madness, yet there is method in it.'

He was marvellous – talk about cool. He told me to lock myself on the balcony and stay there.

'I can't leave you,' I said, as I ran after him to the bedroom. He threw off his jeans and put on his best suit and tie. I ran down the stairs and looked out the back window, one of them was climbing on top of the brick wall, but he did not enter the yard. I could hear the other men shouting that they intended to break down the front door. The man on the fence climbed back, so I unlocked the back door, ran to the outside kitchen to our only phone and called the police. I returned as Greg came down the stairs looking as if he was going to a swanky dinner; the only give-away was the policeman's cosh he was carrying.

He explained that he could protect himself far better if he didn't have to defend me and he asked me again to lock myself on the balcony. I went to the balcony ready to lock myself in if necessary. I was terrified for Greg as I watched five burly brutes lumbering along the street. They began to throw themselves against the front door. I ran down the stairs. Greg stood calmly, cosh in his right hand.

Light streamed through the stained glass, which began to rattle. In a moment Greg was showered with emeralds and rubies. The image was beautiful – it could have been an illustration in a book. I stood transfixed, imagining what would happen if they got in. To my surprise the battering ceased. I ran up the stairs and watched from the balcony as they left, still bent on trouble if their body language was an accurate indicator. They could force entry by breaking any one of the back windows.

I checked on Evan; he was asleep in his upstairs bedroom. I returned to the balcony and saw a police car. I ran down the stairs and called to Greg to open the front door while I stood watch at the back window – they were coming over the fence one by one, armed with hammers and some kind of bars. Two policemen walked down our hallway.

'It's all my fault,' I said, giving a brief outline. They could do nothing unless the men entered the property. 'They're already in,' I said.

'Okay. If they touch the door, open it and then stand back.' This happened as if by clockwork. As they entered the house the police stepped forward and arrested them.

While they were driven off I made a full confession. One of the policemen suggested that a court would probably find that there had been serious provocation. I did not want to lay charges as I accepted full responsibility for having over-reacted. We were advised that the perpetrators would be released the following day.

'If I were you, I'd quit the premises before lunch,' I was told.

I've never worked faster. I packed all night. In the morning I made arrangements to rent the house we were buying. By 11.30 a.m. the next day we were ensconced in our new home. It was only then that I got around to asking Greg why he had put on his best suit when he was about to be clobbered?

'You taught me to look the part,' he replied. 'When I began to wear a suit to work I was given better assignments. Why do you think the police behaved respectfully to us? You looked gorgeous and I did not look like a loser.'

Greg had no memory of his father, so it was a big surprise when Bill Hogg called and asked to stay with us. Greg was in a quandary over the proposed visit. He held very dark fears that his parents would behave badly. It was easy to see that while the little boy in him was desirous of getting to know his father, the adult wanted to be rid of the mind-numbing neglect that their estrangement had caused.

Greg bought three tickets for a musical comedy that night because he wanted to buy a gift for his father. Bill certainly seemed delighted. Shonny then called to invite Bill to have lunch at her house, but did not include us. We fell into each other's arms with relief. Bill said he planned to go to Shonny's for lunch first and meet us for dinner and the musical afterwards. He returned from Shonny's inebriated, but lucid.

Poor Greg, he was embarrassed because he suspected that this was Shonny's revenge. His father was eager to see the show, but asked if he could have a snooze and skip dinner. We cancelled our booking, and I had eggs and bacon sizzling when he came downstairs. He seemed fine at that point and insisted on driving us into town.

He was a very bad driver and halfway through the first act of the show he vacated his seat and did not return. Greg went in search of him and returned making a sign to show he was drinking at the bar in the foyer. At interval we joined him and tried to encourage him to accompany us into the theatre. He did but after fifteen minutes went out again. I don't remember a thing about the show, not even its name, but I will never forget the wounded expression on Greg's dear face as he tried to persuade that man to let Greg drive us home. Bill then refused to return home with us in a taxi, and so we left him there.

We picked Evan up from the baby sitter and I gave Greg a sleeping tablet as he had an early call the next day. About two hours later I heard a commotion downstairs – Bill was falling-down drunk. The front door creaked. I crept downstairs to find chaos and the door swinging wide open, but Bill was nowhere to be found. Around 10 a.m. the next day, a bedraggled Bill rang the doorbell. Looking as if he had slept in his car he said he had lost our key. I offered him a shower and breakfast which he declined; he had important business elsewhere. He went upstairs and came back down carrying his luggage.

'Do you want to leave a message for Greg?' I asked.

He shrugged. 'I said all I had to say yesterday.'

The Circle of Silence

I did not see him to the door. We never heard from him again. Even though Greg had told him how wonderful it was to have met him and how he loved having a son because he had always wanted a family life. Greg was absolutely devastated. We decided not to speak about him again as it was too painful.

There was every excuse for Bill Hogg's alcoholism, which I did not discover until 2009. At the age of 18, having joined the army, he worked in communications in Bougainville. He and his fellow servicemen were not armed or guarded, even though they came under constant Japanese attack. Vulnerable in every way, lacking food and equipment, they slept in the bush spread out for safety. One night a large contingent of American soldiers moved into the area and slept in a cave. I don't know if the Aussies knew this, I don't think they could have because if they had they would have taken action to prevent what followed.

The young Americans were being tracked by a large Japanese force. When they were asleep the Japanese went in with all guns blazing. The Australians heard the attack and witnessed the aftermath – there were no survivors. The 'incident' was hushed-up and the witnesses sworn to secrecy. Bill Hogg never recovered from the massacre and the trauma of the cover-up.

Little did we know the parallels the poor man would have to suffer over his own son's murder. However, a new life was soon on offer to salve Greg's wounds from his father. In 1969 he was selected to work for the Australian Tourist Commission in San Francisco.

FOUR

Once we had decided to go to America I suggested it might be a good time to have another baby. Greg was horrified.

'It's true,' he exclaimed, 'women forget! I'm never going to let you go through that again. Honestly, Shirl, you must have forgotten.' I had forgotten that post-operative complications had forced me to spend three weeks in the hospital. Carrying the baby had been easy; I suffered no discomfort at all. I even rode my bike until the last two weeks of the pregnancy. When Greg brought us home from hospital all the buildings and the traffic looked so huge I was alarmed. By comparison our apartment was an oasis of calm and Greg took such good care of us that I recovered quickly. When I suggested another baby the look of horror on his face coupled with my memories scared me so thoroughly that we never spoke of it again..

Greg went off to inspect Australian tourist destinations, leaving me to pack and store our furniture. Before he left I made him a dressing gown based on a djellaba, as Greg had been warned that accommodation could be primitive in some of the places he would be visiting. I chose brown, cream and black cotton stripes – he looked like an eastern potentate. He had also asked for a tiepin that might act as a conversation starter. I also ordered a beautiful black sheepskin coat in which he looked splendid.

We had a romantic dinner together the night before he was to fly out to America via Fiji. I gave him a brilliant matrix opal tie pin with a dark base and wonderful orange flecks. He started in surprise and I thought he looked guilty, but it was illogical so I did not remark on it. Then he fumbled in his pocket. Out came an interesting piece of amber.

'Um, I got this for you, Shirley Pearly,' he said, using my Grandfather Venn's nickname for me. I was touched.

His first letter to me raved about the djellaba. His luggage had mistakenly gone through to San Francisco while he stopped over in Fiji. He would have sweltered in the winter clothes he was wearing, but as he had carried the djellaba in his brief case he had a great time wearing it, and even wore it sailing. Everywhere he went he created a sensation. The Fijians said they had never seen a white man so beautifully and sensibly dressed.

Our house was rented out to relatives of friends. Greg had suggested we should let Shonny look after the place as landlord in our absence, so I arranged for the rent to be paid into the bank holding our mortgage and I left money in a separate account for any repairs that might need doing, so there wasn't much for her to do.

Evan and I travelled to the US on the *Oriana*. Evan, who was two-and-a-half by this time, engaged in shipboard activities with verve and vigour. He entered the fancy dress competition and I dressed him as a sunflower. He wore his black tights with my black t-shirt tucked into them, and I made flower petals from yellow paper and sewed them onto an elastic band that framed his face. Easy peasy. His body represented the stem and he held a green leaf in each hand and his dear little face formed the centre of the flower. He won first prize. When the other children came forward to accept their prizes, some were so badly behaved that they tore the wrapping apart and threw the toy on the floor. Evan took his prize, walked backwards, solemnly thanked the judges, then came and gave it to me. From then on wherever went he was congratulated for being a perfect gentleman.

Because of rough weather the *Oriana* was diverted to Canada and we were booked to fly to San Francisco. In the airport Evan was excited at the prospect of flying and seeing Daddy again. Our luggage was despatched down a tunnel and Evan moved towards it. As I gently explained that it was not a slippery-dip I heard a woman say, 'Keep watch on those two, Walter, they train the children to attract your attention and then they steal your luggage.'

The well-dressed woman was speaking to her black uniformed chauffeur, who looked extremely embarrassed. I realised she was speaking about me. I've never been more surprised in my life. I gaped at her and then at Evan who was standing quietly holding my hand. I could feel my jaw dropping as I looked at her face, which was screwed up into something akin to hate.

'Are you accusing me? Are you insane, Madame?' She stuck her nose in the air, and I walked away muttering like an evil dwarf. This was the first time I had been insulted by someone who was working on assumptions and it would not be the last.

There should have been film of our arrival in San Francisco as Greg had arranged for a dear colleague to record it, but he used up all the footage recording airport scenes. It was a very joyous occasion, anyway. Greg was absolutely elated and I sensed a huge change in him, which was confirmed by the fact that he wanted to take us to China Town right then and there. Greg, who used to complain that fussing with food was a waste of time and wished he could just take a pill, was transformed. He was keen to try all kinds of food. I soon realised that he had become adventurous in every way – I told him I thought he must have been bewitched by the Wicked Witch of the North in Australia.

'Her name is Shonny,' he said, shame-faced.

When we first arrived we stayed in Sausalito, which was a fine introduction to California. Moored outside were hundreds of houseboats and ocean-going yachts, and we could see San Francisco rising white and magical through our bedroom window. Greg reacted with shock when he saw the ring I had designed for the unusually shaped stone he had given me. When I asked if he did not like it he explained that he had picked it up on a beach. It was just a piece of beer-bottle worn smooth by time and tide. I liked it all the more.

We soon rented a duplex in San Rafael, a suburb over the Golden Gate Bridge. The flower-power era was waning. There were no footpaths in our town – you were supposed to drive. Finding a way to occupy Evan had been troublesome in Sausalito, as the parks there were locked to keep drug addicts out. Evan had been without the company of children since our arrival. On our first Sunday in San Rafael we took him to a park that was opened each weekend. As we approached the huge metal gates, Greg stopped in mid-stride.

'Evan will be terrified with all these strangers,' he said. But Evan was running ahead of us and as he burst though the huge black gates he called, 'Hi guys, I'm here.'

We were now living the American dream. Greg did not have to work long hours and we spent the weekends driving around California in his first car. Though we travelled widely our favourite haunts were the Valley of the Moon and Yosemite. We went to the movies often. On one occasion, Greg, who used to cringe when I asked people to stop speaking during films, stood up in the cinema to confront a woman who continually rustled her cellophane package of sweets. 'Good heavens, Madame,' he said, 'are you building a nest?'

We enrolled Evan at a pre-school for very young children, FYT. It was a revelation. A few weeks later as we were driving through San Francisco Evan called excitedly, 'There's Daddy's bank,' and he spelled out the words Wells Fargo Bank. Our friends were astonished, but I was not.

FYT gave children a marvellous start in life. Classes were held for all the usual subjects as well as reading phonetically. If a child lost interest in a lesson, they could go to any one of the play stations and occupy themselves until they chose to rejoin the class. 'Children cannot learn if they do not want to learn' was FYT's motto. There was no scolding, no tears, just a calm atmosphere that encouraged learning. I expressed surprise that every piece of pottery made by the children was fired, no matter what it was. 'How would you like it if something you made was tossed back into the clay box as if it was worthless?' was the response.

School started at nine, but the playground was supervised from 7 a.m. to aid working parents. There was a ten-thirty outdoor play period and lunch was served at midday. The children sat in groups of eight around a table and took turns to be the host of their table. Their duty was to introduce the guests to each other and make sure they had everything they needed. After lunch the children slept on their own little mattresses and covers. I would receive a call when Evan woke. Because I did not have a driver's licence, he came home in a taxi and quite a lot of the drivers were charmed by him. They said he asked the most perceptive questions. Unfortunately, Evan was later diagnosed as asthmatic in America, which Greg handled brilliantly.

For the first time in my life I was a woman of leisure. Greg delivered Evan to school and travelled on to the city by Greyhound bus. The housework was finished half an hour after Greg and Evan left in the morning. I now had a drying cabinet and washing-up machine – they were still a novelty in Australia. I sat in the beanbag in the corner of the living room drenched in sun and read to my heart's content. When I discovered the free library in the Marin County Civic Center, designed by Frank Lloyd Wright, was down the hill and around the corner, I continued my lifelong study of textiles that had started when I won the dressmaking and embroidery sections of the Royal Adelaide Show when I was thirteen years old.

Greg had adventures, like meeting baseball player Joe DiMaggio (who had been briefly married to Marilyn Monroe in the late 1950s), and I met Earl Conrad, who had ghost-written Errol Flynn's autobiography.[1] Earl told me fascinating details about Flynn, but it's not for me to pass these on. While I cuddled Evan on my lap Earl surprised me by making a prediction.

'When you are no longer side-tracked by looking after your family, you are going to write.' I did not take this seriously.

---

1 My father had met Errol Flynn while he was in Sydney looking for work during the Depression. Flynn was then unknown, a charming young Tasmanian who invited my dad for a nightcap on his ocean-going yacht. My father had never met anyone with better manners or who possessed such natural charm. They became friends and met frequently, but soon Flynn prepared to set to sail for New Guinea – before his creditors or admirers caught up with him. He tried to persuade my father to accompany him, but Dad declined as he was engaged to be married. They did, however, meet for a farewell dinner. After a riotous night, my father watched Errol sail away at sunrise to an uncertain future.

Friends had always said my letters should be published but I knew enough about writing to know what was needed and I could not see it happening.

'Nevertheless, Shirley Pearly, I agree with Earl,' said Greg. 'You will write when you find the right subject.'

News anchormen were a recent phenomenon in American television. The most talented were not chosen for their looks and the really good-looking ones were performers not journalists. Greg watched them avidly and it became obvious that this was a role made for him because of his talents, news background, appearance and photographic memory. Six months before his contract was up with the tourist commission, Greg's work was criticised. In articles he had written about skiing in Australia he stated that, though we have the same amount of snowfall as Switzerland, it is spread over a wider area. He had listed all the places suitable for skiing. He had also written a series of articles about Aboriginal culture and history, but he was informed that this would be rejected for publication – Aborigines did not exist and any future articles had to state that Australia had the same snowfall as Switzerland, full stop.

When he called to tell me, I was consoling. 'That's why the Australian directors employed you; they wanted your standard of writing. Tell them if they insist on editing out indisputable facts they cannot use your name.' He was immensely cheered and asked if I would really support him. 'Of course. Stuff like that won't do your reputation a bit of good.' I put down the phone and started packing. He was sacked by the end of the week.

Greg called Shonny to arrange for her to ask our tenants to vacate as soon as possible. She said they had left the house several weeks before without paying their rent. At our last get together with Errol Flynn's biographer, Earl Conrad, we discussed the possibility of an Australian rising through the ranks to the lofty

The Circle of Silence

heights of an anchorman in America. Earl asked how many subjects Greg had passed for his B.A., the lowest requirement for the journalism course at Columbia University.

'Complete your B.A., get some TV experience in Australia, do the course and you will be in like Flynn.' Before we sailed off into the sunset Greg applied for the course at Columbia.

We docked at the Port Melbourne wharf, and our friends were charmed by Evan's American accent and by the way he called me Mommy. He was given a toy and when he was asked if he knew what it was called, he replied in a perfect American accent. 'Oh sure, it's a battery-operated rocket.' He was just three years and six months old.

We were denied access to our house as our tenants had failed to advise us in writing when they vacated the premises, so technically they still held the lease. We were informed by their solicitor that Shonny had repeatedly ignored their requests for repairs. They owed us a considerable amount of unpaid rent but they claimed Shonny had ignored the water damage to their bedroom. There were three other bedrooms, so we were not impressed with their argument, and I had left Greg's work address with them, yet they had never contacted us.

Shonny resented being asked to explain how this calamity had happened. She flew into a rage whenever Greg tried to talk to her. When Greg asked her what had happened to the money we had left for this purpose, she breezily replied, 'Oh, this and that. Those tenants of yours caused me huge travelling expenses. What did you care, living the life of Riley in America?'

My friends Liz and Robin Archer came to our rescue. They were wonderful to us while we waited to gain legal access to our empty house. While we stayed with them Greg started work in the newsroom at Channel Seven. We called Evan in to watch his daddy's first broadcast. Moments after Greg began to speak he cried out in distress, 'How is Daddy going to get out of that little box?'

When we gained access to our house, the refrigerator had been disconnected after having been left filled with food. After removing the stinking, rotting mass the interior was so damaged we had to throw it away. All kinds of irreparable damage had been done to skirting boards and doors. Our neighbours told us they had gone down on their knees and given thanks to God when they heard we were coming home. Wild parties and terrible arguments had raged night after night after night. We took our tenants to court just for the rent and won. It was a very nasty experience. The magistrate made certain that they paid their court expenses there and then, but we were left in limbo. I was so naïve; I had no idea that the only legal course open to us was to garnishee their wages. They agreed to pay weekly so it would cost us as much as we received. That part of the legal system is a fraud – no wonder our tenants had looked so smug in court.

On the day we moved back home I found a poor skinny little grey cat shivering in the backyard. When Greg saw me feeding her he objected.

'We are not going to feed a menagerie,' he said, remembering my predilection for taking pity on various creatures. I gave the cat a noble name, Empress Theodora of Byzantium, and I forgot to mention to Greg that we were to be blessed with a royal litter, not at all the kind of thing that would have pleased the original empress, since she had started life as a prostitute. However, Theodora lived up to her opportunistic namesake for in the morning she caught a mouse in our kitchen in front of Greg.

'Oh, well,' he said, 'she can stay if she earns her keep.'

When the kittens were due I worried because I was being trained at the Blood Bank for night duty and I thought I might not be there when the kittens came. One night Theodora leapt onto our bed. She had never tried that before and she was very, very frightened. I reassured her that everything was normal for a situation of that kind; she settled down in the cradle of my arm purring her little heart out, much to Greg's annoyance.

The next day Greg had the day off, so I persuaded him to at least make sure she had enough water. He was not pleased. While he made exasperated noises offstage, I tucked her into her wicker box lined with a soft rug before I left for work. When I returned Greg was very excited. He had watched four kittens being born and was absolutely devoted to them. 'That one's mine,' he said, pointing to the kitten with black and orange stripes. We gave one away when they were weaned and kept the black and white one, and the one he called Tiger, as he supported the Richmond footy club.

When I started the night shift at the Blood Bank I almost killed Greg. This happened repeatedly when something I said made him laugh. Unfortunately it always seemed to happen when he was drinking something. I rode my bike to work because it was faster than public transport, especially in the mornings when I had to get back to Albert Park to collect Evan from the babysitter and take him to school. Greg had covered a large square torch with red cellophane and sewed it onto an elastic strap to wear on my back as he believed I was more likely to be hit from behind than head-on. I had grown my hair long in America and I did not realise it flowed over the light until I paused at the intersection of Swanston and Flinders streets. A man waiting for a tram called out, 'Hey lady, your hair is on fire.' When I told Greg this he laughed so hard he inhaled a large amount of cocoa.

We settled down to a strange routine. As I returned from taking Evan to school, Greg would be leaving for university. I was supposed to sleep until I collected Evan, but of course it was not always possible. I started work at 8 p.m., after cooking for Evan and delivering him to the babysitter. It was a gruelling routine, but we needed the money for house repairs and we had agreed to return to America so Greg could study at Columbia.

Greg helped write the six o'clock news and did stand-up reports. Especially brilliant at thinking on his feet, his photographic memory was his greatest asset. In a very short time he wrote and presented the eleven o'clock news and produced, wrote and anchored a regular weekly political discussion program called *This Week*. His political acumen was considered remarkable by John Maher, who sent him out on dangerous assignments, such as reporting bushfires and complex accidents. Maher said Greg was reliable and did not take silly chances – he didn't have the gung-ho attitude that made so many reporters a danger to themselves.[2]

Greg's ideals and work practices were too ambitious for some of his fellow workers: he always arrived for work half an hour early and never left until everything was done. Some preferred to get the work done as fast as possible then leg it down to the pub. They dismissed him as an eager beaver.

Can you imagine how this gorgeous, ambitious, hard-working man annoyed them? He was very fond of John Maher and he put a lot of affection into that relationship as he had with Corbett Shaw, the news editor at 3AW. They took the place of his father. Greg liked his workmates and admired Brian Naylor because he was astute and always did his homework. John Maher was anti-intellectual. He despised academics and gave Greg a hard time over his studies. Greg was forced to take his holidays in order to sit his exams and John had issued a warning: if he refused an assignment in order to sit for an exam,

---

2 Greg had always admired Ed Murrow, the anchorman in the 1950s of CBS's *See it Now* program. I had admired Fred Friendly, Murrow's producer. Together they had exposed Senator Joseph McCarthy's witch hunts against perceived communists in America. In doing so they risked their liberty.

he would be dismissed. If Maher called on an exam day I told him that Greg had already left for Melbourne University – they were the good old days before mobile phones.

Though I was permanently tired, I was very happy. Greg was moving towards the realisation of his dream. He had more confidence, purpose and a dignity which was new to him. We had an agreement. I would do everything to help us return to America and he would help me go to Iran when he was established. I had been reading about Iran for many years and since researching weaving in Frank Lloyd Wright's San Rafael library, I wanted to study nomadic flat weaving. I had always had an interest in textiles but it expanded when I took possession of my Darling Street apartment long before I met Greg. I had bought a four-shaft loom and taken lessons with a member of the Handweaver's and Spinner's Guild of Victoria. That of course led to the purchase of a spinning wheel and coupled with my research in San Rafael, I began giving private lessons in both San Rafael and Melbourne.

In 1974 I was asked by the producer of a Channel Seven children's television program if I could appear on camera using a spinning wheel. After completing the segment he asked if there was anything else I could do. I told him there were many ways of spinning: drop spindle and the Indian charkha, for instance. 'I know a man who spins on a pencil. You can knit raw wool without bothering to spin it.'

'Anything else?' he asked, somewhat surprised. I explained that there are hundreds of ways to weave. Every country in the history of the world developed unique textiles and embroideries. The inkle loom makes wonderful ribbons and the four-shaft loom weaves just about anything.

'Anything else?' There was American Indian beadwork and knitting, knotting, netting. He then offered me a regular segment on *This Week Has Seven Days*, and made it attractive by agreeing to pay me $100 for every four programs, which we would film on one morning. It was a very good career move, as the program was broadcast to fifty-five stations around Australia. It was not long before I was better known than Greg in some quarters.

The policy was to film straight through without rehearsal. There was no allowance for mistakes and no opportunity to edit, unless I filmed away from the studio. In that case I had to cut the film. My little segment was successful because I demystified the art of craft and I publicised craft events around Australia. It led to so many offers of teaching assignments and weekend workshops that I had been able to leave the Blood Bank.

I loved looking after Evan full-time and teaching was satisfying. I was only sorry that, though I was constantly invited to teach the teachers, the education department refused to allow me to teach their students. When I investigated the possibility of studying to gain the qualifications, I was told by several craft teachers that they couldn't possibly have me in their class – they used my program for their own teaching inspiration. I was offered regular work at Prahran College of Advanced Education, and I began to conduct weekend workshops in country Victoria, The National Gallery and I held private classes using our front room (the former shop) as a studio.

I had loved living in San Francisco and looked forward to New York, but a year before Greg was due to sit his final exam I began to take a realistic view of the difficulties. I would not be allowed to work in America and a year without income would place huge pressures on him. We had already learned what a disaster renting our house could be. Even though Greg had made very good contacts in America and he was selling freelance articles to American magazines, the money he earned would not be enough to support us. When we decided to return to America I had suggested we should sell our house, but he could not stand the thought of losing it, nor could I. I suggested to Greg that I was prepared to stay in Melbourne. I could manage the house payments and earn enough to support Evan for a year. That would leave Greg free to concentrate on studying. He was amazed I would do that for him, but he was not keen on the idea.

'I'm not either,' I said. 'But the time will fly. Remember how wonderful it was when we met again in San Francisco?' We would not have to worry about Evan's safety either. This hit home for Greg, as having witnessed some nasty incidents on his travels in America, he was already concerned for our safety, to the extent that he had decided to learn to shoot.

Leading up to Greg's impending departure, our lives chugged along happily except for the pressures endured by any family where both parents work. The only time we had arguments was when I had worked the night shift at the Blood Bank and we had to leave messages for each other. Now we slid seamlessly into an acceptance that Greg was going to America without me and Evan. I spoke regularly to Shonny and was relieved that she showed minimal interest in us. That is, until the day she accused me of having an affair.

'With whom,' I said, laughing. I had made a djellaba for a male friend of Professor Henry Schoenheimer, Greg's uncle, and that's what prompted her accusation.

'He told Henry you are gorgeous.' Touched by her concern, I assured her she was wrong.

'It was an open invitation,' she said.

'Which I ignored.'

Every time we spoke she repeated her suspicions. I found this endearing, as I knew she was worried about Greg. An affair is dangerous because you cannot know how your lover will behave – he might be jealous and do something stupid that could ruin your marriage. I knew this had happened to her.

I realise now that there were plenty of warnings of the disaster about to engulf me. For example, we were having a rare lunch together and discussing the necessity of Greg having an operation on his nose. An old football injury caused him difficulty in breathing, which did not help his asthma. He didn't like the shape of his nose, which I thought was fine but, as he was about to endure an operation, he wanted to know if I would mind if he spent some of our budget to change the shape as well as the internal structure.

I made a joke about it, which as usual caused him to spit his beer as he burst out laughing. Inevitably, some liquid shot up his nose, causing him to choke and splutter. When he was able to speak he looked at me in surprise and said with wonder in his voice, 'That was very funny, Shirl.'

Even as I responded, I failed to understand the seriousness of what I was saying. 'This is terrible,' I said. 'If I had made that joke when we first got together, you would have taken it for granted. You're reacting as if you don't know me.'

His face drained of colour. He spoke in glowing terms about how grateful he was for all my support and hard work. A moment of quiet reflection passed. 'Marriage is not equitable for women,' he said, 'but I will see to it that you will have a gold-plated wheelchair, Shirl.'

My reply got him laughing and choking again. 'You can keep your wheelchair. I want a lapis lazuli bath and a Maserati with a gorgeous chauffeur.'

Greg was also becoming obsessive about certain things. Though his appetite for different food had improved vastly in America, he announced that he was now going to become a vegetarian. This had nothing to do with animal liberation: it was to establish the cheapest possible method to sustain himself during the year at Columbia. Because I did not want to cook one meal for Greg and another for us I began an enthusiastic study of vegetarianism.

About six months before he was due to leave for New York, Greg told me he had been having affairs. I remember

The Circle of Silence

every sound, every word and every feeling sweeping over me as I tried to take it in. I had been reading in bed. I stared stupidly as he removed his socks and put on his pyjamas as if it was a normal day. I knew exactly what he had said; I just couldn't believe it. He stooped to pick up his clothes and then gave me a puzzled glance. I must have looked as stunned as I felt because he suddenly looked guilty. 'I ... I'm sorry.'

If I had been standing I would have slumped to the floor. 'You said "affairs".'

He had received phone calls while he was on duty at night from women who said they had champagne on ice and were wearing a black nightgown. He found it impossible to resist. He was running several of these women at once and was concerned that one of them might phone me. He seemed completely unaware of the gravity of the situation. I could scarcely think let alone be logical.

'It sounds as if you've only told me *because* they might call.'

He actually sounded annoyed. 'I'm trying to protect you!'

I felt like a cork bobbing on an ocean and the distance between us widened. I was disgusted, but at the same time I did not want to be moralistic. The source of Shonny's suspicions hit me with a radiating force. 'Shonny knows, doesn't she?'

The guilt in his eyes shocked me almost as much as the confession.

'Did she tell you I was having an affair?' He nodded. 'And you believed her, you idiot.'

No one at university knew he was married. He tried to explain how a girl would come up to him, place her hand on his crotch and say, 'I want you'. I actually laughed at this.

'Well of course any man would find that irresistible,' I said, 'but don't go thinking it's an excuse.' One of these girls told him that her life stopped when he was away from her; when he returned she came alive again.

'I know it's ridiculous,' he said, 'but I get caught up in it.' Two of these girls were planning to follow him to America.

'Oh well, that settles it. I'm definitely not coming with you,' I declared.

I made a lot of mistakes. For one thing this had happened before. Soon after our return from America Greg told me he had been having an affair with one of my friends. I was furious with them but forgave him as long as we had nothing more to do with her. It was a wrenching loss for me because I really liked her and I worried about her little boy who was the same age as Evan. His father had a terrible temper, which he took out on the child. I could not understand how I had forgotten this former fall from grace, or that I had blamed my friend and forgiven my husband.

As weeks went by I realised we were lying to our friends by omission. We weren't admitting we were breaking up. Denial again. Greg believed he would overcome what he called his weakness and then there would be no need to tell anyone. I even defended him against Shonny's unreasonable criticisms. Months flew by while we wrestled with our feelings. In the end I insisted on consulting divorce lawyers.

I told my lawyer I did not want support from Greg until he either returned to Australia or was fully employed overseas. I wanted him to be free to study full time. I wanted the house and I would sign any document agreeing that if he returned to Australia, he could borrow on it to get a place of his own. My lawyer was horrified. She said I should stop him from leaving the country and force him to accept his responsibilities.

His lawyer said I was lying. I would get the house anyway and then sue for support. Once you seek advice from lawyers, there is a good chance you will end up being nasty to each other. We had been doing well on our own, so we agreed to pay our respective legal fees and drop the idea of a divorce. Greg tried to make me promise to join him in America. He would send for us as soon as he landed a job. I was horror struck.

'And what will you do with the two ladies who are pursuing you to New York?'

His reply left me speechless. 'I'm not clairvoyant.'

He was worried about money. He came up with a crazy idea that he was going to live in a van in New York to avoid the expense of renting; he was determined to put up with any discomfort in order to succeed. I thought he would be swamped with offers to share an apartment. He was really unhappy as he anticipated complications with the women in his life. I suggested he should try living in a van in Melbourne so he could find out how horrible it would be.

A few days later he arrived home with a van and he packed up a few belongings. I suggested he should visit Evan at every opportunity and continue to use our laundry and bathroom facilities as he needed. That meant we saw him often as a result and it was not long before he admitted that I was right, that living in a van, especially in New York in winter, would be dangerous and nasty. It was time he left home anyway as staying with us was tantamount to lying. We agreed to tell Evan together, but it didn't work out that way. Evan came downstairs one morning and asked if Daddy was at another all-night party. I knew nothing about this cover story and it was clear to me that the child did not believe it. I decided to tell him the truth. We sat together in our beanbag where we spent a lot of quiet times together. I stressed that we wanted to stay friends and that Greg loved Evan just as much as ever. His response surprised me.

'I'll be the same as everyone else now.' Apparently live-in dads were a rarity in his class. His dear little face broke into a smile as he hurried off to school to tell everyone the news.

Greg was understandably furious until I asked him to put himself in my place if I had been at an all-night party. He was deeply ashamed. This was one of his most admirable qualities; it takes a lot of courage to admit to one's faults.

Soon after he left, Shonny called me. She was furious and blamed me for kicking him out. She had been covering for him and resented this bitterly. If he was out with one of his partners and another wanted to talk to him she had to lie. 'I don't remember half the time what I have said to them,' she complained. 'I'm scared I'll trip myself up.'

No matter how I defended myself, she maintained that I was the guilty party who had broken up the marriage by refusing to tough it out in New York. Now I had thrown him out so he would be forced to live in a van. From then on her resentment surrounded me like acrid smoke – if we had been living in the fifteenth century she would have accused me of being a witch.

Our separation was the most difficult thing we had ever done. We agreed that there must be no arguments and no hint of anger or nastiness to distress Evan.

One of Greg's favourite staples was a custard I had invented based on polenta made with milk and served with fruit. He would sit on the edge of his seat while I made it. When it transpired that he was trying to live on raw vegetables, I told him he was being too fanatical.

'I can do without criticism. I'm getting enough from Shonny.' Once he had eaten the polenta he calmed down. 'I don't understand what's happening to me,' he said. 'I'm determined to succeed in America even if it means losing you and Evan.' His eyes filled with tears. I felt he needed to consult a psychologist, and although I most certainly did not excuse his behaviour, there is a kinder way to explain it.

Inventors are traditionally obsessive, so are scientists and musicians. In fact artists and scholars often need to be single-minded in order to succeed. Who would criticise Marie Curie or Henry Ford?

'You've grown up with a supremely obsessive mother,' I said. 'But you're smarter than her and kinder. You are right, I do understand you. When it comes to us getting back together the Flynn Syndrome makes it unlikely. I don't believe you will ever overcome your problem with sex.'

I had taken over the house payments, was cleaning a couple of houses as well as teaching and doing the TV show, and I had already contributed towards the huge fees for Columbia. I was furious because I suddenly understood why he was so broke. He must have been spending money on those bloody women.

'I have done everything I can for you,' I said nastily. 'Would you like me to find you a couple of houses to clean?'

After a long silence he said, 'Please, Shirley, don't do this. You've got to promise you'll never divorce me. I'll get control once I succeed. Please promise you'll give me another chance as soon as I can support you.'

'I won't promise any such thing,' I said. 'I have no desire to marry again, so you don't have to worry about a divorce. If marriage with someone as kind as you used to be hasn't worked, nothing will.' My anger had nothing to do with any of that; I had seen that he wanted to use me as a shield in order to indulge himself. 'How do you suppose we would live together? As brother and sister? I've got a brother, thank you, and I'm not going to be your mum.' I told him to bugger off and stop doing a Shonny. It was time for him to deal with reality and make an effort to understand me.

By the time we met again I had calmed down. I remembered all the lovely things, like when we were first married and how I used to consult him before buying anything. He always said, 'Do whatever you want. Buy what you want to buy. As long as you are happy, I will be happy.'

We planned how to keep in touch. I had agreed for Evan to

have lunch with the two main women in Greg's life (on separate occasions, of course, as they each still thought they were the only one). Evan pinched them cruelly.

'Dad's already beginning to let me down,' he said upon his return from the first unfortunate occasion. I felt terrible; I should have known that our perceptive little boy would object to being lumped in with strangers.

Greg asked why I did not believe he would get control of his failure to resist the ladies, as he put it. My answer went along these lines: 'You are irresistible. You will always be irresistible especially in another country where you will have the added attraction of being different. At eighteen you were too pretty; at twenty-seven you look wonderful. By the time you are sixty you will be better still.'

By then I understood my own mistakes. By working nights at the Blood Bank I had freed him to live the life of a bachelor. He had few responsibilities towards Evan and his schedule was taken up by study, attendance at university and working full time at Channel Seven. I had thought our relationship was strong, but I failed to take into account the effect on him of his media image and his childhood.

Greg's trouble was that he *loved* women in the same obsessive manner that he loved his mother. The other problem was that women loved him. Exposure on television had changed him. When a male attempts to denigrate him I point out that they would give anything to be idolised and pursued by hoards of beautiful women. He was the incarnation of Shonny's thwarted ambitions. Imagine living with that lively, beautiful, insanity all his life? It's a wonder he was so grounded and I submit it as a testament to his intelligence, kindness and strength of purpose. I'm not out to eulogise him, I want to portray him accurately – warts and all.

FIVE

On 11 August 1975, just thirteen days before his twenty-eighth birthday, news of a terrible civil war in Portuguese Timor was widely broadcast. Greg volunteered to go to report on the situation. If the aggressor was Indonesia it could mean that an expansionist military dictatorship was moving closer to our shores. Though Greg did not expect an invasion of Australia, the historical facts were undeniable.

The island of Timor is narrow; volcanic eruptions forced huge jagged ridges to rise up in the central highlands like the spine of a mammoth. Besides Portuguese, Hakka (a Chinese speech) and thirteen indigenous languages, plus many dialects, are spoken. The lingua franca is *Tetuñ* (pronounced *Tetu*, the final nasal vowel is swallowed).

The country is a fascinating ethnological puzzle which had regional princedoms and regional kings called *liurais*. The *liurai* was responsible to a district administrator who operated through a lesser official called the *chefe de suco*. Under the Portuguese colonial system the people wore exquisite hand-woven sarongs called *t'ais* or, in the case of the males, a *leipa*. People lived in small hamlets and were skilled hunters, especially with the bow and arrow. Their flora and fauna were unique.

Even though Portugal had colonised the country in the sixteenth century, they interfered only marginally in the lives of the East Timorese. Though treatment of perceived wrongdoers was harsh, the same rules were applied to all. Offending officials were demoted and returned to Portugal in disgrace. In short, the Portuguese generally respected Timorese customs and culture.

Portuguese married into Timorese society. They had outlawed slavery, the *criado* system, which for political reasons is still described as slavery today, but it did prevent the poor from becoming destitute. Although a male *criado* or female *criada* served the master or mistress for life, they were not indentured for money. Depending on the head of the household, *criado* children attended school, ate with the family and were able to marry into that family, though they had to earn their keep. In order to climb the social ladder people had to speak fluent Portuguese and convert to Catholicism. Despite this, animism persisted in Timorese society, and the rich pattern of tribal life and art was unique. Their unwritten literature is likened to the Norse sagas.

During World War II the island of Timor was considered the gateway to Australia. After the war, Portugal returned to claim their Timorese colonial outpost. Having been decimated by what the Timorese called the Australian war with Japan, the East Timorese, although they desired independence, were unable to resist Portuguese military authorities. Twenty-nine years later, in April 1974, the Carnation Revolution was launched in Portugal and the dictator Marcelo Caetano was deposed and banished. All the Portuguese colonies began to plan for self-determination.

In Portuguese Timor three political parties formed: *União Democrática Timorense* (Timorese Democratic Union or

UDT), largely made up of conservatives who had prospered under Portuguese rule; *Associação Popular Democrática Timorense* (or Apodeti), originally called the Association for the Integration of Timor into Indonesia, but because of adverse public reaction, it was swiftly renamed the Timorese Popular Democratic Association; and *Frente Revolucionária de Timor-Leste Independente* (Revolutionary Front of Independent East Timor or Fretilin), the political party with the majority of supporters. The differences between the political parties were minor until a covert Indonesian military organisation, Operasi Komodo (named after the Komodo dragon), was established to destabilise Portuguese Timor. Strategies employed by the organisation included transmissions from a propaganda radio station into East and West Timor; hit and run attacks against the shared border designed to convince the western Timorese that their eastern brothers were a threat and vice versa; and Indonesian spies infiltrating businesses in Dili and presenting gifts with 'no strings attached' to *liurais* and individual church leaders to convince them of President Suharto's goodwill.

Fretilin's stated aims, meanwhile, were based on the universal doctrines of socialism and democracy, including the right to independence with a program of progressive autonomy to be overseen by the Portuguese. Fretilin leaders told Australian officials on a fact-finding mission they 'would need a lengthy timeframe of about eight to ten years in order to establish an efficient political and economic infrastructure'.

Propaganda painted the Fretilin political party as a front for communism. Even today certain Australian bureaucrats, politicians and members of the Australian military assert that the Timorese were either communists or were about to become communists. Remarks by Indonesian Generals Ali Murtopo and Yoga Sugama to US ambassador David Newsom would eventually be revealed as a strategy of disinformation carefully designed to smooth the way for an invasion. The Portuguese half of the island of Timor was rife with rumours; people lived in dread, not knowing who to trust. Some Timorese believed that the Indonesian government intended to improve their lives; the majority favoured home rule.

The lead-up to what was originally called a civil war remains as poorly understood today as it was in 1975. Some experts bet a bob each way by referring to a civil war and the UDT Coup in the same breath. I intend to call proceedings in Dili what they were – a coup. The term 'civil war' was used to provide justification for the Indonesian invasion.

On 11 August 1975, the UDT political party seized control of the airport and the radio station in the capital, Dili, they arrested the police chief and seized the water purification plant and the Marconi Communications Centre, then arrested the leaders of the Fretilin political party. Portuguese officials, believing BAKIN (Indonesian intelligence agency) propaganda that Fretilin was planning to overthrow the Portuguese government, began to quit the country. UDT officials were said to be plotting to arrest their own leaders. Senior members of UDT were believed to be in Indonesian-controlled Western Timor, conspiring with Javanese generals. The Portuguese governor called an emergency meeting and issued instructions to all Portuguese officials and Portuguese military to stand aloof from both UDT, and Fretilin. Some Portuguese military officers were suspected of secretly supporting UDT and at one time a small contingent from the Portuguese garrison marched from Baucau to take control of Dili.

On 5 September 1975, in the eastern part of East Timor two youths – one of them Abel Guterres – went to see an

The Circle of Silence

Australian Hercules aircraft at Baucau airport, where they encountered a drama. Upon being told by the pilot that he was under orders not to bring Timorese to Australia, the airport manager Antonio da Silva ordered his ground staff to block off the runway. He then raced to his office and collected a hand grenade. The situation was tense because two Indonesian warships patrolled the coast day and night. In an inspired move da Silva re-entered the aircraft and announced that if the pilot refused to save Timorese lives he would blow up the plane. The pilot agreed to do as he was told and Abel Guterres seized the opportunity. It was not an easy decision; there was no time to farewell his mother, his family or his friends. His decision, as will be revealed, almost certainly saved Gutterres's life and we who worked with him in the diaspora could not have managed without him.

Confusion was as widespread as it is in any country undergoing bewildering threats and changes. Loss of confidence and suspicion was skilfully manipulated to appear as if the country was on the edge of a civil war and Fretilin was cast as the guilty party.

The ticker-tape machine at Channel Seven churned out disturbing reports. Greg began to research the situation — for example, he interviewed Cliff Morris, a member of Australian 2/4th Independent Company who had fought in Timor in World War II and praised the Timorese for their decency, kindness and loyalty. But Greg's boss, John Maher, wasn't remotely interested in Australia's closest neighbour. Channel Nine not only sent a cameraman but Kerry Packer and Gerald Stone, Chief of staff of Channel Nine news, went with him. At the time and afterwards, Packer steadfastly refused to discuss the reason for his involvement. As they waited in a foxhole

Stone reported on TV that there was no fighting apart from the odd shot.

Eleven days after the UDT tried to seize control, the fighting arm of Fretilin, known by the acronym Falintil, rallied, put down the attempted coup and restored the peace. At Channel Seven, John Maher began to take an interest in East Timor.

Greg had to pass his last subject for his B.A. and he wanted to be in New York by the end of the year. He had made a lot of important contacts in America and intended to take up every opportunity to publish articles while studying there. He was already reading the books for his first term at Columbia. But he could not resist the opportunity to go to East Timor, especially as reports of hit-and-run attacks on the border continued.

Maher's wanted journalists to send was his senior reporter, David Johnson. Greg made copious notes in order to brief David, but when David was unable to take the mission, Maher offered the assignment to Greg.

I knew Tony Stewart, sound recordist, and Gary Cunningham, cameraman, very well, as Greg had worked on many assignments with them. After completing any particularly trying assignment Greg always brought them home for supper. I kept a supply of salami and cheese, or soup in winter – their favourite was pea and ham – for such occasions. I always got up to make the coffee but I was usually too tired to stay up long, so I only ever heard about their adventures when we lunched together at a Port Melbourne pub called The Flower, or at the Station Hotel in South Melbourne.

I was impressed with their plans for Timor. They hoped to gain access to a cross section of the population in order to represent all sides equally. Although it was their primary job to try to expose the culprits, they knew they would be very lucky to achieve that in the short time they were given. They felt John Maher's allocation of three days was not long enough, but before their departure Greg did gain permission to stay longer if they were getting good footage.

If Indonesia was responsible for the hit-and-run attacks along the border, Greg did not expect to be deliberately harmed because of Prime Minister Whitlam's greatly lauded friendship with the Indonesian president. If one of the newly formed Timorese political parties was responsible, they might end up in gaol, but it was difficult to imagine being harmed by the Timorese, who had given their lives for the Australian cause in World War II. The numbers of Timorese murdered by Japanese was estimated to have been forty to fifty thousand, some say eighty thousand.

I did not want Greg to go. Though his exam was several weeks away anything could happen to delay his return. If he missed the exam he would have to wait another year to attend Columbia University. I was also nervous because John Maher had made it perfectly clear that to return without a full report would be unacceptable. The team knew they could rely on each other to stay out of harm's way. Although Greg was the leader they had minds of their own and did not hesitate to express their opinions. They all agreed no story was worth dying for. However, depending on who was staging the attacks on the border, they might get to break the biggest news report of their lives.

I remember Greg demanding, 'Don't tell me after all these years you think we will take chances?'

'It's got nothing to do with that, Greg. If you did, Tony and Gary would give you a thick ear, I know that. You're supposed to be going to America – and as they say in the home-of-the-brave: keep your eye on the doughnut and not on the hole.'

Greg responded angrily. 'Even the feared North Vietnamese did not harm cameramen or journos covering their invasion of South Vietnam.'

Tony, the youngest of the group, made a tired old joke journalists use to belittle each other's ambitions: 'Which award will we deign to accept?' Huffing on his fingernails as he polished them on his lapel, he got the bollocking he expected.

As I sipped my wine, I thought how lucky Greg was to have such a dedicated crew. Gary, who had a prodigious appetite for life, love, food and alcohol, said something funny about double Dutch, a play on words, and we all laughed. I wonder now if other family members behaved as I did at that moment: when the die is cast you enter into false gaiety. There is nothing you can do and so you try not to spoil the expectation that everything will turn out well. The team were told the government would get them out if anything went wrong.

As we arrived back at the house Greg stopped to take in the beauty of our little neck of the woods. He turned in a circle, his arms outstretched. As he took in the vista he whispered, 'Evan's school, the park, look at the sun on the trees, Shirl.' A tremor flicked up and down my spine as I saw his outstretched arms cast the shadow of a cross on the footpath. I told myself not to be dramatic as we walked inside to make coffee. We then sat in the back garden and I confessed to him that I had contributed to our break-up. I had been in denial; there were plenty of signs, I just didn't want to see them. We stared at each other sadly.

'Perhaps we should have sold the house and gone back to the States together,' I said. 'You were in your element in America.'

'Would you sell up now?'

Birds twittered in the lemon-scented gum we had planted together. I did not think I could ever trust him to remain faithful and I would never allow myself to be dependent on anyone again, for Evan's sake as much as mine. I shrugged. 'Who knows what will happen. When you complete your studies and get a good job, if you can afford to pay our fares, I will bring Evan to see you. If you take your holidays I will leave him with you and go to South America by bus. But he won't be coming to live with you until he is at least seventeen, no matter how successful you are.'

At this time of his life he was very happy. His health had never been better and, though he did not boast, he just loved being the object of desire. I did not blame him for that. He was at the pinnacle of his powers. His legendary photographic memory gave him a very useful advantage and his news reports were insightful and interesting. I reassured myself that by Christmas he would be in the Big Apple. He mentioned the black sheepskin coat I had given to him for our original stay in America and he thanked me for it again.

'I should think so,' I said, 'it makes you look like a Persian prince.'

We talked then about the dark side of the East Timor assignment, how their reports might be muzzled.

'We could end up in gaol,' he said. 'Can you imagine conditions in a third-world prison? I could die without medication. Don't leave me there, Shirl. Do everything. Sell the house. Get me out.' He then handed me the tiepin I had given him when he left for San Francisco. 'Take care of it. It's very precious to me.' He also said he could not be married to anyone else. 'You think like a man.'

'Depending on the man,' I said, laughing derisively. 'If I'm like Sir John Monash or Fred Friendly, I would be honoured, but this could be the most disgusting insult you could say to any woman.' He burst out laughing and was almost asphyxiated when his coffee shot up his nose.

Some memories stay with us forever. I will never forget Greg's last visit. He was quietly confident that the visit to Portuguese Timor would be successful. He wore new navy blue baggy trousers and his old safari jacket. I joked that the trousers suited him better than the ridiculously tight jeans and very short shorts he favoured. He explained to Evan that there was nothing to worry about; it was not a long assignment. He would only be gone for three days unless he was getting really good information. He told me he was troubled by Shonny. She had been demanding to be interviewed on any and every subject on Melbourne radio stations. She thought she had special rights because her son was a 'TV personality'. Greg had been warned about this, which was embarrassing in itself, but he had to ask her to stop and this had initiated several very nasty scenes. On the eve of taking on what could be the biggest news report in the Pacific since World War II, her anger was the last thing he needed. But he still loved her unconditionally.

'You're going to have a cot-case on your hands when Shonny dies,' he said. 'I won't be able to cope.'

We sat in the sun watching Evan pouring pretend tea for the Empress Theodora in a cup from his china tea set. I poured a little of Greg's coffee into the toy teapot and filled it with milk. The father and his adored son sipped their coffee together. I wondered if Greg's love for his mother was based on the fear that she would desert him when he was a child, and now he was about to leave his own son. I said, 'He'll be here when you get back.'

Greg had tears in his eyes.

'What happened to your idea that you would die young?' I asked.

'I've been meaning to talk to you about that,' he said. 'I've decided I was wrong about the time and right about the fact.'

* * *

The Circle of Silence

My last conversation with Greg took place before he left for the airport. He called to tell me about his will. 'If anything bad happens, you are my legal next-of-kin. The insurance is huge. It costs a thousand dollars a day for each of us. That's nine thousand dollars for three days.' I interrupted to tell him I did not want to discuss money but he was buoyed. 'I've never felt better in my life,' he said. 'After this assignment there is only one subject to go and I will be on my way to America.'

I tried to think of something fresh to say, but I could only think of tired old clichés. Silence was the last thing I wanted. While I dithered he continued. 'I want to thank you for your support.' I felt sad because we were slightly self-conscious. The last words I ever said to him were, 'Good luck, Greg. We'll be thinking of you.'

Later I walked Evan to school. The Empress followed us. We had always been charmed and mystified by the cat's behaviour. Was she guarding Evan? I reminded him how his dad had been opposed to cats or any pets, until he saw Tiger being born. 'He's a real softie at heart,' I said. We smiled fondly at each other and imagined Daddy flying over the ocean and landing in a tropical island. It was 10 October.

The phone was ringing when I arrived back home. It was Shonny. She'd had a premonition that Greg was in danger.

'Of course,' I said. 'Worrying is what mothers are for.' She wanted me to call John Maher and demand that he bring Greg home. I tried to end our discussion as gently as possible. There was no way I was going to interfere.

'Greg doesn't take chances,' I said. 'Remember John Maher told us he was sending him because of his good news reporting record. Can you imagine the future? He's so lucky to know what he wants, and if anyone can succeed in America he can. He's a different person there, Shonny. Try to be glad for him.'

When he did not return as planned because he was getting such good information, I called to warn her. She was more certain than ever that disaster was waiting to strike. I did share her dread, but I tried to be reassuring. 'He won't take any chances,' I reminded her.

SIX

I came downstairs early in the morning to make coffee. I'd caught the flu and had slept badly. As I switched on the radio I took my temperature – 101 degrees Fahrenheit. No wonder I'd had nightmares! The ABC played one of our favourite songs – 'Our Love Is Here to Stay' by the Gershwin brothers.

> *The more I read the papers*
> *The less I comprehend*
> *The world and all its capers*
> *And how it all will end.*
> *Nothing seems to be lasting.*
> *But that isn't our affair;*
> *We've got something permanent,*
> *I mean in the way we care.*

The announcer was summing up the news items in a breakfast-bright voice. He mentioned missing journalists.

Missing. What terrifying images that word conjured. The black-edged dead and missing columns on the front pages of

Adelaide's *Advertiser* from the war reappeared to haunt me with sad memories of my cousins and the lads from our district; their mothers' anguish over those long-dead victims welled in my chest threatening to choke me. I walked to the phone ... it seemed to take ages. My hands shook as I looked up the number. My call went straight through to the ABC newsroom. The man who had just made the announcement refused to tell me what I wanted to know: 'Who is missing?' He was annoyed to the point of rudeness and ticked me off for wasting his time.

'I only want you to tell me what you've already broadcast,' I said. 'My husband might be one of the missing journalists.'

'In that case you would have been notified by the Department of Foreign Affairs.'

'I haven't heard from them. For pity's sake, you've already broadcast it.'

He clicked his tongue, sighed and repeated the assertion that I was wasting his time. He sounded frightened rather than angry.

'Please tell me at least if the missing men are from Channel Seven.'

'So call Channel Seven.'

I told him the newsroom there would be closed; John Maher did not start work until eleven. It was just after 7 a.m. The wait would be torture. As an answer to that he hung up. I realised he had already told me what I wanted to know. My husband was missing and that horrible bastard did not have the courage to tell me.

I replaced the receiver and went back to the kitchen to wait for a telephone call from the Australian Department of Foreign Affairs. That call never came. I remember walking outside to look at the garden; memories that normally beguiled me now had the power to hurt. I went back inside. On that cold October morning I poured a glass of Greg's whisky and drank it neat. I felt Greg was already dead. I told myself to stop being dramatic, but then I heard the voice of the ABC man who had refused to help me. He was reading the news again. Five newsmen were missing in Portuguese Timor. Five?

A second team from Channel Nine – reporter Malcolm Rennie and cameraman Brian Peters – had arrived in Balibó, but at the time I wasn't aware of this. I wondered briefly about the condition of the roads. Could there have been a car accident? Greg's last words to me repeated in my mind. *Get me out*.

The door to Evan's bedroom opened. He bounded down the stairs, skipped across the living room and threw his arms around me. 'Hi, Mum, I'm hungry.'

In his book *Butir-Butir Budaya Jawa* (*Items of Javanese Culture*), the self-elected president for life, General Suharto, stated, 'There are five categories of lies which are not punishable. First, those you tell in a social gathering; second, those you tell your bride on your wedding day; third, those you tell to protect your wealth; fourth, those necessary to protect your life; and fifth, those you need to protect your family.'

I did not want to lie to Evan. But what could I say? He was only eight years old. Why frighten him? On the other hand it would be cruel not to prepare him, especially since my feeling persisted that Greg was already dead.

I tried to explain the situation without crying, and then added, 'Daddy is probably hiding. He cannot call us as the telephone box is on the other side of the road and he cannot risk being seen.' My heart seemed to break in two as the expression in Evan's eyes showed his trust in me. I told myself Greg would approve of this lie – 'Why meet trouble head on?' he used to say. I walked Evan to school accompanied by the Empress.

I had decided against calling Shonny. Why worry her? Later that morning she told me she had also heard the early news and did not call me for the same reason.

I had heard General Suharto denying any plans to invade East Timor, so there was some comfort in that. Greg's words circled in my head: if he was arrested and held without medication he would be unlikely to survive an asthma attack. 'Imagine conditions in a third-world prison? If I'm arrested do everything to get me out. Sell the house. Don't leave me there.' Those words revealed the tensions and dynamics in our relationship. They were comforting then and have comforted me ever since. Our separation had not shaken his trust in me.

In the three and a half decades to come I would learn some very bitter truths. If you want to establish what really happened in the past, you should return to the original reports before politicians, diplomats and public relations experts use weasel words to describe something that is likely to affect trade – especially if the trade deals are with a country that is implicated in murder, an atrocity, a full-scale massacre or genocide.

Back then I was too shocked to cry, my mind filled with memories of a very energetic and alive Greg. Tears don't help, anyway. They leave you more exhausted than before. Grandpa Venn used to tell me if you looked up your tears would go away. I would do a lot of looking up over the years to come.

In the days that followed I felt as if my face was set in a grin like an orange slice. Even thinking Greg might be dead made me feel disloyal. He couldn't be dead. At the back of my mind his voice repeated, 'Don't leave me there, Shirl.' I called John Maher several times and left messages asking for details of the other missing men's relatives. Someone rang back and said John was frantic with worry. I must wait until the situation cleared. I got the feeling that I was expected to stay out of what the voice on the other end of the telephone called 'this muddle'.

'It may be a muddle to you,' I replied, 'but it's a nightmare to us, especially to Greg's mother. Can you imagine her suffering?'

His tone of voice reminded me of our schoolmaster when he ticked off a recalcitrant pupil. He alleged that the families' contact phone numbers were private. 'I am not sure we are at liberty to divulge them.'

'Well, I am asking you to personally see that they receive my phone number with a message that I would like to meet with them, as they might want to show a united front.' Silly me, that was never going to happen.

Reports varied. Some said the men had been murdered by Indonesian troops dressed in civilian clothes. Others said they had been killed in crossfire. One claimed that the body of a white man had been found some distance from the house the journalists had slept in. I began to receive calls from concerned neighbours and strangers, but nothing from Maher or the Australian government. Some kind people wanted to bring me groceries but I had not learned then that the griever has a duty to accept charity.

I listened as Greg's fans expressed their grief: 'Greg came into our living room like a member of our family.' In the eyes of many he could do no wrong. He was perfect. I wondered how they would feel about me if they knew we were separated. Each time I agreed to do an interview at my house I asked the reporter if he knew we were separated. Each time I received a negative reply. I wondered if I should keep my mouth shut, but not one word of our separation appeared in the press, for which I was grateful, since this might have detracted from the tragedy.

One listener called in to a talk show I was on and she was particularly disturbing. She criticised me for not doing more. Feeling defensive, as if I had done something wrong, I said I was hoping our government were doing all that could be done and that I had a little boy to protect – perhaps she would do me a favour by asking the prime minister what he was actually doing.

While Neil Davis was eulogised for staying when the North Vietnamese invaded South Vietnam and for having crossed the line to report the other side in other conflicts, Greg was being criticised for aspiring to the same aims. He would even be criticised for carrying a sealed letter for the Fretilin commanders; in journalistic circles this is called 'shmoozing the talent' or doing minor favours in return for access. It's a common ploy used by professional journalists wanting access. Greg was no dupe. We later heard that he had intervened when Falintil soldiers were going to execute a captured militia/mercenary and saved the man's life, a step that could well have jeopardised his relationship with Fretilin and his filming access. He would not compromise his humanity. Any accusation of partisanship ignores the realities of doing journalism in a tough environment.

Critics insulted Brian, Malcolm, Gary and Tony as if Greg led them around like puppets on a string. I did not know the Channel Nine team but I knew Tony and Gary very well. I know exactly how they interacted; they were a practised team. Nevertheless John Maher also hastened to blame Greg, even for wearing the safari jacket he had insisted Greg must wear for stand-up reports – the jacket in question was the one Greg wore on our camping and walking holidays.

Shonny was critical of me. It was all my fault. I had badgered Greg to take up study. I should have refused to go to California. I had thrown him out and forced him to live in a van like a homeless person. I was the worst thing that had happened to her in the whole of her life. I felt like striking back: most of her accusations were nonsense, but how could I expect logic from a mother whose heart was breaking? I took the brunt of her anger with as much grace as I could muster.

One day when Evan returned home from school he was furious. That morning he had been met by a group of children who chanted:

The Circle of Silence

Ding dong your dad's dead,
King Kong bashed his head.

I couldn't think what to do. If I kept Evan at home he would hear the misery in my voice as I answered incoming calls. That night I took him to his favourite eating place, Taco Bill.

The phone rang early one morning, I'm not sure which day – time was a blur for me. I ran downstairs to answer it, hopeful of good news. I was told the Australian Journalists Association was to hold a commemorative service in a park for the men.

'What makes you think they are dead?' I responded.

The voice on the phone, claiming to be a reporter for the *Sunday Press*, sounded surprised. 'But, haven't you been told?' He then slid into a gaggle of words – he was very worried about us, Greg had been a good friend to him. He talked rather a lot about their friendship. Greg had never mentioned this man to me. His long-winded chatter exhausted me. I felt I needed to lie down and give in to misery . . . then came the cruncher. He wanted to come right then and take photographs of me. I explained I wasn't feeling well and he said that in that case they would come and photograph Evan.

'Definitely not.'

'In that case we will follow him to school; he won't even know we are there.' At that I slammed the handset down.

The next call came from someone from Channel Seven I did not know. I was expected to go to Tony Stewart's parents' house to discuss another funeral. No one from Channel Seven offered to go with me. I felt abandoned.

My brother called. He wanted to do something useful. On the spur of the moment I asked if Evan could stay with him. I told Bruce about the call I had just had.

'Evan can stay with us as long as you like,' he said. Hearing that was like winning Tattersall's – a burst of sunlight on a dark winter's day, a life-belt in a storm. Evan could go to school in Adelaide and live with four cousins he adored. I was jubilant until I realised I simply could not send him away with false hope.

When I studied psychology I had learned that it was important not to cry when telling children about the death of a loved one. If you cry it could add to an already fearful situation. Evan was playing with his toys so I asked him if he could wait for breakfast while I had a shower.

'Yes, Mummy.'

The trust in his voice and his face demolished my composure. I wept under the shower, then dressed and put on make-up in case the prospect of black mascara running down my face might help me not to cry. I walked down the stairs to find that he had lit the fire and was holding a glass of orange juice he had squeezed for me. I can't describe my feelings; that such a lovely little boy would have to deal with the possibility of his father's death was just too terrible to contemplate. We snuggled together in the beanbag, our memento from our happy times in California. I don't know how I found the words. I can only remember the last two sentences: 'All the time we have been worrying about Daddy no-one has been able to hurt him.'

Evan tried to hold back his tears. 'Remember what Daddy told you,' I said, cuddling him. The best thing Greg ever did for our son was to tell him to go ahead and have a good cry if he wanted. 'Don't listen to silly people, who tell you otherwise,' he had said. So even though I held back crying myself, Evan then cried with passion and abandonment. I think I died a little that day. Grief lodged in my heart like a black stone. I mourned for myself, for Greg, for poor Shonny and for the suffering of my eight-year-old son.

The Circle of Silence

I asked if he would like to fly to Adelaide and stay with his cousins. His answer was a revelation: 'Can I take your handbag with me?' How can we ever know what is going on in the minds of such young children? I reassured him he could and told him he could stay there as long as he liked. If he wanted to come home after the weekend he could. If he wanted to stay a whole week he could. I would leave it up to him. He became very excited about travelling alone and carrying Mummy's handbag with a coterie of adoring air hostesses to spoil him.

I believe Bruce and Jill's understanding and generosity saved my sanity and perhaps more than my sanity. They had also saved Evan from living with long, drawn-out grief. Grief takes on a persona whose needs are paramount. Grief requires quiet and solitude. Grief demands rest, lots of rest. At the most grief requires a cup of tea given without talk, without advice, without weeping. Grief does not need platitudes – suffering is increased when anger and dismay refutes statements like 'everything will be all right'. That other misnomer, 'closure', is insulting in its banality because it really means, 'shut up and go away'.

The day Evan flew out of my life I went to bed and slept fitfully between bouts of frantic weeping. I lost all sense of time and fell into such a deep sleep that when I returned from the void I had no sense of location. The Empress Theodora and her daughters were making a racket and as I came fully awake the traffic seemed to purr in unison with them. I padded downstairs in Greg's voluminous dressing gown, feeling comforted and secure wearing it. In a flash I knew what I would put on that day – the brown sweater I had knitted for him while I was in hospital after Evan's birth. I wore it for months, even when the weather was hot enough for shorts and sandals. It was imbued with Greg's presence.

The next day I travelled by tram to a meeting about the funeral at the Stewarts' house. I realised how lucky I was. June

Stewart, Tony's mother, beautiful in her frailty, had four children to contend with. Her little girl was still in nappies – I hoped that the children would bolster each other in the coming years. I remember those proceedings with cruel clarity. We were expected to make decisions as if an announcement had been made that the journalists had died. Shonny was not there; I asked if she was coming. No-one knew. Had she been asked? No-one knew. I felt lightheaded and stupid when I asked, 'Why are we doing this?' June stared at me, 'They are not coming back.'

'So what do you know that I don't know?' My question was received with uncomfortable silence that made me feel everyone thought I was too stupid to face facts. The priest hurriedly suggested it was necessary to know everyone's preference.

'But not everyone is here,' I protested. He cleared his throat and glanced at this watch. Disgusted at what appeared to me to be indecent haste I said, 'Greg is not religious, neither is Gary. If the Cunninghams don't mind, since Tony is a Catholic, I suggest an ecumenical service in a Catholic church.' And that was the end of the meeting.

I was finding it hard to sleep and as I hovered on the edge of wakefulness something kept bothering me. It was not until Evan left that I was free to think deeply about Shonny. I realised we were both suffering from guilt. Her last months with Greg had been fraught with recriminations and anger. I also felt guilty for other reasons. Some of Greg's fans eulogised me for being his suffering widow. This made me feel untruthful, but I did not really want to tell them we had broken up. People can have very strange reactions to news like this. Just one unkind thing could be said and they could easily turn against Greg.

I blamed myself too readily for our break-up – Greg had admitted to me that my offer to stay in Australia had caused him

The Circle of Silence   91

to suspect I did not love him any more. I felt guilty and thought I had no right to object publicly about what might have been murder simply because we were separated. I also felt shame when I was accosted and offered sympathy. I did not understand that I was feeling this until one day at the South Melbourne Market I met a friend who told me how sorry she was. As she pressed a bunch of flowers into my arms I saw a lady I knew who had lost her husband and her son in a car accident. Her face was devoid of expression as she walked by like a zombie. Here was me being showered with flowers and solicitations while she was not. It was a valuable lesson. This was Greg's tragedy, not mine. If he had been killed, he had lost everything. I was alive.

I still hoped the two news crews were being hidden in the same valiant manner that had driven the Timorese to help Australian soldiers in World War II.

I missed Evan dreadfully but he was fully occupied and very, very happy at his new school. Bruce told me he was worried when he went to pick him up that first day. Would he fit in? Would he be bullied? The teacher said he'd had two fights and had won both.

I was doubly grateful that Evan was in Adelaide when calls came from women grieving for Greg – they were cruel and judgmental, accusing me of forcing Greg into an unsuitable and unsavoury marriage and then kicking him out so he had to live in a van. They said I was spiteful and accused me of grasping at every opportunity to make money out of the tragedy.

I did not even try to explain that I never asked for or received payment for my interviews, nor later for my activist work. These people have to take their socks off to count to twenty and still today, some believe I have made a business out of Balibó and East Timor. They think this way because they would never do anything without payment.

A commemoration was organised in a park, and the day

before this was held the reporter from the *Sunday Press* called again. He wanted to know if I was going to take Evan along. I said no, it was unsuitable for a child. He asked, had I told Evan that Greg was dead? I did not answer, instead I told him how Evan had lit a fire and made orange juice when I had the flu, then I hung up.

There was a huge turn out. The day was bleak and we were deluged with wind-blown rain. I knew quite a lot of the journalists there. Some were clearly moved. I was touched by them but not by the proceedings. I knew that some of those speaking about Greg actually loathed him. They were probably jealous because they could not keep up with Greg's energy, but you would have thought they were in love with him that day. I guess they were caught up in the glamour of speaking in public and delighted with their own rhetoric, no matter how fraudulent. I had to grit my teeth in disgust and revulsion.

As we shivered in the rain Shonny told me she had been rushed to hospital the other day, which was why she didn't attend the meeting at the Stewarts' house. I asked her if it had been an asthma attack? Her eyes narrowed.

'It was something I was told about the deaths. I'm not going to tell you, so don't ask.' I recognised the symptoms. She had a secret and it was all hers. I was suddenly very worried for her, and for my vulnerability. No matter what fantasies she cast, I was honour bound to suffer them in silence. I told her how sorry I was about her suffering, and asked if she had any more news.

'You would know if you weren't so busy basking in his reflected glory,' was her response.

The next day the *Sunday Press* carried an exclusive interview with Shirley Shackleton, who had invited the reporter into her home. 'As she spoke, her little boy placed a protective arm about her.' What a clever boy he was, since he was in Adelaide. I guess he must have had an India rubber arm.

* * *

I had expected advice from the Australian government and I was anxious to know what they were doing to establish the facts. I was so naïve. I actually thought that our prime minister, Mr Whitlam, cared about Australian citizens. True, Gary was a New Zealander, and Brian Peters and Malcolm Rennie of Channel Nine were British. But in that case Whitlam should have sought assistance from the British and New Zealand governments. I asked Channel Nine for contact details of the British families and frequently called Canberra to see what was being done. I might as well have saved my breath on the latter. I wanted to get Greg released from prison. At the time I did not realise I was in denial. I had convinced myself he was rotting in a death hole.

That morning my mother called to say she had dreamt I was in danger. She was worried about my plans. 'Promise me you won't forget you are all Evan has now,' she said.

My father called half an hour later, 'I have to be quick,' he said. 'Doreen's in the garden. She's frantic. She thinks you are going to be murdered and then they will come after us.' I asked him to call her to the phone. While I waited I realised that we were all going out of our minds — my mother expected to be hunted down and murdered! — so I tried to be reassuring.

'They got Greg,' she replied, and the fear in her voice was palpable. Just as a normal person can twist a statement to suit their bias, so can the paranoid. After that conversation I hit a very low point. Through my mother's delusions I was able to understand the disconnect driving me: the complex process of denial was not that far removed from paranoia.

News broke that both teams had sent film out with Jose Ramos-Horta, then the Timorese minister for external affairs. It showed

Indonesian warships moored on the wrong side of the border. I was invited to an interview on ABC News. I was expected to publicly clarify matters on which I was simply not qualified to comment. I took a chance and called Bob Hawke, who was federal president of the Labor Party at the time, for advice. I knew he had a reputation for being entrepreneurial, and a straight talker. He explained the Spanish Civil War was the perfect analogy here. The US had sent American volunteers to fight in Spain and this ploy was echoed in the case of Timor, proven by the film footage. Warships cannot volunteer. I understood what he was saying. It appeared in my mind as if it was printed in indelible ink.

The ABC team came to offer their condolences to me. They said they had not waned to withdraw but their insurance had run out and they were forced to leave on orders from management. The fact that they left was frequently held-up as evidence that the ABC crew were wise and the Balibo Five were not.

The day after the ABC interview a woman who declined to give me her name called and asked who was training me. This was followed by a call from the editor of the women's pages in the *Age*, whom I knew from my public relations days. 'People are asking who is paying you,' she warned. 'Watch your back.'

The battleships film gave me chances to vindicate the 'Balibo Five', as they were now being called, though some of the interviews were minefields. No matter how carefully I chose my words or stated my sources, there was a good chance I would be dismissed as an irrational, emotional widow. This mainly happened with males working in commercial radio and despite all my years of dedicated research into East Timor, it can still happen today. Many years later I would learn that the Indonesian navy were not violating any law at the time. Though their presence was ominous no one knew enough to correct me.

SEVEN

Adelino Gomes, a Portuguese reporter, brought out Greg's last report. It is iconic for it shows Greg's remarkable breadth of skill, honesty and sensitivity. It has been described by David Bradbury, a documentary maker and supporter of Timorese independence, as immortal, unique, a transformative and powerful presentation of Greg's feelings. In an email to me, he said:

> the impact of that meeting the night before on Greg [in the hut] is so fresh, so intense in his immediate consciousness-forming response as he presents it to camera the next morning that short of living the experience himself, no one could ever match its dynamism. It must have been an electrifyingly charged moment for Greg and the others when the men and he met and they rose to their feet to say, 'That's all we want, camarade journaliste!' That moment has stayed in my consciousness forever. And Greg's wonderful poetry, so out of context of what was expected of

the straight newsman of the day about being able to reach out and touch the fragrance of the night ... truly remarkable.

At the same time, I found out from Shonny that I was not pop-ular with Gary Cunningham's father. Shonny said he had made vile accusations but I simply did not believe her. I suspected she was telling me what she thought of me. Years later some of his letters to the Department of Foreign Affairs and Trade (DFAT) were released through freedom of information (FOI). They make surprising if not offensive reading — grief does terrible things to parents. Mr Cunningham actually wrote to the government insulting his son's intelligence and blaming him for his own murder. In another letter he revealed his absolute loathing of me. I was quite shocked by it all. Didn't he know I was asking for a full judicial investigation into the cold-blooded murder of his son? No wonder I was treated like a pariah in some quarters. I was being white-anted from within and these particular little carnivores had voracious appetites. As one academic said to me recently, 'You got exposure when others could not. They were jealous of you. There's a lot of it about.'

Back then I was deeply hurt. It takes much time, effort and emotion to do interviews. There is nothing glamorous about it. It was easier then because most interviews were done live. It's a dangerous enterprise now because editors can cut your words and are able to change the meaning of your carefully chosen phrases. I could have given up, especially when I was told that Shonny was also writing letters complaining about me to the government. This lack of solidarity helped those whose interests were served in covering up for the murderers.

Shonny even called one day to say that one of Greg's girlfriends was up in Indonesia posing as his common-law wife.

'She isn't letting the grass grow under *her* feet. Imagine when he comes home and finds out what you've been up to.'

'Imagine when he comes home and finds out how you are treating me; have you thought of that?' I wasn't proud of my defensiveness, especially as I was driven to such cruelty.

Vivid memories of Greg playing with Evan, the love shining from his face, re-focused me. He was Evan's father. What harm would my innocent son suffer if these lies persisted? Greg, who would not hurt a mouse, was powerless to defend himself. When would his detractors admit who the aggressors were? I could not make any claims other than request a full judicial enquiry. It had become my mantra: 'I want to know what has happened to my husband and his colleagues.'

Channel Seven informed me that they were going to hold an ecumenical service. I had read that Mr and Mrs Rennie were on their way home to Scotland and had to be taken off their ship by helicopter to bring them back to Australia, so I assumed I would meet them at the funeral. My parents flew over with my brother, Bruce, for the service. I went to the church with our friend John Sydney. By the time we arrived nearly everyone was already inside. The church was packed and since no seating had been arranged for us we thought we might have to stay outside. Then John saw an empty pew just four rows from the front. He guided me there and we sat down. Though I was overwhelmed with sadness I thought I was all cried out.

The priest I had met at the Stewarts' house hissed at me, 'You can't sit there!' He spoke as if addressing a wayward child. I could feel my eyes and mouth opening wide. 'Come on, move!' he barked.

'Do you know who this lady is?' John asked. The priest did not recognise me.

'We met a week ago at the Stewarts. I suggested this service,' I said as dryly as I could. At that he gaped and proceeded to tell us we were sitting in the place reserved for the premier of Victoria.

'He must have the whole pew,' he said. He appeared to be brushing a fly away as he told me to go to the side of the church. Even though he had recognised me, it didn't make a scrap of difference. I was in the way.

John, thankfully, found a place in front of Shonny. She looked dreadful. She was alone. I did not ask where her husband was but I thought it strange he was not with her. She was stripped like an insect whose wings had been pulled off by pitiless children. The lines on her face looked like scars. I touched her hand; it lay in her lap like a dead fish. Someone asked if she was going to take communion.

'There's no point,' she replied, hopelessly. 'We might as well not be here, we don't count.'

'But it's a blessing, Shonny,' I said. 'You don't want cameras stuck in your face.' But that was probably what she had expected. To see her sucked dry of all her sparkle, staring about with a peculiar blankness, mournfully, helplessly, was terrible. In resolving to make an effort to show my sympathy, I whispered, 'I hope you will visit us soon, Shonny. There are so many things you can tell Evan about Greg that no else knows.' I could not tell if she had heard. Her eyes remained as vacant as a moonscape.

Members of the congregation and some choirgirls lined up to take the sacrament. The girls behaved beautifully but the priest did not think so. He emitted a high-pitched squeak that reverberated around us like an irritated bat and whispered furiously, 'Hurry up, come on. Get a move on.' John burst into hysterical giggles and I joined him. I should have laughed outright because the effort to restrain myself made me feel quite sick.

Among the many strangers asked to speak, not one voiced the obvious – the deceased had been murdered. The eulogies, the music, the total lack of coffins gave the proceedings the quality of an odious sham. Once again I felt divided. Politeness should have had no place there; if the devout truly believe in God's love, surely the simple truth could have been stated. The omission made a mockery of the reverent phrases and tones. 'No,' I reasoned with myself, feeling weak at the knees at the thought of actually saying the words, 'They are trying to pay respect to five absent corpses.'

Corpses! That revolting and pathetic image lodged in my brain and stayed there for most of the ceremony. I don't remember a thing until John shook me and asked me to stand. My brain stayed in limbo while I tried to recall where I was. I thought I must be delusional, but slowly my consciousness returned and I wondered again if anyone had noticed there were no coffins. Everyone behaved as if the deceased were present. Could no one see the absences as an insult to the memory of Gary, Tony, Brian, Malcolm and Greg? Were Shonny and I the only ones who recognised that pomp and circumstance made the proceedings an insulting farce? If this was not a sinister plot – an unforgivable act of treachery to cover up the murders – why did no one demand answers? Well, of course, no one could state what was obvious, because it was unbelievable.

As we left the church Brian Naylor appeared at the top of the steps. We were told to clear an area as Channel Seven News filmed Brian, the official mourner. Clicking her tongue like an angry animal Shonny glared at him. He had the grace to look uncomfortable.

I caught sight of my family and asked Shonny to come over and see them. I waved and smiled and turned back towards her. She was walking swiftly in the opposite direction. I made my way through the crush, trying to keep as low a profile as possible without being rude to well-wishers. I had not told my parents that Greg and I had split up. I had intended to tell them at Christmas when I was due to visit them in Adelaide. They adored Greg. His tragedy multiplied my mother's fears. Whenever Greg's name was mentioned my dad burst into tears. The treatment we received, the lies, the insensitivity, were more damaging than the death.

My family had to leave immediately for the airport. Considerate as ever, they did not even ask to stay with me. They showed their love and sympathy with their gestures. I wanted them to be selfish for once in their life and demand to come home with me. As I took my mother's hand, she patted mine, 'Yes, I know, Shirley, but you must learn to put yourself first. You've taken on a huge task. Look after yourself and don't worry about us or anybody else.'

I never agreed with my mother's later diagnosis of schizophrenia; I had always maintained that her problems were a perfectly normal result of her terrible childhood. My parents, who never put themselves above their children's needs, were now giving me the space to grieve by flying back to Adelaide, but they maintained daily contact. This was a very hard lesson, like learning to accept charity when the occasion demands. I murmured something inadequate and watched them walk slowly away as if they were carrying huge loads on their shoulders, their heads bent forward in misery.

I looked for Shonny. If there were to be any hope of healing the wounds there would never be a better time than now. I found her at last, bludgeoned by anguish. It was clear that her subterranean struggle was threatening to drown her.

I was frightened for her. 'Come and have a drink, I'll tell you about Evan.'

Her face lit up for a split second and then the lights went out. 'When the boys come home they won't thank you for wishing them dead.'

'Listen, Shonny, we have to work together on this.' Another small intention flickered in her eyes and then died like an insect that lives for a moment.

'You're getting all the credit.'

I was stunned. What had I done to cause such enmity? I had asked for a judicial inquiry to establish the circumstances of her son's death. I wanted to ask her not to refer to them as boys. They were being denigrated for being young and inexperienced as if that excused an act of murder, if it was murder. Even the youngest, Tony Stewart, who was twenty-one years old, used his considerable accomplishments with a skill equalled by few. I wanted to shake her and tell her to grow up. But envy ruled her. What a fool I had been to think she appreciated all I was doing. I should have remembered she liked to be the centre of attention. The core of her wild accusations held the key to her agony – she could not tell the difference between the truth and her blatant fantasies. She had cast herself as a tragic heroine. Anyone 'grabbing the limelight' was, ipso facto, a mortal enemy. *She* was the victim. It was *her* tragedy, not Greg's.

Years later I discovered to my cost that certain people who made my life hell adopted the same, selfish stance. They had made it their tragedy. Back then I could not see a way to help her. Anything I said, no matter how innocent, was twisted to suit her bias. I did not want to increase her pain and anger. Was I the only person who understood what ailed her? When reality is not attractive, imagination produces gods and enemies, saints and sinners. Shonny was constructing a closed circle devoid of reasoning. She required sycophants to reinforce the naïvety of her illusions. Didn't they see they were making things worse by being over-sympathetic? She needed us; she needed Evan; she needed reality.

I made a desperate attempt to get through to her. 'What do the government officials you are dealing with do for you?' I asked.

'I've been told I can call one of them at home any time.'

'That's very good. Who is it?'

Her eyes flashed. 'Oh no, you're not going to get your greedy little mitts on this. It's mine.' I recognised the 'I've got a secret' syndrome. I was seized by an insane desire to slap her, which then changed to a feeling of brutal coldness. This reaction was as much from fury and dissatisfaction with my own shortcomings as from disillusionment with her.

'But what has he actually done for you?' I asked. Her face twitched; a combination of guilt and indecision appeared in her eyes. She was trying to understand. 'What if he is schmoozing you, Shonny, in order to shut you up? Don't let him.' The sun shone through a gap in the clouds. 'What's happened to us? We used to be friends, Shonny.'

I don't believe she was ever able to understand the wider picture, and I dared not say anything further to her – she was so fragile. Time might heal; this was probably our only hope. To my surprise she said she would give anything for a drink, and so we walked together as if we were normal people out for a stroll. I forget now where the Channel Seven wake was held but on our way there she asked if I had seen her interview on Channel Ten and when I said I had not, she made a crack suggesting I was not interested in anything she was doing.

'I was cleaning a house,' I said. Seeing her astonishment, I added, 'I'm earning my living.'

She laughed. 'And here's me thinking you spend your days chatting up your press mates and drinking champagne.'

'I have never called the press.' She was genuinely surprised.

'Of course you have.'

I could have done without this complication. If I told her why I would never ask for an interview, she might think I was admonishing her – people who do that get a reputation for being a pest, as she well knew. 'You will have to trust me.' I said. 'I have never and will not ask anyone to interview me.'

'Anyway, I didn't have to ask to be interviewed.'

I said nothing that would spoil her moment of triumph, though I felt like disabusing her. Channel Ten had invited me to do that interview and I had suggested they might prefer to speak to Greg's mother. When they agreed I had asked if they would provide her transport to and from the studio.

As we left the church grounds someone I did not know came and shook my hand. He whispered, 'Don't ever give up,' and thrust an envelope into my pocket. When I opened it later the handwritten note stated, 'You have friends everywhere.' Though I was intrigued by the secrecy, I was grateful for the additional message which gave me contact details for Malcolm Rennie's parents who were staying in a Melbourne motel.

Two of my friends were at the wake so we sat with them and Shonny behaved very well. We parted on good terms. There were some more attempts by people who did not know me very well to warn me off speaking in public, saying I would wind up dead, I would go crazy, it wasn't fair to Evan, etc. I was horrified by these predictions but I did not feel I had the right to give up. I told them it was not open for discussion; besides, I was attending to Evan's basic rights.

After the stress of the funeral I thought there was a

possibility that no one in the future would know what Greg, Tony, Gary, Malcolm or Brian had looked like. I asked channels Seven and Nine if I could buy copies of the best photographs they had of the missing men. I was told I would be contacted and warned against upsetting the families. I realise now that this is how they kept we families apart, to prevent us from forming a united front.

    I contacted Jack and Mina Rennie and invited them around for afternoon tea. That was when I discovered that they had not been invited to the Channel Seven funeral and Channel Nine had held a funeral to which none of us were invited. The Rennies were as amazed by this as I was. They said they would have loved to have company. Their sadness was tangible and they needed to talk about their son. I will always remember Mina's pride when I asked why Malcolm didn't have a Scots accent? Her eyes shone as she said, 'My beautiful son was BBC trained.'

I decided I would still go to Adelaide at Christmas and bring Evan home at that time. First we would celebrate our reunion by having an adventure — we would travel home in sleeper accommodation on the overnight train. The day I purchased our tickets I received a telephone call from a man who described what he was going to do to me. I was not quick-witted enough to put the handset down. I could not believe what I was hearing. I'd had a few strange calls over the years, but those poor devils were heavy breathers. This was different. The threats were terrifying. I slammed the phone down and called the local police. When he called again the line was intercepted, which worked well on one level, but I still felt very vulnerable. It was hard enough to get to sleep since the murders without having to deal with the threat of torture. I walked around the house trying to imagine how a killer might get in and I almost cancelled my plan to bring Evan home.

At least the women who constantly called to accuse me of not doing enough to help Greg were dissuaded when their calls were intercepted; in fact, they never called again. So often in my life something that seems to be a disaster turns out to be a plus.

Two days before I was to leave for Adelaide I received a call from our life insurance company. John Menzies, who I knew from my days at Gallery A, came straight to the point. He was horrified to have to tell me that Greg had cancelled the policy several weeks before leaving.

'I thought I was going to bring you a lovely big cheque,' he said. 'How are you going to manage?' I was too distraught to respond straight away. I could not believe that Greg had done that. Trailing blood from wounds of resentment I asked how much they have given him as a refund on the cancellation. A little over three hundred dollars. It is the only action of Greg's I cannot understand. The amount of the policy was one hundred thousand dollars.

Until that news broke over my head like a tsunami I had failed to see myself as a single parent. I now wished I could leave Evan with Bruce and Jill, where he would be protected from the calamities buffeting me. I took the phone off the hook, swallowed a large dose of sleeping tablets, curled up on the couch and slept for twelve hours.

Sleep has to be one of the most wonderful forms of healing humans possess. The familiar sound of the nearby Town Hall clock pealing entered me like a countdown cure-all as I dozed off. The solution to one problem was the solution to the other. I consigned the loss of financial security to the Never Never. Make of that what you will, but by far the most valuable lesson

I learned from this was that the only loss that mattered was the loss of Greg's life, not the money. I now had a new mantra, 'It's only money.'

I cannot remember exactly when I received a call from someone who said she was speaking for John Maher. She told me a girl in the Channel Seven lobby was demanding the keys to Greg's van, claiming his mother had sent her. Until it was established that the men were officially deceased all matters such as ownership of property were in abeyance. I spoke calmly and firmly and told her to 'Tell her to go away, and make sure no one is given access to anything belonging to Greg.' After replacing the receiver I shouted with vigour. 'And tell the bitch to mind her own bloody business.' This episode was destined to backfire in another unbelievable Monty Python event four months later.

Shonny called me within the hour. She was hysterical.

'I've found out the Channel Seven payout will be three hundred thousand dollars. And you will get it all. I warn you, Little Miss TV personality, I will drag you through every court in the land for my share.'

'If they were going to pay that much it would be all over the front pages of the *Herald*.' She remained unconvinced.

'You're going to be a very attractive proposition now.'

'I always thought I was; that's why Greg married me.' A very long silence followed. 'Rest assured, Shonny,' I finally said, not bothering to hide my irritation, 'I would give you sixty thousand. I would pay off the house and my debts. I would invest one hundred thousand for Evan's education and keep the rest to bring him up.'

'Will you put that in writing?' she asked.

I sighed. 'On one condition. You must never mention money in public. If you do I won't give you a cent. The moment

The Circle of Silence

money comes into this, the tragedy of the journalists will fly out the window. We would get lots of sympathy. I don't need sympathy, I want justice and I won't have Evan growing up in a world that ignores murder, if it turns out to be murder. You can take it or leave it.'

Once again she tried to convince me of the truth of the allegations she had made previously against Mr Cunningham. I still did not believe he would have been mercenary, but I did not know enough or care enough to argue. 'Okay, Shonny,' I said. 'Whatever you say.'

I did not know how to help her. I could do nothing to dispel her desolation. It would take a miracle to mend the rift between us. I was disgusted with her for letting something as juvenile as jealously force us apart. Frustrated and overtired I was deeply ashamed of my own impatience. My flaws were equal to hers. I blamed *her* for causing *my* distress. Because of her I had to acknowledge my own wretched weaknesses. And yet I knew she was a sick woman, so why did I expect sanity from her? How could I be so callous? Opposing feelings raged in me: I should have been kinder. Why the hell wouldn't she be distraught? Australian government agents were manipulating her and I was resentful that she had never once asked about Evan; I had not even dared to tell her he was in Adelaide for fear of being accused of having chucked him out. I was frightened by the changes in me too. I was not used to being judgmental, and I had always believed I was understanding and patient. My deepest shame was that I felt sorry for myself for the first time in my life. I wondered if this was going to destroy the old me. Would I ever find a way of avoiding self-pity?

Channel Seven called to say that John Maher, Ron Casey and Brian Naylor wanted to visit me at home. They arrived and as they drank the coffee I had prepared for them, they stood in a circle with their backs turned against me. I sat on the couch with my hands clasped in my lap waiting in dread for the news. They chatted amiably while glancing at me from time to time. Their behaviour was insulting; the strain terrible. I began to shake and felt like I was going to vomit. I excused myself, went to the kitchen and drank some Alka Seltzer. On my return I was asked how much I owed on my house, and assurances were given that Channel Seven would 'take care of it'. They nodded like three wise monkeys. After thanking me for the coffee they turned to leave.

'Is that all?' I stammered.

John Maher spoke very fast in response. 'You know, Shirley, the cost of the insurance was huge, absolutely huge. It was nine thousand dollars.' Ron Casey glared at John then grabbed his elbow and pushed him roughly while stammering an abrupt goodbye. They got stuck between the sliding doors on the way out. Brian Naylor seemed to mirror my thoughts: they were there for six days, not three and so the cost of insurance should have been eighteen thousand dollars. We watched in amazement as they struggled to get through. They finally did, and Brian followed them into the front room. I walked after them and noticed someone had forgotten his suitcase. I picked it up and ran out into the street. Their black limousine was already drawing away from the kerb. They must have moved like lightning to get in! I held the case aloft to catch their attention. Brian Naylor gaped at me through the rear window. I waved the suitcase as the car roared off at speed. I waited at the kerb thinking they would return for it.

After a while I went inside and placed the case near the front door. As I cleared away the coffee cups I noticed that someone had stirred his coffee with the sugar spoon and had placed it back in the sugar bowl. I suddenly felt dizzy. Greg

The Circle of Silence

hated that habit. I remember sitting down and staring stupidly at the sugar-encrusted spoon. Why on earth had they come? Apart from 'hello' and 'yes, we'd love a coffee', they had hardly spoken to me. I felt humiliated. I might just as well have been the tea lady.

Later that night while washing the dishes a terrible thought struck me. I seemed to float though the rooms to the suitcase. The surroundings disappeared and the size of the case increased. I felt I was hallucinating. My ears buzzed, which was weird because there was no sound. I remember opening the latches on the case. They made a noise like a shot. I lifted the lid and stared at a plastic shower bag. The unfamiliar case contained a jumble of articles, a used tube of toothpaste and other toiletries, a couple of shirts and a pair of underpants and one of Greg's notebooks wrapped in his yellow Channel Seven t-shirt. There should have been more than one notebook and most of the pages had been torn out. I turned each page. Who had torn out the missing pages? Amazed that such ordinary things had the power to hurt I picked up Greg's electric razor and stared at it as if it was a live thing. A single whisker was caught in the blade.

Those bastards didn't have the decency to tell me that the suitcase contained all that remained of Greg's earthly goods.

I never heard another word from them about paying off my mortgage. What I did finally receive was a cheque for forty thousand dollars, plus a letter instructing me to sign the enclosed document, stating acceptance of the terms. I was supposed to sign a form agreeing that not only would I never make a legal claim for more money, I would sign Evan's rights away too. If I did not accept the offer by return post it would be withdrawn.

The bank manager was twice as shocked as me. He said he was surprised by my composure. I shrugged. 'They're businessmen,'

I said. 'It's their business to give me as little as possible.' He called his lawyer who explained: 'If Mrs Shackleton goes to the Supreme Court she will certainly be awarded one hundred thousand dollars. The case would take years to come to court; she would be harassed and worried; and the costs she would have to pay would be at least sixty thousand, leaving her with forty thousand.' He also confirmed that I would commit an illegal act if I signed away Evan's rights.

The bank manager asked if I would pay for a telephone call to allow him to ascertain if Treasury would honour the cheque. He said he would not tell them anything except to identify the number on the cheque and the name of the institution that had issued it. He needed my permission to ask for the money to be sent to the bank immediately by telegraphic transfer. 'If we can pull that off, they can't claw it back.' I dimly remember agreeing.

The brutal coldness of these dealings was only eclipsed by the miserly estimation of Greg's worth and by the wonderful support I received from that temporary bank manager. I was in another nightmare. I wanted to wake up. I wanted to get out of there. I wanted to give in and have a good cry. I also dreaded the inevitable confrontation with Shonny about the money. By the time I arrived home the phone was ringing. I heard the bank manager's excited voice saying, 'The money is in your account, Mrs Shackleton.'

That night I tried to recover from what had happened by studying Greg's photograph. His kindness and generosity was fully evident in his beautiful face. You cannot quantify the loss of Greg to his family and no amount of money could measure how precious his life was to him. But the day's vile events were nothing compared to the criminal suppositions that were circulating about the Balibo Five.

The clock ticks as I
hold your photograph.
How does it feel to be
forever youthful
enigmatic, imprisoned
behind your walls of glass?

… you remain calm, remote
perfectly preserved
like an amaranth flower
blistered by fire.
Love Lies Bleeding
behind your walls of glass.

EIGHT

Around the time I learned to disregard my blows of misfortune, something really bad started. Greg, Tony, Malcolm, Brian and Gary began to be blamed in the press and elsewhere for their own murders. Midway through 1976 I received an anonymous phone call alleging that the Australian diplomat Sir Keith Shann was claiming that the Australian news reporters were wearing Fretilin uniforms when they were accidently killed in crossfire. Shonny received the same information. There was a good chance that we were being set up to encourage us to make fools of ourselves, so I decided to ignore it. Shonny told me she tried to have it published but everyone was afraid of defamation. I also felt I had to protect the other family members. Imagine giving information like that to the parents of the murdered men?

Seven years later Shann made a public statement. Now, he claimed to have seen photographs of the journalists manning machine guns. 'They shouldn't have been in Balibó,' I heard him say on the ABC news, 'they asked for it and they got it.' This became the catch-cry for an evil group of self-appointed apologists who in time became known as the Jakarta Lobby. My letter to the editor published in the *Age* on 16 October 1988 kept me busy answering phone calls from people who loved the fact that I had challenged Shann to prove his allegations or shut up.

Quite a number of journalists told me that they knew Australian government officials who claimed to have seen the photographs. They were unable to be published because the journalists looked dead.[1]

Even today some people blame the Balibó victims for their own murders. If you followed the carping criticism to a logical conclusion you could imagine they committed suicide. In response to the claim that they should not have been in Balibó, you could blame all murder victims this way. Quite obviously if they had stayed in bed on the day that they were murdered, they might have avoided their professional killers. But they were doing the job they were sent to do.

They were originally allowed only three days to complete their assignment because of the cost of insurance. They did not remain in Dili, as they needed to go to the border to report on activities there. To do otherwise, as many did, would have meant that they would be forced to rely on second-hand information and this would have left them open to spreading propaganda. They were not sent with camping equipment and Greg may have refused to be lumbered with it if it had been offered. They already had enough gear to carry with film stock and cameras and sound recording equipment.

---

1 James Dunn, former consul to Portuguese Timor, in a radio interview in 2009 with Warwick Fry, revealed that he had spoken to an eyewitness who said that though the uniforms were in perfect order, the bodies of the newsmen had terrible wounds. James Dunn's interview can be heard on: *http://vensol. blogspot.com/2010/01/remembering-balibo-author-warwick-fry.html*

José Ramos-Horta told me that he'd heard them discussing, as they tried to sleep on a cold hard floor, how shocked they were by the first-hand evidence they were recording. He had overheard them making a solemn pact to take up Timor as a cause.

To the lies circulating that they wore military uniforms, they didn't. They wore yellow Channel Seven t-shirts, identical to the ones worn blithely by Channel Seven reporters for years after their murders, without ever once causing those wearers to be murdered. Some fool claimed Brian Peters wore military trousers in a Darwin pub a week before he left for Timor. Did this vile seeker of publicity not know about reject clothing stores? You should have seen his self-important, chest-swelling performance as he pretended to have damning evidence against Brian. You might have thought he should have worn a dress. According to Mal Waldon, a Channel Seven reporter at that time, John Maher complained that Greg wore military clothing. As I said before, Maher's instructions to Greg was for him to wear his safari jacket while filming reports from Timor. This hardly constitutes a uniform.

In 1975 a young inexperienced journalist wrote, 'The Channel Seven team were young, inexperienced and fresh from chasing trams in Melbourne.' Thirty-three years later at a dinner held in my honour, Hamish McDonald, by then foreign editor of the *Sydney Morning Herald*, made a fine speech and admitted that he had been on the 'other side' when these attacks were being made on the Balibo Five. He had spent the intervening years researching East Timor and had collaborated with Professor Desmond Ball on their excellent book *Death in Balibo, Lies in Canberra*. But others guilty of spreading disinformation have never admitted to their role in denigrating the five men, and some opportunists still seek to make money by publishing fraudulent claims.

The biggest lie was that the Balibo Five had been killed in the crossfire of warring factions. Though it did not take an over-abundant intelligence to recognise that this was a self-serving political excuse, it is still in use today. The village had been deserted for much of the previous year because of the murderous attacks by the Javanese that had also occurred all along the border. The journalists were alone in Balibó, having refused to retreat with Falintil. This should have ensured their safety – had Falintil stayed there would have been fighting, and Greg would have urged Falintil to go.

The lesson here is that if you are a journalist who makes an exclusive report on a big story you will be deemed a hero; if you are murdered to prevent you from reporting one of the biggest stories in the world, you will be decried by creeps and opportunists. It's called blame the victim.

I received a long telegram from Senator Don Willesee expressing shock and regret over the killings. Apart from public expressions of their opposition to the invasion of Indonesia by parliamentarians Tom Uren and Senator McIntosh, this was the only expression of sympathy or telegram I received from any government official, ever. Senator Willesee's daughter, Geraldine, would give evidence at a coronial inquest held more than three decades later that until the day he died her father had suffered remorse for his government's betrayal of the Balibo Five.

What could be more callous than to withhold information about the murder of a loved one? We know now that the Australian government not only knew the men had been murdered, they had also withheld all relevant information from the families for two weeks. Former ambassador to Indonesia Richard Woolcott is on record as stating that he knew more about the Armed Forces of the Republic of Indonesias' [ABRI's] plans regarding East Timor than the top Javanese generals had known.[2]

Three now-declassified cables reproduced on the UNSW@ADFA website show that Australian officials were informed in advance of the Indonesian attack on Balibó.[3] These were all sent from the Australian embassy in Jakarta to Canberra between 13 and 16 October 1975:

> We have received today, 13 October, more details of the Indonesian assistance to anti-Fretilin forces ... The main thrust of the operation would begin on 15 October. It would be through Balibó, Maliana and Atsabe. The objective is to complete the main operation by the middle of next month (including the occupation of Dili). It is possible, however, that because of the problem of Indonesia's providing logistical support without being observed and the setting in of the wet season that the task won't be completed until sometime in December. The President in approving the budget had made it clear that 'no Indonesian flag' could ever be used in the operation.
>
> President Suharto has recently authorised a significant increase in Indonesian involvement ... The stepped-up operation begins today, as you know. Tjan has now given the following additional details about it. All Indonesian forces operating in Portuguese Timor will be dressed as members of the anti-Fretilin force.

---

[2] Richard Woolcott, *The Hot Seat: Reflections on Diplomacy from Stalin's Death to the Bali Bombings*, HarperCollins, Sydney, 2003; Richard Woolcott, *Undiplomatic Activities*, Scribe, Melbourne, 2007.

[3] *www.unsw.adfa.edu.au/hass/Timor/2/index.html*

They have been assembling in Atapupu. Initially an Indonesian force of 800 will advance Batugade-Balibo-Maliana-Atsabe . . . It is of course clear that the presence of Indonesian forces of this order will become public. The Indonesians acknowledge this. The President's policy will be to deny any reports of the presence of Indonesian forces in Portuguese Timor. We are not in a position to assess the likelihood of success of the Indonesian operation. The Indonesians are confident. They estimate the Fretilin armed force at 5,000 including reservists. If difficulties arise Indonesia will, we assess, escalate its involvement to overcome them. Meanwhile Indonesia will continue to portray its policy in as favourable a light as possible on the diplomatic and public presentational level.

Foreign Minister Malik's agreement to talk with his Portuguese counterpart is part of the pattern. As seen from Jakarta, we need to address ourselves to the attitude we should adopt as fighting again increases in Portuguese Timor, which it should do from today. On the basis of the Townsville talks, President Suharto will assume that the Australian Government will make every effort to give Indonesia what support and understanding it can. The Prime Minister's statement in the House of Representatives on 26 August confirmed this assumption. An example of the Indonesian Government's confidence . . . is the extent to which it keeps us informed of its secret plans. There is no doubt in my mind that the Indonesian government's fundamental assessment is based on the talks between Mr Whitlam and President Suharto in Townsville.

I had a long and very frank discussion with General

Benny Murdani last evening, 15 October. General Murdani had returned the previous day from a visit to Timor, including Batugade. On the operations which were launched yesterday, 15 October, General Murdani confirmed what Tjan had already told us and which we reported previously. In these circumstances I can only repeat my earlier comments that, in the next few weeks, we are going to need steady nerves and to keep our assessment of our longer term interests in this region in front of us.

If only we had known that Richard Woolcott had been advised seven days before Greg's twenty-eighth birthday of Indonesia's intention to invade Portuguese Timor. He sent a secret cable to the Australian Department of Foreign Affairs on 17 August 1975, telling them to 'leave events to take their course ... and act in a way which would be designed to minimise the public impact in Australia and show private understanding to Indonesia of their problems'. He admitted that this was a 'pragmatic rather than a principled stand'. He continued: 'I wonder whether the [Australian] government is aware of the interest of the Ministry of Minerals and Energy in the Timor situation. It would seem to me that the Department might well have an interest in closing the present gap in the agreed sea border and this could be much more readily negotiated with Indonesia ... than with Portugal or independent East Timor.[4]

A most dramatic event in Australia's political history wiped every other calamity off the agenda of every media outlet in

---

4 Quotes from Brian Toohey and Marion Wilkinson, *The Book of Leaks*, Angus & Robertson, Sydney, 1987, section on 'The Timor Papers', pp. 143–95; *National Times* (Sydney), 30 May, 6 June 1982; Richard Walsh and George Munster, *Documents on Australian Defence and Foreign Policy, 1968–1975*.

Australia. On 11 November 1975 the Whitlam government was dismissed by order of the British queen, the titular head of the Commonwealth of Australia. While Australians protested I wondered if this might turn out to be an advantage. Whitlam was bitterly opposed to the old empires, despised the Portuguese, the Dutch and the British, and was infamous for his assertions that Indonesia could do no wrong. I might not be right about a lot of things but I was right about him. In possession of an oversized ego to suit his monolithic proportions, he was destined to become an effective weapon in Suharto's hand. With the help of hindsight it seems evident to me that he betrayed the Balibo Five, the Timorese and the Indonesian people because he thought Indonesia could do no wrong. When stripped of his position and title, he became an ordinary man. He looks important and is sharp witted, but it seems obvious to me that he cared nothing for the Timorese or for Greg, Tony, Gary, Malcolm, Brian or journalist Roger East who would be murdered by Javanese troops in Dili on 8 December 1975.

Surrounded by memorabilia that made Greg's presence in our house distressingly tangible, I opened a telegram from Jakarta with shaking hands. I cannot exaggerate the hope that flared in my heart. Were they alive? A Doctor Will, claiming to be the Australian consulate medical officer in Jakarta, stated that he had been given the remains of the journalists to identify and the most he could say was that they were 'possibly human'.

My knees buckled as I tried to make sense of those words. Even though DNA testing was not the exact science it is today, a sliver of skin, a strand of hair or part of a fingernail is sufficient proof to distinguish a human being. I burst from the house like a lunatic, muttering insanely. I walked along the beach crying out my rage and frustration. Why had the remains been sent to Jakarta at all? The oh-so-truthful Indonesian dictator had repeatedly denied any intention or right to invade Portuguese Timor. Why weren't the remains sent home?

That same morning I received my first phone call from a government source, in this case DFAT. It contained elements of black comedy. Did I want the bodies brought home? It would cost me forty-eight thousand dollars: 'Do you understand, Mrs Shackleton, that you will have to pay?' I tried to understand the implications. Why was this creature trying to frighten me? Trying to think made me dizzy. This could not be happening. My hands shook as I picked up the telegram and read it again. I did not want to get Doctor Will into trouble. The creature at the other end of the telephone obviously did not know that I knew what constituted 'the bodies'. Possibly human?

It was a trap the enormity of which I could not fathom. I was frantic. My body wanted to shut down as I imagined the scene at Melbourne airport as Australian family members waited to take delivery of the bodies of their loved ones. I felt doomed because I could not allow that to happen. I also knew I did not have the right to make decisions for anyone but myself. All the energy drained from my body as I foresaw the delivery of the remains to the already traumatised parents. They would be expecting five coffins.

The voice on the other end of the telephone was either annoyed or frightened. This was a ghastly reprise of the newsreader who had refused to tell me that five journalists were missing. I took a deep breath. 'Are they in five coffins?'

'Ah . . . [a long silence] . . . er, no.'

'Are they in five suitcases?'

'No.'

'Are they stuffed in a shoebox?' An even longer silence ensued. Taking a deep breath I read out the telegram without divulging the writer's identity. 'In other words,' I shouted, 'the bodies could come home in a matchbox in the pilot's pocket.' With mounting fury I said they could do what they bloody-well liked because what they had up there wasn't my husband or his colleagues, as they were definitely human.

The Circle of Silence

I see so clearly now that I played into their spotlessly clean hands. They recorded: Mrs Shackleton has given permission for us to dispose of the remains.

Today I would call a press conference and hand out copies of the telegram to tell the world about the threatening phone call from DFAT. They actually told the other families that I had given my permission to have the bodies interred in Jakarta. This turned them against me. Perhaps eager to dispose of what must have been a terrible embarrassment and a whole heap of paperwork, Ambassador Richard Woolcott arranged a hasty funeral in the Kebayoran Lama cemetery in Jakarta. There was only one coffin. The date was 5 December, which did not mean a thing. Its significance would be revealed two days later.

In the days following the murders at Balibó, Alan Renouf, head of the Department of Foreign Affairs, tried to save all Australian nationals in Dili through the auspices of the International Red Cross. He sent a no-nonsense message on 1 December 1975 to Ambassador Woolcott, as soon as the date of the proposed invasion was revealed:

> You should make it clear to Mr Tjan (and others, if you think it desirable) that we expect the Indonesians to exert effective influence to see that the lives of Australians are not endangered. Any repetition of the experience of the five journalists would have a grave effect on public relations in Australia and would damage relations far more severely than that episode. In the circumstances, we look to the Indonesians to get guarantees from the Timor parties, Fretilin aside, that they will respect the lives of Australians, who will be readily identifiable. (You will appreciate that we do not find persuasive the Indonesians' arguments about their lack of influence with the non-Fretilin parties) . . .

This message included a list of the names of Australian citizens in East Timor at the time. Mr Renouf disclosed the above message at the Glebe Coroner's Court in 2007 and also admitted that he and Woolcott had a serious disagreement back in October 1975 because of the murders at Balibó. Mr Renouf might just as well have spoken to a pot plant.

In the lead up to Timor's invasion, Angola, a former Portuguese colony in Africa, had declared its independence from Portugal, and thirty countries recognised the new African nation. The Fretilin political party then unilaterally declared that East Timor was an independent country on 28 November 1975. This was partly due to the impending fall of Atabae, an important mountain base in what was an undeclared war being waged by Indonesia. UDT and Apodeti members, Portuguese civilians and apolitical Chinese disposed of their assets and fled. Although the caretaker Fretilin government repeatedly appealed for help, no nation responded.

In the rarefied atmosphere of Melbourne some Australians sought to pass secret information to me. They seemed to think I could do something with it. They were terrified of being found out, but since they refused to sign an affidavit attesting to the evidence, I had to explain that I could not use it. All of it proved to be true. The allegations were as follows:

- In June 1974, José Ramos-Horta had received written assurances from Adam Malik, the Indonesian minister for foreign affairs, stating that his government respected East Timor's right to self-determination.[5]
- Since October 1974, BAKIN (the Indonesian intelligence agency) had operated a subversive organisation called

---

5 This is quoted in Robert Elson, *Suharto: A Political Biography*, Cambridge University Press, Cambridge, 2001.

Operasi Komodo – appropriately named after the komodo dragon, the giant monitor lizard, a survivor of carnivorous dinosaurs of 130 million years ago. Operasi Komodo was created to destabilise Portuguese Timor. The methods included clandestine hit-and-run raids upon undefended villages using bazookas and hand grenades, infiltration to cause political unrest and the establishment of a radio station to broadcast false reports throughout Portuguese Timor.

- In September 1975, a captured Indonesian corporal disguised as Timorese claimed he had been told by his officers that he was operating in West Timor. Surprised to discover he was not in his own country he said, 'We came to kill communists.'

It is evidence like this that Greg and his colleagues went to gather.

Two days after Fretilin declared East Timor an independent nation on 29 November 1975, a bevy of Timorese led by João Tavares, the self-styled Integration fighter, were flown to Bali. At the Bali Beach Hotel, one day after Timor's declaration of independence, four representatives from UDT, Apodeti and two other minor political parties – KOTA and *Partido Trabalhista* – signed a document declaring that the majority of Timorese desired integration with Indonesia. Any document prepared by a foreign power and signed by Timorese without official status on foreign soil could not be said to represent the will of the majority, yet judicial validity was claimed because the document was grandly titled The Balibó Declaration. Appealing to the criminal minds of the collaborators and those who were financially coerced to use this deception, the perpetrators laughed and toasted each other as two letters were added to transform Bali into Balibó.[6]

I must mention here that the political party Fretilin had won local elections in February and March 1975; their literacy campaign that had spread into villages had been one of the reasons for Fretilin's success. Long before Balibó, Whitlam's policy of appeasement towards *Operasi Komodo*'s subversive activities bore the stench of collaboration. Being in possession of information like these allegations was a burden for me. There was a lot of opposition to unpalatable truths about East Timor and the media were either too busy or too frightened by the immense power of the Jakarta lobbyists to stand up to them.

In those dark days I thought the relationship between our two countries would have to be skilfully managed or Australian children like my 8-year-old son could be fighting Javanese in the future. I then watched as lies and cover-ups over the next twenty-four years ensured that confrontation with Indonesia became inevitable. However, that was way in the future and some of us were hard put to keep our sanity in the present.

In late 1975, Maureen Tolfree, Brian Peters' sister, had flown to Sydney in an attempt to get information unavailable in England. Years later, while we were staying together at Clifton College in Bristol where she worked, she wept while telling me her story. Her mother had disappeared when Maureen was 14 years old. Her brother had died, and her father was almost destroyed by both tragedies. Petrified the authorities would place the three surviving brothers into care, Maureen left school to look after them. She scrubbed and ironed their clothes and sent the boys

---

6 This is quoted in Antonio Barbedo de Magalhaes's *East Timor, A People Shattered By Lies and Silence*.

out in perfect order. As she scoured the house and worried about her father's health, she was haunted by the possibility that he would die, too.

Maureen felt she had lost a beloved son as well as her brother when Brian disappeared. When she came to Australia after it was announced he was 'missing', she was lonely and miserable, cut off from the rest of the Australian families and stuck alone in a Sydney motel. Then she received two terrible shocks. Her father had had a heart attack in England and a journalist friend of Brian's tipped her off that a funeral was to be held in Jakarta. She took the first available flight to London via Jakarta.

She cried all the way there, thinking she was going to put Brian to rest. When she told an Indonesian air hostess about her troubles the hostess promised to enquire about the address of the cemetery. An act of kindness? Perhaps, but upon landing the passengers were told to remain seated until further instructions. Armed Indonesian soldiers marched on board and ordered Maureen off. As she scrambled to collect her in-flight luggage they kicked her overnight case along the aisle and advised her to follow their orders. She was hustled across the tarmac to a small bare room with a table and a telephone. A cultured voice asked what on earth was she doing in Indonesia? Before she could finish explaining about the funeral, the speaker claimed to be the British consul. She was urged to take the first available flight to London because she was in terrible danger. Eyeing the weapons held by the circle of soldiers surrounding her and seeing their hostility she did as she was told.

This terrifying encounter left her feeling she had been duped, and she suffers still because she did not even ask for the name of the so-called consul. It could have been anyone. We consoled each other. Sixteen years later an English activist sent me a glossy photograph of the funeral. All the 'mourners' were embassy officials. Not a single family member was present. We were not invited.

Since the photographs I had requested from the dead men's employers were not forthcoming, I contacted people who had been at the funeral services. It was a long shot and it paid off. As photographs were printed on the programs (I was not given a program on the day), I had them re-photographed and then sent them to every major newspaper in Australia with their names and details attached to the back of each photograph with sticky-tape. They are the photos that the press still commonly used of the newsmen today.

The funeral in Jakarta gave me no peace. I remembered vividly Greg's request to me: if he was arrested and held without medication for his asthma he would be likely to die. 'Can you imagine conditions in a third-world prison? Don't leave me there, Shirl. Do everything. Sell the house. Get me out.'

I found the work phone number for Gary Cunningham's father. I wanted to encourage him to help me to persuade the five families to form a united front. My idea was to take turns in doing all the interviews I was being offered. His secretary asked me to wait on the line. Half an hour later I blew Evan's scout whistle to attract her attention. She answered my question reluctantly. Does Mr Cunningham have any intention of speaking to me? No.

I sought advice about holding an official inquest and was told by three lawyers that there was no way in Australian law that would allow this. Whitlam was dismissed thirty-six days after the atrocity at Balibó, and he claimed that this prevented him from taking any action regarding the Balibo Five. Malcolm Fraser, the new prime minister, was able to claim that he was not in power when they 'lost their lives'.

* * *

For a year before the tragedy at Balibó the Javanese military had conducted a terror and destabilisation campaign in the border regions of East Timor. Its aim was to generate atrocities that could be falsely attributed to pro-independence East Timorese forces. The Javanese would then be able to invade under the pretext of 'restoring order'. Greg and his colleagues' assignment was to find out whether the incursion was a Javanese invasion and not an uprising of disaffected Timorese. If the Balibo Five had wandered into crossfire on an active battlefront, as the Javanese maintained, it may have been a foolhardy risk. But they didn't. They were murdered. Not in the heat of battle but in cold blood.

In November 1975, Roger East, a renowned Australian reporter, published his concerns about the Australian government ban on travel to Portuguese Timor in a local paper. A few days later the Australian government ban was lifted, on 5 November 1975. Roger immediately left for Portuguese Timor. He had thirty-three days to live.

At fifty-two-years-old Roger was planning for early retirement. The last thing he needed was a cause, but his forensic journalist's nose had sniffed the breeze and detected the stench of treachery. Keeping track of events all over the world was a difficult habit to break. Some news reports emanating from Portuguese Timor did not add up. Spokespersons for the newly organised political parties UDT and Apodeti believed that 'incorporation' with Indonesia would be mutually beneficial.

He researched the history and established that there was scant historical, religious or cultural affiliation between Portuguese Timor and Indonesia. An invasion would breach the United Nations Charter and contravene Indonesia's own constitution. José Ramos-Horta met Roger in Darwin and offered him directorship of the East Timor news agency, ETNA.

Roger's published reports are prophetic. He wrote, 'Fretilin would embrace an offer of a UN supervised plebiscite in the knowledge that it would win by the handsomest of margins. The mortar that binds them is the singular and irrevocable process towards independence. East Timor will settle for nothing less.'

East also interviewed eyewitnesses to the Balibó murders. These were the first credible accounts of the event and although they differed in some detail the consensus of all those interviewed was that the five had been deliberately murdered. Channel Nine's Brian Peters was shot while still filming the advancing Javanese. Channel Seven's Gary Cunningham, Greg Shackleton and Tony Stewart and Nine's Malcolm Rennie died with their hands in the air in the universally accepted sign of surrender.

East's writings about the general situation in East Timor were iconic in their brevity and accuracy. As stated on ABC radio's *Hindsight*:

> The major news wires, Reuters and AAP, were led to believe that East's Balibó exclusive came about because of his close association with Fretilin, which, according to the propaganda at the time, made Roger East a communist and his fledgling news service, ETNA, a mouthpiece for Fretilin. Roger wrote about it in a letter to his brother Bill:
> *And by the way, it seems the agency AAP, which has almost a monopoly on news down under, has been upset over its correspondent here missing some of the stories. They've notified the big papers I am the 'official news agency for Fretilin', which has nicely scuppered me. News by me [in Australia] will now get scant attention,*

The Circle of Silence

but what you lose on the swings you pick up on the proverbial merry-go-round. The Portuguese news agency is accepting my copy, also France-Presse, both based in Lisbon. I am now chasing the Japanese agency Kyodo and TASS. We also intend having a go at TV documentaries. Plenty of work, but very little pay. So be it. [7]

---

7 'Roger East – Australia's Forgotten Journalist', *Hindsight*, ABC Radio National, 14 December 2008.

NINE

There is an underwater channel running the length of the Indonesian archipelago, which ends at the eastern tip of the island of Timor. Suharto knew that by taking over the whole island he would control the choke points to the Indian and Pacific oceans. Since American atomic submarines required access to both the Pacific and the Indian oceans, the dictator believed that this fact alone would be a *persuasive* argument in his dealings with the Americans – in Mafia parlance it provided Suharto with a protection racket.

On 6 December 1975 the US president Gerald Ford and his secretary of state, Henry Kissinger, left Jakarta and witnessed the aircraft they had donated to the Indonesian Government on the tarmac. Warships and landing barges were also at the ready. Paratroopers, marines, pilots and foot soldiers had checked their gear. The mothers of the men of the armed forces would have died from heart attacks had they known what their beautiful sons were about to do. If they'd had the opportunity to ask what was the point of this exercise they would have been assured that their son's mission was a proud one. They were to destroy communists and Portuguese to prevent them from causing harm to innocent civilians in Timor who had begged the Suharto regime to come and save them. Suharto's reign had already seen the murder of millions of perceived communists in Indonesia. But the simple truth is captured in five succinct words: it was a land grab.

A memorandum (published in the *Nation* magazine fifteen years later) underlined the fact that Kissinger's deputies had told him that the use of American arms for purposes of aggression was illegal under a treaty between the US and Indonesia. Kissinger had rebuffed them, asking, 'Can't we construe a Communist government in the middle of Indonesia as self-defence?' As a CIA official later put it, there was no evidence that Indonesia was ever threatened by communism. An American State Department testimony in 1977 established that 'roughly 90% of the military equipment made available to the Indonesian Army in the 1975 invasion was American supplied'.

The Indonesian generals should have done their homework. Back in the eighteenth and nineteenth centuries resistance to European, Topasses (black Portuguese) and Chinese political interference took many forms. In 1726, when historic battles took place in the mountains of Cailaco, four thousand Portuguese troops were contained by a Timorese army of less than one thousand. When the naturalist H.O. Forbes travelled in Timor in 1882, he reported that the Timorese had learnt many of the customs of the Portuguese, in order to 'outwit them more effectively'.[1]

---

1 Cited in John G. Taylor's chapter in Peter B. R. Carey and G. Carter Bentley (eds), *East Timor at the Crossroads: The Forging of a Nation*, University of Hawaii Press, Honolulu, 1995, p. 29.

On 7 December 1975, in the newest independent country in the world, East Timor, tens of thousands of babies and toddlers slept. Old men, youths and women of all ages tried to sleep. Insomnia had been prevalent since the first hit-and-run attacks had claimed thousands of innocent lives. Some prayed to God, to Jesus or to Mary, the sainted mother of Jesus. A handful of Muslims prayed to Allah. The majority prayed to their animistic gods. They might as well have prayed to a boulder, for men with hearts of stone expected to celebrate their 'manhood' upon the morrow.

With invasion looming, one Australian in Dili did not sleep. Roger East had made the momentous decision not to abandon the Timorese. The radio link with Darwin would provide the only way of reporting events to the world when the Javanese waged their undeclared war. This was the anniversary of the day that the Japanese had bombed Pearl Harbor. That in itself might provide an insight into the pig-ignorant cowboy fantasies of the warlords who boasted that they would be in Balibó for breakfast, Dili for lunch and Baucau for dinner.

Just under six weeks after the murders at Balibó, at four in the morning, the people of Dili felt vibrations to a magnitude of a hundred plus on the Richter scale. Citizens leapt out of bed and ran outside before they were properly awake in the practised manner of earthquake drill. The blasts were just the beginning of a concentrated naval barrage that threatened to burst eardrums. Terrified parents covered their screaming children's ears and tried not to panic.

When the barrage ceased some thought they saw big, multicoloured flowers floating in the sky. Dom Jose Ribero, the bishop of Dili, thought the paratroopers dangling beneath their camouflage parachutes looked like angels, 'But when they landed they behaved like devils. The soldiers who landed started killing everyone they could find. There were dead bodies in the streets – soldiers were killing, killing, killing.'

Baba Do'ok, the huge sacred Lulik drum, boomed over the countryside. The invasion message it bore had been sent only three times in the previous four centuries: the first to invade were the Portuguese, then the Australians, and then the Japanese. Terror and panic swept the streets. Hercules C-130B aircraft flew overhead, firing rockets into the stricken crowds. Buildings exploded; roof tiles shattered; splintering timbers, metal and shards of glass pierced human and animal flesh. Timor ponies galloped screaming through streets strewn with dismembered corpses.

Falintil snipers fired on descending paratroopers. Citizens ran forward to help seize enemy *nanggala* knives, hand grenades, ammunition and M-16 assault rifles. Once they gained a foothold, the Javanese shot every civilian they came across. Some were puzzled by the haphazard manner of the drops – even with scant knowledge of military tactics the enemy made costly errors – paratroopers were dropped directly over Dili. As if to illustrate the point, three paratroopers hit the power lines. What could be more futile and demoralising than to die in an undeclared war? These were fit and healthy boys with their whole lives before them. What could their evil masters hope to do with the land they were sent to conquer? How can you tame soil?

Plumes of smoke blacked out the early morning sun. Enemy soldiers employed a brutally efficient tactic: they fired without warning at unarmed civilians attempting to give themselves up. Rich or poor, ignorant, educated, friend, enemy or neutral, all died together. Some lost their hearing, some went mad, some were too shocked to do anything other than stare in disbelief as their sanity drained slowly into an epicentre of silence. They made easy pickings.

In Michele Turner's *Telling: East Timor*, a woman named Eloise talks about that day:

> In the afternoon some Timorese came and told us everyone must come to surrender at headquarters ... Once we got there they divided us: the women and children and old men to one side and on the other young boys [and men] ... Then an Indonesian screams an order and we hear machine guns running through the men. We see the boys and men dying right there. Some see their husbands die. We look at each other stunned. We think they are going to kill us next. All of us just turn and pick up the children and babies and run screaming, wild, everywhere ... [Later] my sister went to look for her husband and son. On her way she met a friend, crying, who told her, 'Don't bother going there. I have just seen my cousin being eaten by a dog. They are all dead. Only the dogs are alive there.' [2]

When the church bells ceased to ring Javanese soldiers continued to run amok. Timorese men trying to protect their daughters and wives were shot. The females were raped – if they screamed, the Javanese were driven into frenzies of excitement and they fought each other to mount their victims again and again. 'If a woman lay mute and stiff, she was shot from the anus to the head,' Fatima Gusmao told me in Darwin in 1986.

Falintil's orders were to resist initially but to do everything possible to survive before withdrawing to the mountains. Roger East intended to go with them. He had faced a grim future, for the going was certain to be very tough indeed. He would

---

2 Michele Turner, *Telling: East Timor, Personal Testimonies 1942–1992*, University of NSW Press, Sydney, 1992.

The Circle of Silence

be hounded by numerically superior forces and could not carry anything that would slow him down.

High above the city, plumes of black smoke turned the sun into an ochre smear. Open drains were clogged with blood. Outside the city, people trying to escape the violence were forced to eat grass, pumpkin leaves, tubers and gourds. Lack of water was a constant problem; they had to lick dew from the grass. Old women, young women, teenagers and very young girls were forced at gunpoint to help the victorious Indonesian army to celebrate their victory. As one decent Javanese soldier would say to me in 1989, 'We have our share of thugs in uniform.'

The 'festivities' continued all night. The females were told they were sure to be pregnant with Javanese babies. Some young girls committed suicide when their condition was confirmed.

The next day, 8 December, the sun rose on a ruined city. Even at the seaside the salt air was tainted with the smell of blood, excrement, cordite and clove cigarettes. Hundreds of murdered Chinese were piled on the beach. Though the Indonesian public would be told the usual cover story – that they were shot because they were Christians engaged in anti-Muslim violence – the truth was they were targeted merely because they were unarmed civilians.

Wreckage of landing craft littered the shoreline. Bodies in uniform floated face down in blood, entrails and vomit. In between volleys of shots, shrieks and the deafening roar of helicopters, the usually bustling seaside was enveloped in surreal silence. A crowd of one hundred 'witnesses' were roped together at the entrance to the wharf. Isobel Lobato carried her son, 4-year-old José. A voice croaked, 'That's Lobato's wife. My God, they can't shoot her.' Nicolau dos Reis Lobato, the vice president who was at that moment fighting a rearguard action, was destined to raise a most remarkable resistance army.

The demeanour of a large group of shell-shocked citizens chosen at random and being marched along the seafront changed dramatically when they realised they were heading towards a line of people being shot on the wharf. Some lost control over their bowels; others were so dazed they moved like zombies. Most wept openly; others, too frightened to make a sound, clung together.

A sergeant using a pistol as a baton conducted proceedings as members of East Java paratrooper battalions 501 and 502 did the killings. When they were shot some fell into the water; others hit the wharf. The witnesses were instructed to count and cheer as each volley of shots rang out. The sergeant stood on the bonnet of a jeep to record the 'tally' on a clipboard – he screamed at the crowd to shout out the numbers as if they were scoring goals at a soccer match. If they failed to ape the right degree of enthusiasm, he shot one of them with his pistol.

Soldiers clubbed and kicked a tall, fair man whose hands were tied behind his back with wire. Such momentous defilement seized everyone's attention; even the enemy were awe-struck to see a white man being treated so brutally. Between sharp, wheezing gasps he shouted, 'Roger East. I'm Australian, a journalist.' He was kicked and clubbed. He wore shorts and a white blood-stained shirt and was barefooted.

A fin sliced through the surface of the water, moving in ever decreasing circles towards the wharf. When Isabella's son was ripped from her arms, she wept inconsolably. The child stared about too stunned to comprehend what was happening. An elderly Chinese man was ordered to tie a length of plumber's pipe to the body of his son with parachute chords. Other Timorese were forced to weigh down the dead with building materials and rocks so they would sink. Working with care as if his son was still alive the father tied his limbs to a metal plumbing pipe. The soldiers laughed at his efforts and one of them sauntered forward and pushed the boy over the edge of the wharf. The father seemed mesmerised as he stared down at the sea until he too was shot and his body kicked into the sea.

Roger East was ordered to turn his back on the guns. Everyone was struck by his dignity as he turned to face them instead. Still shouting that he was 'not Fretilin, an Australian, a journalist', he was shot, some say in the face. As he fell into the sea the soldiers moved to the edge of the wharf and shot at him until he sank.

At the handing over of a bribe by a son of the *liurai* of Atsabe, a relative of Isabella's, young José Lobato, was spared. Isabella was ordered to strip naked. She removed everything except her black panties without uttering a sound. She was knocked down from behind and bayoneted. Pleading to be spared, she was shot in the back and pushed off the wharf. The following day her body was seen floating face down next to that of Rosa Muki Bonaparte, a feisty young member of the Fretilin political party.

Semo ho Espirito Santo, Rosa Muki Bonaparte.
Semo ho Espirito Santo, Isabella Lobato.
Semo ho Espirito Santo, Roger East.

Most of the civilians who were slaughtered that Sunday morning were chosen simply because they had no political affiliation to send the required message – do as you are ordered on the instant, or you will die. And the torment was not over for the witnesses. They were formally pardoned and assured that they would be safe as long as they showed that they had 'learned their lesson'. The sergeant, still clutching his clipboard, demonstrated how to bow when addressed by important personages such as himself and other representatives of the New Order. The crowd made deep obeisance. In stumbling *Tetuñ* he addressed them: 'Now you are Indonesianised.' Smiling and clapping his hands he proclaimed triumphantly. 'Me teach good, but,' he said, wagging his finger like an actor in a side-splitting comedy, 'you can be dead.'

Indonesian national flags were distributed and television cameras zoomed in for a close-up. 'For Indonesian Television News,' shouted the cameramen as if they were speaking to deaf and mentally impaired people. 'Smile, smile. Show how happy you are to be liberated from Portuguese oppression.' Some tried to smile. Their expressions resembled sudden spasms of pain. The cameramen appealed for help; the captain threatened to kill them all on the spot. After a semblance of a smile was finally achieved, the cameramen recorded the cheering citizens.

They were instructed to walk to the airport where they would be issued with identity passes. If anyone disobeyed the masters of the New Order, they would be shot. On the long walk a boy was seen offering a coconut to a soldier. The soldier took the coconut then shot the boy, he dropped to the ground, his legs shaking violently while the soldier calmly drained the coconut. People cowered in disbelief when they saw women on their knees pleading for the soldiers to stop the senseless killings. People in the open were easy prey; they were shot as they kow-towed. Soldiers continued to rape females of all ages; none were spared in the glare of the corrosive sun.

The surviving population waited all day under hot sun without food, water or toilet facilities. The sun was setting when they were told to go home. Not one ID pass had been issued. People were too frightened to speak as they waited for permission to pass through a series of hastily erected road blocks manned by heavy machine guns. Buildings in the centre of the city were fortified with razor wire. People with mad eyes searched among human corpses for missing relatives. Bloated remains of Timor ponies buzzed with flies.

Upon reaching their homes they understood why they had been sent to the airport. All the doors and windows were gone; fly-wire frames had been ripped from their hinges. Carpets were gone. Nails and scraps of underfelt littered floorboards. There was no furniture; kitchens had been stripped. All light shades and bulbs had been taken. All food, crockery and utensils were gone. Sinks, taps and bathroom fittings had been torn from walls. Beds and clothing were gone. Books and children's toys were gone. What couldn't be stolen had been destroyed. The Marconi Centre was destroyed and even the water purification plant had been bombed. Jeeps and trucks drove at break-neck speed, tooting horns. A seemingly endless line of trucks loaded with their possessions was down at the wharf.

That night bullets whizzed through windows followed by gusts of drunken laughter. This was an indication of things to come. True to their lust for money the Javanese stripped the hospital. The X-ray machine and operating tables were sold to Indonesian hospitals, along with all linen, equipment and instruments. In the overcrowded wards enemy soldiers took precedence, though they too suffered from the lack of equipment. Timorese without family to look after them died of neglect.

Trucks waiting at the blood-soaked wharf loaded the loot onto ships that had brought the infantry in. In the months that followed hundreds of thousands of ponies, goats, pigs, dogs and chickens were *acquired* for the live animal trade in Java. The Javanese commandeered all donated supplies of Red Cross rice; what they could not sell to starving Timorese they sold in Bali and other islands in the Indonesian archipelago.

The next day the phone went wild. Did I know a Roger East? Did I know anyone who might know him?

'Why, who is he?'

'East's gone west,' quipped one cynical so-and-so. I had grown used to limiting my rage so he got away with this smart remark. Roger East was the sixth Australian journalist deliberately murdered by Indonesian soldiers. This spoke volumes to me. That's it then, said the old familiar voice in my head. This cannot be officially ignored. I was in for a severe disappointment. If the Balibo Five were stuck in a hole out-of-sight out-of-mind as far as Jakarta lobbyists and DFAT were concerned, Roger East was non-existent.

It was not long before the denigration began: Roger East was a communist and an old hack ready for the scrapheap. He was hopelessly naive, a waster and a drifter and he had been found wanting during World War II. Nevertheless I took advantage of every opportunity to protest about his death and the deaths of the other journalists, and the murders of the Timorese. I could speak about Greg until the cows came home and I was certainly given many opportunities by the media, but the barrage became so intense that I could no longer see the old joke: when a man screaming in agony bashing his head against a brick wall is asked why he keeps doing it, he says, 'It feels so wonderful when I stop.'

On 8 December 1975, the phone had begun to ring. The media wanted me to make meaningful statements. East Timor had been invaded by Indonesian forces, starting with a huge parachute drop on Dili and Baucau. I did my best but I was mainly frustrated by my ignorance. I knew any invasion was sure to be bloody. I tried and failed to suppress the horrible images forming in my mind. I imagined the United States would denounce the invasion at the United Nations. Citizens of the world would hold public meetings demanding support for East Timor. Hunger strikes in England, the birthplace of the Magna Carta, would be common and all Western governments would ostracise the Indonesian dictator. All that was needed was a little bit of humanity.

On a shortwave radio that was crackling and waning, I heard explosions and gunfire in the background. Fretilin member Alarico Fernandes's voice broke through the static: 'Indonesian forces have been landed in Dili by sea . . . they are flying over Dili dropping out paratroopers . . . Aircraft are dropping out more and more paratroopers . . . A lot of people have been killed indiscriminately . . . Women and children are being killed by Indonesian forces . . . we are going to be killed! SOS, we call for your help, this is an urgent call.'

The December invasion was promoted as a success in Indonesia. Actually it was a failure, but it would be a long time before that could be determined. Falintil put up a spirited resistance against overwhelming numbers; it took five months before the Javanese breached Falintil defences. Their remorse as they ran away to fight again another day, leaving their families to the mercy of the enemy, is horrible to contemplate.

In the years to come the Javanese continued to employ starvation as an extermination weapon. Napalm and deadly chemicals poisoned plant food and water supplies. Public beheadings, the mutilation of genitalia, burying and burning victims alive, the use of cigarettes to burn victims, the slicing off of ears was widespread, and systematic executions, arbitrary detention, torture, rape and sexual slavery prevailed in a culture of impunity in Indonesian-occupied East Timor.

Two days before the invasion, José Ramos-Horta, the Timorese minister for external affairs, had been ordered to leave his family and friends so that he could represent East Timor to the outside world. It was a daunting task. Seen from the perspective of a small, neglected country about to be blown apart by war, Ramos-Horta was on a mission impossible. The shy 25-year-old arrived in New York in the depth of winter. He was the youngest foreign minister in the world and his initial task was to persuade the United Nations Security Council to allow him to address them.

He would suffer homesickness and frequently lacked the funds to buy decent food. He regularly received death threats. In Indonesia and Australia, attempts were made to defame and discredit him. He would reject numerous bribes (including one from a Commonwealth ambassador who offered to secure a favourable vote for East Timor at the United Nations upon payment of two thousand Australian dollars). He would learn to live without a real home, furniture or a car. He carried the hope and fatigue of a man forced to live permanently in transit, while his Indonesian counterparts luxuriated in five star hotels supported by bevies of Western public relations consultants.

TEN

In the summer of 1978 José Ramos-Horta's sister, Maria Ortensia, was killed by a US Bronco aircraft flown by Indonesian forces in East Timor. The same year two brothers, Nunu and Guilherme, died. Nunu was killed by bullets fired from a US-designed M-16 automatic assault rifle made under licence in Indonesia, and Guilherme died as a result of a rocket and strafing attack by a US-supplied helicopter on an East Timorese village. No wonder their mother Dona Natalina Ramos-Horta said on the ABC in 1999: 'People who behave like that [the Indonesian military] are not civilised.'

Semo ho Espirito Santo, Maria Ortensia Ramos-Horta.
Semo ho Espirito Santo, Nunu Ramos-Horta.
Semo ho Espirito Santo, Guilherme Ramos-Horta.

On 22 December 1975, José Ramos-Horta achieved a remarkable victory. The United Nations Security Council handed down a unanimous resolution (384) calling on Indonesia to withdraw all its troops from East Timor 'without delay'. The precious paper was in José Ramos-Horta's hands, but that was all it was, a piece of paper. It was worthless because Indonesia behaved as if it did not exist, and world leaders, by remaining silent, gave tacit approval to the illegal Indonesian occupation of Timor, known now by its Indonesian name of Timor Timur (or Tim Tim). Another silent circle and one that destroyed all hope for the Timorese.

The two generals in charge of the 7 December invasion, Murdani and Kalbuadi, were forced to admit secretly that without continuing US logistical military support there was a good chance their troops would be beaten.[1] When the home of the brave granted Javanese requests for support, the victorious generals ordered a second invasion. On Christmas Day, while the rest of the world celebrated peace on earth and goodwill to men, twenty thousand Javanese marines obeyed their orders to 'show the enemy your fangs' and 'submit the aborigines to our will'.

At the United Nations, Indonesian representatives claimed that brave Indonesian 'volunteers' had responded to entreaties from terrified Timorese to free them from the 'Fretilin terror regime'. If only the world had known about this report written by the CIA operative, Philip Leighty:

> We are sending the Indonesian generals everything they need to fight a major war against somebody who doesn't have any guns. We are sending them rifles, ammunition, mortars, grenades, food, and

---

[1] Javanese generals had underestimated Falintil's fighting prowess and skill with modern weapons. Since Portugal was a member of NATO, some Falintil weapons were superior to those of their Javanese counterparts. Falintil had light infantry weapons: G3 automatic rifles, Second World War Mauser rifles, grenades, bazookas, mortars and Mercedes-manufactured troop transport vehicles. Besides, it was traditional for every Timorese male to be trained for three years in compulsory military service and they had been very well taught by their Portuguese officers.

The Circle of Silence

helicopters. You name it; they get it. And they get it direct. Without continued, heavy US logistical military support, the Indonesians might not be able to pull it off. No one cares. No one gives a damn. It is something that I will forever be ashamed of. The only justification I ever hear for what we are doing is concern that [they] are on the verge of being accepted as a new member of the United Nations and there is a chance that the country in question is going to be either leftist or neutralist and are therefore not likely to vote with the United States at the United Nations.

The bulk of the surviving Timorese population fled to Mount Ramelau, Mount Mundo Perdido and to the main stronghold in the east, the spookily named Matebian – 'The Mountains of the Dead'. Falintil coped with the huge influx of refugees by constructing *umas* (huts) and planting food crops under the cover of darkness. In Timor's climate plants grow fast, but the Javanese made daily raids in an attempt to destroy every vestige of food. At the same time the people suffered daily bombing raids and lack of every comfort.

Wholesale exploitation was forced upon the population. The Javanese seized the opportunity to be everything from judge to torturer and executioner. Thus rapists, pederasts, arsonists, murderers and thieves shook off all restraints and revelled in barbarism. In Dili, all educated Timorese, anyone wearing glasses, any person who had held an official position in the Portuguese administration, including civil servants, teachers and doctors, were murdered. Along with apolitical Timorese they were taken to Areia Branca (a popular beach outside Dili) and shot by a succession of execution squads.

Although a handful of professionals had quit the country and some had retreated with Falintil, the purge was perhaps the most damaging act of all, since it ensured that the country was now bereft of Timorese possessing administrative skills. Details of these atrocities have yet to be recorded as such; their numbers are lumped in with overall deaths recorded as due to 'natural causes' – this was the term that the New Order used in its official documentation for their deliberate policy of mass murder. Later, when the people were driven into concentration camps called 'strategic hamlets' the term 'population losses' was also employed. When the desperate asked questions they were told that their missing relatives had been sent to Bali – this was a cruel lie because it gave hope when there was none.

Timorese could be shot for failing to comprehend orders spoken in the unfamiliar language of the victors. Many were shot for refusing to salute the Indonesian flag: Timorese had to kow-tow to all Indonesians. Women and young girls were raped with such regularity that the people concluded it must be official policy.

The Javanese were now in total control of every aspect of the lives of every Timorese. The Indonesian president was given opportunities to speak to the outside world. 'No power in the world can check the desire of the East Timorese to join the Republic of Indonesia,' Suharto asserted. Yet in one week when twenty-seven thousand Timorese tried to apply for emigration, the emigration department closed its doors.

There was one good piece of news: Timorese priests had opposed a plan to conduct church services in Indonesian. When they made it clear that they were prepared to die, foreign priests supported the Timorese priests and the authorities were forced to give in. Subsequent attendance at churches formed the basis of the claim that the whole country was Catholic – in fact, since the church was the only place where the lingua franca, Tetuñ, could be spoken without an immediate threat of death, people attended in order to hear their own language.

In Melbourne I was able to raise a laugh by claiming that in five hundred years the Portuguese had been able to convert only a handful to the Holy Roman Catholic Church, but it only took the Javanese a few days to convert all of Timor. 'It's a miracle,' I declared.

The audience roared with laughter: 'It's a miracle.'

'The pope will have to beatify the arch-toad Suharto,' cried a young Timorese boy who had lost his entire family. 'Praise the Lord and praise Allah.'

Former Aussie commando Cliff Morris cried, 'Praise the Lord and pass the ammunition.'

Audience enthusiasm rose. 'Allah be praised.'

'The light of the world, be praised.'

'The butcher of Jakarta is a Catholic saint.'

'It's a miracle.'

Knowing what was happening in East Timor was as bad as worrying about Greg had been. I could never have done anything to help him, but the people there now were just trying to stay alive. I could not stop thinking how parents would be suffering watching their children's terror as they starved or died from their injuries.

The Javanese established a naval blockade. No one could get in and no one could escape. However, five months after the invasion, only parts of East Timor could be said to be under Javanese control, because of their cruelty and the valiant resistance by Falintil.

In Australia, four men had made several brave attempts to break the naval blockade encircling East Timor. The subsequent storm in a DFAT coffee mug caused by their derring-do thrust all activists for East Timor into the fray. On their third and last attempt, *Dawn*, a fifteen-metre ex-Army work boat, was packed with Red Cross supplies. Manolis Mavromatis had agreed to sail it to East Timor for eighteen hundred dollars, which did not cover his expenses. Robert Wesley-Smith took a .410 cut-down shotgun and a 12-gauge shotgun. Cliff Morris took his 12-gauge shotgun. The vessel was equipped with two 12-gauge shotguns for use against crocodiles and sharks. James Zantis, a man known for his work providing aid to underdeveloped countries, also had one shotgun.

When they reached the five-kilometre limit they were arrested in Australian waters by coastguards at gunpoint and taken to the Northern Territory Customs House. They were told that they were free to leave. As they stood to go a telephone call came from the caretaker prime minister, Malcolm Fraser. The accused heard him insisting that they must be charged and their ship with its supplies impounded. Subsequently two of the men were found guilty but released on bail. Upon appealing the decision, they faced criminal proceedings in the Supreme Court of the Northern Territory.

'Once that arrogant arsehole Whitlam was sent packing, I expected compassion from the new mob,' Cliff Morris told me. He was found guilty of two offences: 'an attempt to unlawfully export drugs, medicinal and pharmaceutical goods' and 'to unlawfully export firearms'. *Dawn*'s cargo consisted of an odd assortment of domestic medical supplies, such as scissors, adhesive plaster, gauze, ointments, antiseptics, anaesthetics, antibiotics, painkillers and anti-malarial preparations. There were also quantities of baby food and medicine for paediatric use, plus bags of rice.

'Why would Fraser arrest you for providing humanitarian aid?' a Darwin reporter asked Cliff.

'His impending visit to sign trade deals with Indonesia, no doubt.'

Cliff's speech in court profoundly moved the magistrate, who resisted all pressure to find them guilty. He said they were heroes. Soon after these legal proceedings the magistrate retired. John Howard, the minister for customs, refused to return the medical supplies.

I did not expect that I would be invited to speak about East Timor in the Netherlands, England, Ireland and later America. Or to be blacklisted and threatened with arrest and deportation along with José Ramos-Horta, Madame Danielle Mitterrand and Archbishop Desmond Tutu if I attended the Second Asia Pacific Conference. I wrote an article which was published in the *Canberra Times* stating that 'they had nothing to fear from me: I wear hats with flowers, I'm so short I look as if I'm standing in a hole and my only weapons are words'.

Over the following years, when it became apparent that I was not going to shut up, I was vilified. I also received phone calls from several more characters wanting to divulge information – they certainly knew about the workings of government and ASIO. Still they continued to call. They accused Whitlam of truckling to the Suharto regime to the extent that the Indonesian dictator assumed (correctly) that the Australian prime minister had intended to abandon the Timorese, and they warned me about a secret organisation of corrupt Australian academics, diplomats, businessmen, politicians, editors and opportunists known as the Jakarta Lobby.

The enormity of the invasion made my former life seem meaningless. All my adventures, pursuit of pleasure, the books I had read, the films and plays I had seen, my love of art and travel seemed feckless, especially when I remembered the image of the shadow-crucifix Greg had made on our last day together.

It flared into my mind repeatedly: this image haunted me and became part of my life.

If he had lived, Greg would have fought in the UN for East Timor. I believe Tony, Gary, Brian and Malcolm would have joined him. I could do nothing less. Many years would pass before we learned that the attack on Balibó had involved five battalions – that's three thousand troops. The border town was attacked with machine guns, bazookas, tanks and aircraft. The Javanese had been ordered to wear uniforms without insignia and to carry older, Soviet-made weapons so as not to be identified as Indonesian regulars. In other words if a Javanese was killed he would be identified as a Timorese communist. This enabled Suharto to hide his losses. Pity the poor soldiers who knew that this would be their fate when they died. The Javanese already held Batugade, but the three-pronged attack on Maliana and Balibó had been massive.

The invasion caused a profound change in me. From that date on I was never going to be the same and, in fact, Australia was never going to be the same if the implications proved to be right. Common sense made me realise what a fool I had been to believe anything my government had alleged about Greg's murder. True, I had objected to obvious lies, but I thought they were mistakes made through incompetence. Now I knew ASIO must know more than had been admitted and they must have known about something as momentous as an Indonesian invasion. Timor was closer to us than Tasmania. ASIO operatives were only pawns in Whitlam's hands. Words like *criminal silence*, *collusion* and *conspiracy* circulated in my head to the extent that I thought I must be going mad. Despite all that our wharfies and other Australians had done to help Indonesia get rid of the Dutch, Australians were no more than dead meat to their supreme commander, General Suharto.

* * *

In November 1978, when Malcolm Fraser invited President Suharto to visit Australia my letter was published in the *Age* asking our Prime Minister to inquire of his honoured guest what had happened to my husband. Many times then and since I have been assured that the visit failed to take place because of that letter.

Author Michele Turner called me after one of my interviews. She knew a lot about East Timor so I invited her to dinner. She arrived wearing a beautiful cream suit. I was struck by her good looks and vivacity. After working for Social Security she had taken a year off to record the experiences of the unemployed. Her book *Stuck!* had been a great success. This had encouraged her to write another book, and the subject was to be East Timor. I lapped up all she was telling me about her research; this was what I had lacked and she seemed to know everything.

Through her I made contact with members of the Australian forces who had fought there in World War II, including Cliff Morris, whom Greg had previously interviewed. Cliff spoke Tetuñ and he was producing a travellers' dictionary in Tetuñ–English and English–Tetuñ. I remember asking who would want to holiday in Timor? He replied with a laugh that some people might love a holiday in Hell. We made a list of all those we would send on such a holiday; I leave it to you to guess their names.

I accompanied Michele to several interviews for her wonderful book *Telling: East Timor* (1992), which taught me how to be relentless in pursuit of truth. One Timorese interviewed for the book said his teeth had been kicked in by a Javanese during what he had been told was to be 'a friendly chat' by Prabowo, Suharto's son-in-law. When Michele made her subject describe the boots, right down to the tiniest detail, I thought she was being cruel. But as the man spoke I could see that just the telling of his torture was beneficial and, once the interview was over, he actually smiled and said he had never told anyone before. From the description given Michele was able to deduce that the torturer had worn P.T. Denok boots, which added weight to the victim's testimony. Michele told us about P.T. Denok, the cartel set up by General Murdani, and gave us details of his other East Timor enterprises, such as the export of marble, and the acquisition of coffee plantations and many buildings.[2]

The naval blockade supported by military aircraft continued until 1989. Timorese in the Diaspora worked double shifts to pay the bribes necessary to bring a relative to safety and, though they tried to attend demonstrations, these could be divisive – in a curious anomaly, while all political affiliations were redundant inside East Timor, resentments over the so-called civil war raged in the West. Accounts of the aftermath of the invasion were hair-raising, but Timorese refused to go public for fear of retribution against their families in Timor. There were no

---

2 Here's a little insight into corrupt circles within corrupt circles. The Murdani monopoly would lose favour in 1990, which enabled Siti Hardiyanti Ruckmana, the daughter of Suharto, also known as Tutut, to *acquire* P.T. Denok's East Timor coffee cartel. This simply replaced the existing cartel and continued the unfair price paid to Timorese coffee farmers. Further, there was long-term damage to coffee crops by P.T. Denok's enforced practices, which damaged plants beyond repair. In 1998 the *Washington Post* revealed that USAID's Indonesian partner, NCBA, funded the East Timor Coffee Project without reporting its connections to Tutut and her shareholder husband Lieutenant General Prabowo Subianto and the puppet governor Osoria-Soares.

The Circle of Silence   153

set routes for escapees and the naval and air force blockade was almost impregnable. Some talked about chemical and biological warfare being waged by the Javanese, but the numbers they claimed had died were doubted by the media.

You could go mad worrying about the Timorese. I had imagined fleeing to the mountains during World War II; now my mind worked overtime – what if I was in the mountains with Evan? How could you remain sane when you have lost everything that makes life civilised? Even if you avoid being killed in the bombing raids they are a form of torture. The blockade was backed by a torrent of media disinformation. If there had been any means of escape Timorese would have fled from their homeland by the tens of thousands. The telephone system had been dismantled and even when it was reinstated some were arrested as they emerged from the telephone exchange. They were never seen again.

A lump had been found in my left breast but mercifully it did not get larger over time. A wide strip of white hair grew at my temples. I frequently caught Evan watching me as if he was deeply concerned. I was all he had now.

One day a neighbour told me to go and sit on a beach in Queensland; he said it was obvious to everyone, including Evan, that I was completely worn out. He offered to take care of my son.

Instead of Queensland, I decided to go to Iran because I knew my neighbour was right – I needed a break. I had been studying that fabulous country for years and since I had spent time in the San Rafael library I had become fascinated with nomadic weaving. Never in my life had I been judged so harshly. My critics operated entirely on supposition. For example, when I asked for sleeping tablets, one GP announced: 'What can you expect, Mrs Shackleton? You've gone after the money.' He assumed I was highly paid for interviews I was doing for East Timor.

Before Balibó I had time to read and enjoy my life. The impact on my psyche was a nightmare. I wanted to escape, not just for a holiday but for life. Timor held me firmly in its thrall – like many others I could not give up when the Timorese were fighting so valiantly.

A neighbour knew David Stronach, the director of The British Institute of Persian Studies in Tehran, so I arranged to stay there. In a very short time I had made the necessary arrangements to board Evan with friends and so there was nothing to stop me. Though I felt guilty on several levels I could not wait to go. I arrived in Tehran on 28 September 1976, on the first day of Ramadan, the most sacred Islamic religious observance. The dark streets were deserted except for black-clad mullahs moving like shadows through moonlight. This would have been a romantic scene if it had not been for all the shonky imitations of Western high-rise buildings in the land known for its fabulous architecture.

The British Institute of Persian Studies was an impressive building situated on a large piece of land including gardens and a swimming pool. Best of all, the library was filled with books about Iran printed in English. I met some wonderful people including anthropologists, zoologists, archaeologists and I even spent some time with Sir Max Mallowan without knowing who he was – a most famous Egyptologist and married to Agatha Christie.

I went to see Ali Baluk Bashi who had the power to issue a permit for me to visit a nomadic tribe. A woman travelling alone! This was simply not done in Iran. 'You could be arrested and beaten for trying to escape a brutal husband.'

'Surely, Mr Baluk Bashi, you have laws to protect women from being beaten.'

'Surely not, Mrs Shackleton, she probably deserves it.'

After that poor start, I will always be grateful to Mr Mashrouteh, an authority on Persian architecture, art, craft and history. Thanks to his generosity I saw silk being spun by hand from cocoons and natural dyeing processes using indigo, pomegranate skins, saffron and cochineal – those unfortunate insects used by the Incas to produce bright scarlet when they weren't using human blood. He also promised to take me to the original mines (if I returned) to see cobalt blue shot with violet that provides the glaze for the blue tiles cladding their mosques. In Isfahan I watched a man sitting on a dirt floor in a shaft of sunlight painting a miniature and I trailed though markets stacked with silken embroideries, lapis lazuli jewellery, unique instruments, bundles of raw silk, gelims (flat-woven nomadic rugs), lumps of indigo, baskets of rose petals and saffron. Pyramids of sticky cakes, nougat and Turkish Delight were just some of the sweetmeats I remembered from The Arabian Nights.

Fired with enthusiasm, my sketchbook was filled with ideas for weavings large and small. Eager to return to my wonderful life filled with colour and threads, historical research and teaching I was most eager to get home to my most precious jewel, Evan, who gave me a wonderful gift on my return. 'You can go away any time you like, Mummy. If I thought you were not coming back I would be hysterical, but I know you will always come home to me.'

What a lovely little boy he was.

But Iran had been a dream and I was back in nightmare country. Information about East Timor was available for those who wanted to know. I continued to ask awkward questions, but I was flagging. It was such an unequal battle that even suggesting how bad I felt in safe, sunny Australia was an insult to the suffering of the East Timorese. When anyone offered me sympathy in the hearing of a Timorese I would cringe inside. By then Timorese in the Diaspora knew that their families were dying in thousands.

Most Australians had no idea that there was a war on their doorstep.

Early in 1976 a group of concerned Darwin citizens began to operate a secret radio link with the Timorese Resistance Army. They were hunted by Australian Federal and local police, ASIO and, on one alarming occasion, an Australian airforce plane which swooped on Brian Manning, the respected wharfie, and a journalist who were avoiding detection in the bush.

The illegal operation was staffed by undercover amateurs.

Secret reports were passed to members of the Timorese government-in-exile by phone. Since they were stationed in Mozambique, Lisbon and New York, Manning was not surprised to receive a $3000 phone bill which he could not pay immediately. Malcolm Fraser intervened and Manning's phone line was disconnected. He then applied for a licence, which was refused. Brian explains: 'We began to contact Timor independently through OTC. We waited until others had spoken and were subjected to abuse by some licensed users, but eventually they tolerated us.'

This radio link provided the only reliable source of information about the war being waged on the civilian population at that time. The orgy of killing and sexual abuse that had characterised the aftermath of the invasion continued. The severity of the killings all over the country was payback for Kalbuadi's failure to suppress the Timorese resistance. It was understandably galling to the so-called professional soldier to be beaten by volunteer amateurs – several inspiring resistance leaders had demonstrated a flair for guerrilla warfare. Under Lobato's leadership they inflicted heavy casualties in a life-and-death campaign, for which the Javanese having been trained to rely on firepower were taken by surprise. You would have thought they might have learned from experience

The Circle of Silence

at home that rapacious behaviour strengthens the resolve of many surviving victims.

Just the fact that the resistance army was fighting against the savagery encouraged tens of thousands to seek sanctuary behind their resistance army lines. Lobato's organisational skills saved lives. Before the occupation, stocks of food, medicine, arms and ammunition were hidden in mountain regions where armoured divisions could not penetrate. Lobato encouraged his shell-shocked civilians to build housing and produce food crops. Work acted as a spur to hope and many families, separated during massacres and total destruction of their hamlets, were reunited in the safe havens.

Nevertheless the degree of the trauma cannot be underestimated. James Dunn, former consul to East Timor, reported in his 1983 book, *Timor: A People Betrayed*, that a letter written by a Timorese official stated that out of a pre-invasion population of eighty-five thousand in the area of Baucau, fifty-three thousand had joined the exodus to the mountains and, out of thirty-two thousand who had elected to stay, only fewer than ten thousand people had survived.

The secret radio was drafted into the service of the United Nations when the Secretary-General of the United Nations, Kurt Waldheim, decided to send an envoy to East Timor. Winspeare Guicciardi was able to contact Lobato via the secret radio link and he was forewarned of a document prepared for Waldheim's visit addressed to Javanese battalion commanders and administrative officials. All members of the armed forces had to wear civilian dress so that it would appear to the delegation that they were unarmed civilians. Roads had to be cleaned and kept free of military equipment. Answers to questions such as 'What treatment is given to prisoners-of-war? were to be rehearsed. Banners of protest against UN interference were prepared.

The Portuguese offered to provide the Secretary-General with a warship until CIA reported, 'The Indonesians are considering whether to sink the vessel before it reaches Darwin.' (This document published by John Pilger was held in secret for twelve years and was finally smuggled into West Timor under the floor carpet of a car.) A safe landing place was suggested via the secret radio and a plane was made available, but the day before the UN envoy was due to land the Indonesian air force bombed the landing site.

On 4 February 1976, the CIA reported the success of the charade: 'Jakarta has managed, during the UN representative's visit, to conceal all signs of Indonesian military forces.'

In East Timor Alarico Fernandes had surrendered and handed over the radio to the Indonesisans. It now fell to the genius of Andrew Waterhouse, who had created a transmitter out of a ghetto blaster. Agio Pereira recommenced regular contact making tape recordings of the material which included updates on Indonesian atrocities. As usual, the media was reluctant to use the material describing them as unconfirmed reports.

A new operation was set up in Rum Jungle thick with crocs and snakes. When Andrew Waterhouse visited the site he was convinced it was unsafe. As they abandoned camp they heard the rumble of car engines and the Northern Territory police arrived. The renegades were arrested and fined $100 each. Despite arrests and constant surveillance Charlie India Eco Tango calling East Timor operated until Xanana was arrested in 1992. Once he was incarcerated in Cipinang prison he developed other means of communications with Naldo Reis, Kirsty Sword and the Catholic Church.

The Circle of Silence

ELEVEN

The leader of the East Timorese Resistance Army, Nicolau dos Reis Lobato, was killed at Mount Maubuse on 31 December 1978. When I saw a photograph of him, I was stunned by his masculine beauty. Desperation after his loss had sharpened once I saw that photograph. I realised he had been a symbol, a shadow, and I had put him out of my mind because I could not stand to think how he had suffered over the loss of his baby son and wife – I imagined his guilt would have been unbearable. I was shocked to discover I had also put Greg and Tony out of my mind. Gary was not the quiet, thoughtful friend that Tony had been to me; consequently I did not miss him as much as I missed Tony. However, each of their deaths was etched in my heart and now Nicolau had joined them.

    The man who claimed the credit for murdering Greg and his colleagues had been decorated and promoted in 1975. As a result of his involvement in the murder of Nicolau he was decorated and promoted again. In an interview in *Tempo* in 1986 Mohammad Yunus Yosfiah described himself as *orang tempur*, a fighting animal. He went on to say he liked nothing better than to relax at the end of the day while watching a video of Lobato's death. I wondered if he had filmed Greg, Tony, Malcolm, Brian and Gary as they died like dogs.

The true circumstances of Nicolau's death are known only to Mohammad Yunus Yosfiah and his cronies. I tried to gain comfort from Victor Hugo's description of the final, desperate, resistance of some French soldiers at the Battle of Waterloo:

> They could hear in the crepuscular gloom that cannons were being loaded, wicks were being lit and gleamed like the eyes of tigers in the night, making a circle around their heads; all the shot-firers of the English batteries approached the cannons, and then, deeply moved, holding the moment of reckoning hanging over these men, an English general – Colville according to some, Maitland according to others – cried out to them: 'Brave Frenchmen, give yourselves up!'
> Cambronne replied: 'Shit!'

Les Misérables is based upon an ethic about the triumph of the defeated. The exclamation 'shit' is not a lament – it expresses defiance not regret. The use of base language raises the stakes; turns the screw. By robbing the enemy of their chance to be magnanimous, to be human in an inhuman situation, it is a celebration of courage. 'Shit' is a rapier thrust. The men who are about to die will not go quietly.

If rumours that Nicolau shot himself after a half-hour gun battle are true, I see it as a victory, for he knew the heartless enemy's proficiency in stripping living flesh from bone with vivisection knives. He knew about his gentle wife's murder at the hands of these brutal *orang tempur*. It's a relief to know he eluded his enemies, even in death.

Semo ho Espirito Santo Nicolau dos Reis Lobato.

The Circle of Silence

There was every reason to suspect treachery. Javanese used the difficult conditions forced on the Timorese to establish a cruel system of collaboration. Disease and famine were worse than in the previous years.

The Australian government's response to Nicolau Lobato's murder was to present six Nomad Searchmaster planes fitted with ground and sea surveillance radar to the Suharto regime and it agreed to provide facilities to train Kopassus troops in Australia. British Aerospace sold Indonesia eight ground-attack Hawk aircraft. The company director described the sale as 'superb news' and 'a real breakthrough into the South-East Asia market'. Four weeks later the US vice president, Walter Mondale, visited Jakarta to finalise details of the sale of sixteen A-4 Skyhawk aircraft. He commended the Indonesian regime on its human rights record, because plans had been announced to release tens of thousands of Indonesian political prisoners held without trial for thirteen years. The Western bureaucrats, intelligence officers, academics, journalists, editors and politicians known as the Jakarta Lobby continued to make excuses for the Suharto regime.

The Timorese mourned the loss of Lobato. The vast majority of his officers died with him. The Javanese claimed a total victory and, in Jakarta, they lined up to be photographed with Lobato's bullet-ridden body. He had been preserved in some kind of wax that made him unrecognisable, so many Timorese refused to believe that their beloved leader was gone. His baby son, who was taken from his mother moments before she was bayoneted and shot on the wharf at Dili, was destined to be educated in Jakarta.

Civilians and guerrillas made sporadic attempts at resistance with mixed results. When the name Xanana finally emerged some of us connected it with the letters column in *A Voz de Timor* (*The Voice of Timor*), the Dili newspaper that had been an important focus for political debate in those halcyon days before the occupation. A contributor who signed himself Xanana had displayed a persuasive skill in putting the case for caution. Xanana was also the name of a popular song. We knew our heroes sang Lead Belly's 'Cotton Fields' but we dare not believe in the emergence of a new resistance leader on such slender and bizarre evidence. It's as well we did not witness him running like a wild animal from carpet bombing raids and trying to eat grass.

The Fence of Legs Operation or The Encirclements (code-named *pagar betis*) was employed by the Javanese from 1979 to 1980 and used methods reminiscent of the great animal hunts conducted by the British Raj in India in the late nineteenth and early twentieth centuries. The *pagar betis* differed in one small way – the British Raj employed Indians to beat the ground to flush out terrified wild animals as easy targets for sport; the Javanese forced Timorese people to flush out human beings. The Fence of Legs Operation forced thousands of males from the age of 9 to 60 out of their homes; they were not given time to collect water, protective clothing or digging sticks and knives with which to obtain food. There was no mercy for the sick and feeble, and no transport. Thousands of Timorese were driven across the country ahead of soldiers armed with whips, guns, fixed bayonets and *machetes*. The theory that they were to flush out areas where guerrillas were thought to be hiding was spurious. As the human chain tightened, *anyone* hiding in the bush was forced into the open. Mostly these were civilians who had quit their villages to seek sanctuary.

One survivor agreed to tell me something he had witnessed. He was making for Matebian with a family of three; the wife was very ill and they were all starving. The father carried his baby daughter in his arms. They heard a commotion and ran to hide in a rocky formation.

Watching through cracks in the rocks they saw a line of Timorese being forced to form a human chain, beating the ground with sticks. A civilian hiding in the long grass stood and held his hands above his head. Some of the beaters called out to him, telling him to save himself, and they were shot dead from behind. Soldiers then ran forward and hacked at the man with machetes. A woman and three children also emerged and tried to run away. Shots were fired and one of the children fell. A roar of condensed grief and fury erupted all along the line as the Javanese gave chase. What happened to the woman and children could only be guessed from their screams.

The right pincer of the formation then closed in towards the rocky formation. 'We were sure we were going to be discovered,' my informant told me. 'The father then bashed his baby daughter's head on the rock. I have never seen a more loving act in my life. He did it to save her from a far worse death.' A moment like that cannot be removed from the mind. I was too shocked to cry, but tears sprang from my informant's eyes like water in a sudden storm.

As a military operation, *pagar betis* was a failure; as a means of enforcing genocide it was a success. Many Timorese who survived starvation and exposure died on the long trek back home; some were mentally impaired. Grandfathers mourning the terrible deaths of their grandsons were too weak to plant crops and so widespread starvation followed. The repeat of *pagar betis* ensured further starvation and death. My report published in the *Age* in 1990 in which I accused the Javanese of a deliberate policy of genocide was never refuted.

* * *

Indonesia launched a new operation in September 1981. In Jakarta, Defence Operation sources called it the *perang terachir*, the 'final' or 'decisive' war. It involved tens of thousands of Timorese citizens. In their book *The War Against East Timor*, Carmel Budiardjo and Liem Soei Liong say the aim of the operation 'was to drive all Falintil guerrillas and their families from the western and eastern sectors into the central sector where they would be exterminated'.[1] This optimistically named 'final war' was launched in retaliation for increased guerrilla activity, which was something of a miracle since a succession of replacements for Lobato had been captured and killed.

Despite their disarray after the loss of their charismatic leader and the logistics involved, Timorese continued to oppose the detested enemy. Numerous guerrilla attacks were launched during 1980 and according to an ACFOA (Australian Council for Overseads Aid) report in 1981, an Indonesian attack aircraft and three helicopters were shot down during April, another miracle since the Timorese lacked missiles and war hardware which was in abundant supply to the Javanese. The magnifying power of dread for the survivors of the Fence of Legs germinated stupefying fear as civilians realised that the Javanese generals were bent on revenge.

A news report in a Hong Kong-based news agency headed 'The Worst Situation in the World' described the operation:

> The Indonesian army is driving large groups of the male population [of East Timor] in long sweeps through the mountains to eliminate the remaining guerrillas . . . informants conservatively estimate the [total number of East Timorese involved] at 50,000.

---

1 Carmel Budiardjo and Liem Soei Liong, The *War Against East Timor*, Zed Books, London, 1984.

They march in groups of twelve ahead of Indonesian soldiers like African beaters for White hunters. They are ordered to look for guerrillas, shout when they see them ahead and even engage them in struggle. [It is claimed] these human lures are not armed.

The forced march ended with a massacre of the civilian participants. This act of senseless brutality created such hatred for the Javanese that many Timorese lost all sense of fear. As Resistance's new strategies spread over the country, they left their homes to join the fight.

In 1989 I met a Timorese girl who remembered that time vividly. As the number of enemy troops increased in the Mountains of the Dead, thought their parents did their best not to frighten them, the children knew what to expect. 'A stange calm seemed to enter my father and brother, who was sixteen,' she told me. They had survived the *pagar betis*. 'I did not understand a lot of what was said or done, but now I know that though they were very frightened they were still like the tide inside.' 'Like the calm before the storm,' I suggested. 'More like hatred turned to stone. They had lost their sense of fear for these alien troops who were determined to exterminate us.'

Trying to get the Western public to know about or understand any of this at the time was almost impossible until 1984 when Budiardjo and Liong published their book. Their information came from incredibly brave people who risked their lives by travelling to Bali in order to call family members in Australia or Portugal.

Books about the tragedy of the Timorese nation are now legion. Although they were written out of a desire to expose the facts, some are dated. This is not due to a lack of academic rigour. Suharto paid millions of dollars to Western public relations firms to manipulate facts in order to reduce the impact that the simple truth would have had on public opinion all over the world. I have just re-read the notes I made after interviewing Andy Sloan, executive of PR Company Hill and Knowlton. He refused to see me, so I interviewed him by phone. After saying he was tired of nuisance calls he replied to my questions as if speaking to an imbecile.

He told me his firm merely supplied national development information on Indonesia. The company was not involved in any way with political matters. It worked with industries all over the world giving financial, business and investment advice. 'And', he declared petulantly, 'in any case we have lost that account.' He declined to discuss the matter any further. He appeared to me to be ignorant about even basic facts regarding the Javanese occupation of East Timor.

Misinformation had been rife from the start. On 1 April 1977 the front page of the *Age* in Melbourne ran this article by Indonesian politician Adam Malik: 'About 50,000 people might have been killed in the war in East Timor. The total may be 50,000. But what does this mean if compared with 600,000 people who want to join Indonesia? Then what is the big fuss?'

After this statement Westerners deduced that it was probably safe to double the amount and so the figure of one hundred thousand dead went down into the history. The truth is, the death rate in the first four years of the Indonesian occupation was three hundred and fifty thousand – more than half the population. This figure was confirmed to me on separate occasions by three priests – one Timorese, one Spanish and one Italian. And that number did not include babies who died with their mothers. Later I learned that babies and toddlers were not counted in any Indonesian census at that time or later – if they were listed at all they were deemed to be 'population losses'. In other words poor little mites who starved or died from neglect could be written off as having died from natural causes.

The Circle of Silence

However, the following article is typical of the disinformation promoted then and now. It is from a report that appeared in the *South China Morning Post* in 1977 and was published again on 22 November 2005 as a 'Slice of life' article compiled by Virginia Maher:

> Thousands of refugees displaced in eight months of brutal civil war preceding East Timor's merger with Indonesia the previous year were reported to be leaving their mountain hideouts under an amnesty offered by President Suharto. At the same time, the leadership of the scattered remnants of the former Portuguese colony's Fretilin independence movement appeared to have moved into the hands of a younger, more radical and openly pro-Communist faction. From one of its hideouts in almost inaccessible mountains, Fretilin continued to broadcast propaganda, including fictitious claims of victories, misleading listeners in Australia.
>
> In fact, overseas observers permitted to visit the 'twenty-seventh province of Indonesia' were placed under strict military escort and refused permission to go off on their own. So they only saw what Indonesian officials wanted them to see. Gough Whitlam, the sacked Australian prime minister who maintained that his actions in continuing to support the Suharto regime were in the best interests of the East Timorese, was invited to visit Indonesia's 'newest province'. He was flown by helicopter to see corrugated roofing which he claimed had been built to house Timorese; actually they were for Indonesian migrants who had been forced to settle. Spontaneous patriotic demonstrations were arranged to welcome him and he reported seeing Timorese women building roads as evidence of great

progress. He elected to become Indonesia's emissary at the United Nations. Without being invited, he blustered his way into speaking at that august institution in 1989 and demanded that 'the matter of East Timor must be dropped from the UN agenda'. He failed to achieve his aim. In fact the UN upheld the rights of the Timorese for self-determination year after year after year.

The next four Australian prime ministers had meekly followed Whitlam's example. In 1978 the Fraser government attempted to bypass the issue by granting de facto recognition to Indonesia's *takeover* of East Timor, largely due to the oil in the Timor Sea, which Australia wanted to steal. At the end of that year, Foreign Minister Andrew Peacock said in cabinet that full legal or de jure recognition of Indonesia's incorporation of East Timor would be difficult as the issue was very emotional. He said he would 'not actually make clear' that Australia was giving de jure recognition, and that this subterfuge was necessary in order to negotiate the maritime boundaries between Indonesia and Australia. He said he would only clarify the point if the Australian media pressed him. They did, and he had to admit the truth.

Aside from the advantages to Australia of stealing East Timor's oil, the Fraser government's recognition of Indonesia's sovereignty destroyed the aspirations of Timorese for self-determination. The border negotiations took place at the height of the atrocities being enacted at Matebian and other mountain refuges, but the relationship between the Liberal government and Suharto was not all plain sailing, in the same way that Genghis Khan was not all giggles and cuddles.

After Fraser granted full de jure recognition of Indonesia's incorporation of East Timor, successive Australian prime ministers hastened to support the Suharto regime. Labor Prime Minister Bob Hawke said big countries cannot invade little countries and

The Circle of Silence

get away with it, and then he helped big, powerful Indonesia to get away with the destruction of East Timor. Prime Minister Paul Keating – another stand-up comedian – saw himself as Suharto's spiritual son. John Howard would extend Australia's support of Suharto, but finally, when there were no other options, he would reluctantly come to the aid of East Timor.

The way our governments and some media behaved has destroyed the way we Aussies who believe in fairness and the democratic process have come to regard ourselves. Accustomed to being accepted abroad for our hail-fellow-well-met reputation, we suffer criticism and remorse for our leaders' grovelling to Indonesia.

The Javanese were suffering heavy casualties as resistance increased over a wide area from Los Palos in the east to as far west as Bazartete. Xanana, who was now integral for the organisation of the resistance, was a military genius.

Where did Xanana find his courage? As it was from the beginning, not one bullet from the outside world would be sent to aid him – which raises the question: how did he get arms and ammunition? The answer to that lies at the heart of the Suharto regime. Badly paid, disaffected Javanese accustomed to every vice were eager to emulate their leaders. Everything was for sale.

In June 1980, the commanders in Dili planned to attack several targets during a conference staged to persuade international journalists and observers that the resistance had been smashed.

Xanana recommended a coordinated attack on Dili aimed at capturing the weapons needed in order to liberate the maximum number of political prisoners. Though he was not in command he was often forced to make decisions – and a successful action would make an undeniable statement that the struggle for self-determination was as strong as ever. An attack on Dili was such a serious undertaking he offered to work with the Clandestine Network, which was in its infancy (by 1992 one thousand seven hundred secret cells were operating). This network supported armed guerrillas and took part in minor subversive activities. Like the secret radio link that was still functioning in Darwin, the few who knew about this subversive organisation were sworn to secrecy.

'We will never surrender,' he said. 'To resist is to win.' He sent runners to Dili to persuade the commanders in Dili to wait for him to arrive with reinforcements; but the presence of foreign journalists in Dili proved irresistible. Xanana travelled fast. Just before midnight as his battalion approached the city, they heard a series of explosions. The television station and several military installations had been blown up. Taken by surprise, the enemy was unable to mount a response and gunfire continued until dawn, with Indonesian soldiers running around the streets in utter confusion.

Upon being informed that the raid was an unqualified success, Xanana was pleased and excited; he assumed the commanders in Dili did not need his assistance and so he withdrew. Ironically he and his fighters became trapped between enemy lines. They were hunted by thousands of vengeful, humiliated troops who assumed they had cornered the men who had set off the explosions. Pursued from two directions Xanana ended up in a dried-up creek bed, which bent in a way that shielded his volunteers from enraged enemy soldiers racing up and down the river shooting recklessly. The Javanese set light to all the trees, bushes and high grass to smoke them out. Scarcely able to breathe, Xanana took a terrible risk by leading his men back across the river in full view of the rampaging enemy. He has never been able to explain their fortunate escape.

General Dading Kalbuadi flew into Dili to oversee reprisals. Innocent civilians accused of assisting in the raid were murdered without evidence. Their bodies were displayed in the streets. Six hundred people, including children, living near the attack sites were arrested and tortured, and their homes destroyed. Hundreds more were transported to the prison island of Atauro. Two battleships arrived, and tanks and troops disembarked to encircle Dili in a show of force. Hundreds were driven from their homes.

The ferocity of the retribution caused a very bitter Xanana to send runners all over Timor to determine if the people wanted to give in or continue to fight. It was no secret that he doubted his ability for the task. Some of the runners were captured and tortured to death; they had been betrayed for fear of reprisals. I believe it was a very emotional meeting when, after months of waiting, the surviving messengers brought the news that the majority wanted to continue the fight. The 1981 conference elected Xanana president of the Revolutionary Council of National Resistance and commander-in-chief of Falintil.

Tony, Greg, Gary, Malcolm, Brian and Roger died for good journalism. I wondered if I could create a scholarship for one journalist each year to study the journalism course at Columbia University in Greg's place. The scholarship would be named for one of the six each year starting with Greg. A number of radio stations reacted enthusiastically when I told them about it on my interviews, and so I wrote a proposal and submitted it to the ABC, to every radio station and every television station in Australia. I invited David Bowman, a friend of mine from Adelaide, to attend a meeting to discuss the proposal. David had been the editor of the *Canberra Times* and the *Sydney*

Morning Herald. He offered to pay his own expenses to attend the meeting.

My suggestion was for each media organisation to donate a percentage of their profit, which, if my maths was correct, would mean an outlay of less than fifty dollars each year for some country radio stations – incrementally more from TV stations. I had also discussed the idea with Peter Spurge of Esso, who gave an undertaking that his company would take up any shortfall that might occur as the years progressed. I insisted that whoever won must have adequate medical insurance, airfares and sufficient income for decent accommodation. In order to avoid accusations of favouritism I asked for a group of journalists or scholars or both to select the winner from work submitted. I planned to admit East Timorese and Indonesian applicants in a future when East Timor was free.

The first winner was Geraldine Brooks in 1983. The first I knew of her sterling success at Columbia was a desperate phone call from New York. She had come top of the class and had won several important awards but she was distressed because she had been offered employment at the *Wall Street Journal*. The committee insisted, however, that she must return to take up where she had left off at the *Sydney Morning Herald*. She was almost in tears and said she would come home if I asked her to do so. The behaviour of the committee members was ridiculous; her success demonstrated that she had been the best choice. I asked what work she was to do in Australia and was told she would be working on the women's pages. I told her to go ahead and take the job in New York.

Geraldine became foreign correspondent for the *Wall Street Journal* and since retiring she has published several successful books and won a Pulitzer Prize in 2006.

The second winner was Damien Kingsbury. Though he was as free to specialise as Geraldine had been, he maintained a strong committment to East Timor. On the third year I called the Australian Journalists Association to ask when the 1985 scholarship was going to be announced and was told, 'Oh, no one wants to do it anymore. It's been closed down.' I was unable to discover anything further. Too numb and heartsick to start again, I gave up. At the time of writing, twenty-four Australian journalists could have been educated to that standard at Columbia University.

The lump in my breast had subsided, but I was so busy I hardly noticed it. The white strip of hair also disappeared so gradually I hardly noticed. But I had begun to notice a change in some of my personal relations. I occasionally met mothers of Evan's fellow students for morning coffee. On arrival I would be asked how everything was going in East Timor. As I opened my mouth to reply someone would say absentmindedly, 'I had such a dreadful time getting here.' As everyone peered at the menu we would be regaled with information regarding the traffic, the cost of petrol, etc., etc. When I would begin to answer the original question someone else would chime in and say, 'How's Timor, good?'

This phrasing is so Australian it makes me laugh. It covers good manners and stops the reply in three succinct words. If it looked as if I was going to persist everyone would speak at once: 'You didn't have an accident?' 'Oh no, not again.' All attention was riveted on the possibility of a calamity my friends could handle. My mouth would hang open as if I was trying to catch a ball like the clowns at Luna Park.

'Where's that waiter?' someone would ask, frowning as if the waiter was being deliberately withheld from us. I learned not to mention information that would disturb their comfort zone.

Evan received a postcard from Shonny while she was holidaying in Tasmania. I read the opening sentence and then put it down without reading the rest. 'Tell your mother,' it said. When Evan read the message he said. 'Oh, what a rude woman.' I suggested he might like to see her. He refused.

Later, the mother of a friend sent me a message about Shonny. My friend's mother had been travelling to Melbourne when she was accosted by a woman who asked her what she thought of Shirley Shackleton. Upon hearing a favourable opinion Shonny apparently behaved like a deranged woman and accused me of preventing her from seeing her grandson. My friend's mother said I must do something about this. What? I called Shonny's home hoping to talk to her husband Clarke, but the phone was disconnected and the telephone exchange was unable to give me a forwarding number.

In the meantime, the changes in East Timor were cataclysmic. Due to the loss of life, food shortages and continuous bombing raids, hundreds of thousands of civilians left their mountain refuges, only to be forced into heavily guarded 'resettlement camps' where women, children and old people slept on hard ground without shelter, which was disastrous in the rainy seasons. Considering the death toll, these should have been called extermination camps. The Javanese did not kill their victims in gas ovens, nor did they tattoo identification numbers on their victims' forearms, but Australia had allowed a vast depravity to occur.

According to American anthropologist Shepard Forman, 'people used to live in small self-contained hamlets cultivating corn and root crops in patrilineal-inherited ancestral gardens where rice was grown in sculpted and irrigated mountain terraces; with herds of water buffalo, goats and pigs, chickens

The Circle of Silence

and fighting cocks. Their thatched houses were built on stilts in highly defensive positions on mountain abutments.' In *The War Against East Timor*, the authors say that, 'by forcing the people to abandon their homesteads in their widely dispersed hamlets in the mountains, the Indonesians fundamentally disrupted the East Timorese economy'.[2]

The former bishop of Dili, Martinho de Costa Lopes, said, 'If the people of East Timor could live where they like there would be no food shortage.' With forced sloth and deprivation the death rate soared. A pro-integrationist academic, Donald Weatherbee, observed at UN committee hearings that, 'when flying over East Timor by helicopter, one is impressed by thousands of acres of field – for corn, dry rice, wet rice and pasture now going back to waste. There was no fertiliser, rodents destroyed a substantial percentage of crops, there was no regular water supply.'

I continued to travel and be interviewed about Timor whenever the opportunity arose. I went to England several times and attempted to find the family of Brian Peters – I was always unsuccessful. Even Carmel Budiardjo, the editor of *Tapol*, the Indonesia human rights publication, knew nothing about their whereabouts. Whenever I was in the UK I always met Mina Rennie, Malcolm's mother. She believed her husband had died of a broken heart after the death of his son, and over the years I watched her grow more frail and troubled.

I was offered an interview on the BBC with João da Silva Tavares, a pro-Jakarta Timorese. I told Carmel Budiardjo I was very nervous but she replied, 'I think you will make short work of him, Shirley.' At such times support like that is invaluable.

When I arrived for the interview, the staff greeted me with wry smiles. Senor Tavares had pulled out at the last minute.

---

2 Carmel Budiardjo and Liem Soei Liong, op. cit.

By then I was ready for a good clean fight so I was quite disappointed. Tavares was notorious for repeatedly demanding to be interviewed and, though they did not say as much, it was perfectly obvious that the BBC staff knew his allegiances were deeply tainted. They then offered to give the whole airtime to me alone.

That interview was interesting. A very nice woman explained apologetically off-air that the Indonesian Embassy had provided a list of statements that they demanded be read ahead of my interview. I asked if I could see the list. Every item was an out-and-out lie. I was horrified. I asked how long we had and then estimated how much time I would actually have left. As she read out the list, I watched the hands of the clock behind her. My heart beat furiously. When she reached the last statement, I butted in.

'Wouldn't you like to know what really happened?' She was surprised.

'Oh . . . er . . . yes, certainly,' she said. I turned the list towards me and one by one demolished each allegation by the time the hands of clock hit the half-hour mark. Every member of the staff waited outside to congratulate me; I exited the recording studio to thunderous applause. I thought, 'So stick that up your jumper.'

In England I also attended numerous meetings and met people I had only ever heard about – Noam Chomsky, Lord Avebury (Eric Lubbock), Anthony Wedgwood Benn (Tony Benn). My favourite activist drove a London taxi cab and the interior was plastered with East Timor pamphlets. By the time his customers reached their destination not only did they get an earful, but some had actually signed up for a subscription to *Tapol*. Later, the same wonderful man decided to do something spectacular: he built a boat with the intention of sailing it to Dunkirk under the Fretilin flag. He got front

The Circle of Silence 177

page and full television coverage in the end, because it sank and he had to be rescued.

David Scott, founder of Community Aid Abroad, once asked me how so many letters of mine got published so soon after an event. My routine, I told him, was to read the paper first thing and if an item required comment, I wrote the letter and took it into the *Age* by hand so delivery was not problematical. If I was lucky my letter appeared the next day.

On New Year's Eve 1978, Shonny had called and said grudgingly, 'It *was* a good marriage, Shirley.' I felt so relieved and told her all about Evan. She said she was all alone now, 'People only bother with me when they want something.' I tried to persuade her to trust me, although I admit I was still resentful about the way she had ignored Evan. She seemed too tired to express anger and as we spoke her disposition sank gradually into self-pity. I began to think she was drinking heavily. I felt quite faint as she began a familiar tirade against me and all the old resentments surfaced with a vengeance. When she drew breath I said, 'Listen, Shonny, Greg really loved you. That was your greatest achievement. How many mothers do you know whose children adore them? You succeeded.'

You got everything. I got nothing.' I said I was sorry she felt that way. If she was interested in meeting us I would be very happy to see her. There were so many things she could tell Evan about Greg that no one else knew. She refused to give me her new phone number.

'So you've moved,' I said. She would not even tell me where she was living. Her last words to me were, 'I feel Greg was not meant to be born. You were right about the government. They used me. My life has been a complete waste.'

Some years before, a neighbour, Bronwyn Hughes, had told me her mother knew Shonny and she wanted me to know her mother was sympathetic towards me. She was not being judgmental about Shonny, and I liked her all the more for that. When Evan turned 16 in 1983 I asked if he would agree to meet Shonny. I thought he was mature enough to be able to handle her by then. He agreed, so I took his photograph and a letter to Bronwyn. When I asked if her mother would deliver the letter for me, she invited me in for a coffee and gave me a generous tot of her homemade liqueur. I admired her series of teapots ranging in size from a one-cup pot to a six-cup pot, each with its own beautiful hand-knitted tea cosy. Halfway through my coffee she gently told me that Shonny had committed suicide in 1982.

She had jumped from the top floor of the Bendigo Base Hospital. I found out the name of her psychiatrist and called him to make an appointment. He said he would be coming to Melbourne in a fortnight. I asked to see her case notes and he promised to bring them. I was amazed at his anger towards her. He accused her of waiting until Easter to kill herself and when she did, 'She did it deliberately behind my back. She came down outside the children's ward and broke every bone in her body, but she didn't die right away.'

I called him twelve times over the following months and years. He never came. When I asked the hospital for details they said I must apply through freedom of information.

I cannot say I suffered grief: I was too angry at not knowing it had happened. I don't even know what surname she used when she died. Clarke did not bother to contact me either. I tried to remember our first meeting when her house was stuffed with gilded objects and she believed in a golden future. No matter what she had done to me, she did not deserve what happened to her. She did not deserve the lies, the manipulation and the horror. Before the murders I had seen her transgressions as pathetic attempts to idealise her life. Since no one believed her flights of fancy she had done no harm. But now I had to admit that she had done me harm, and yet I still could not blame her. She had become a victim of grief and professional liars.

No question about it, I had let her down, and I had failed Greg. How could anyone not see the blind jealousy driving her? Her suicide is still unfathomable. There must have been a lot more troubling her than a flight from emptiness, grief and the slow erosion of her spirit from old age and sickness. One of Greg's aunts told me Shonny had wanted to get out of the army (almost everyone was in the armed forces in those days!) so she got pregnant – maybe her feeling that Greg was not meant to be born was a result of misguided guilt. She might have expected to be portrayed on the front pages of the newspapers as the tragic mother of her charismatic son.

Guilt and remorse caused me to become someone other than myself for a very long time, and I could do nothing to slow the destructive process. My love for Evan and his loyalty was my salvation. I threw myself into work, though in some ways I stumbled on in a haze of powerless amazement at the terrible news trickling out of East Timor.

Despite overwhelming superiority in numbers and American equipment the first two-and-a-half years had been disastrous for the invaders. The Timorese resistance had maintained almost total control over the countryside. In 1978 the capture of Alarico Fernandes, a member of Lobato's central committee, was followed by Lobato's murder in 1979. Attacks upon Matebian increased in proportion to aid to Indonesia from America, England and Australia. This included a massive series of artillery attacks by OV-10 Broncos, the pride of Rockwell International. They were slow-moving, counter-guerrilla planes equipped with infrared detectors, rockets, napalm (or Opalm, the Indonesian version) and machine-guns designed for close combat support against an enemy lacking effective aircraft capability, such as the Timorese. Tens of thousands of Timorese were trapped on Matebian in daily bombing raids, which turned the mountain refuge into an inferno. The bombing was so intense that civilians and resistance fighters alike saw their friends and relatives blown apart. Xanana describes human limbs dangling from branches and lumps of flesh stuck to trees. When the order came everyone had dreaded – get off the mountain – people swarmed together like birds with broken wings. If they fell there was no time to help them. Women giving birth on the bare earth had to keep moving or risk capture. Some went crazy trying desperately to save a fallen comrade as if by doing so they would save their whole world. Those who reached the lowlands were attacked in an orgy of sadism. Sexual organs, tongues, lips, ears, fingers and limbs were hacked off. Abdomens were ripped open. Tens of thousands died from wounds, hunger, thirst and exhaustion.

In 1983 Colonel Purwanto, the military commander of yet another extermination operation (Operation Security), would admit it as a failure. The new strategy was in full swing at that time. The armed struggle had spread all over the country creating great instability for the enemy. And yet still the Western powers, including Australia, turned a blind eye!

That year Xanana considered a proposal for a ceasefire. Some resistance fighters took advantage of the ceasefire to go in search of their families and it did really look as if a compromise might be agreed, but it was short-lived.

TWELVE

It took me weeks to tell Evan about Shonny. When I did, he could not understand my anguish. He had no memory of her apart from the postcard she had sent from Tasmania.

I called Shonny's friend, Patrick Tennison. He refused to speak to me until I said I would take a taxi to the studio. I wanted to know the circumstances of her death and I also wanted to talk to Shonny's husband, Clarke. I told Patrick's secretary that I had not even been told she had died. When he came on line I asked, 'Why didn't you tell me?'

His reply was curt. 'I believe I was rather busy at the time.'

I wanted to cry. I wanted him to say nice things about her, but all he did was bristle.

'Did Shonny leave a letter for Evan? I asked.

'No.'

'What about photographs of Greg, what happened to them and what about his poems?' He did not know, even though he was managing her estate. He treated me as if my only interest was money. He warned me against going to Bendigo, where she'd died.

'There are people up there who will kill you on sight.'

Shonny was not alone at the end – one person did not let her down. X's kindness in helping her was a courageous act from someone who clearly cared for her. She is buried in Fawkner Cemetery in Melbourne. She was cremated on 16 April 1982.

I have been asked on occasion what happened to her estate, which was considerable. According to her will her money was to be used for 'the encouragement of education of journalists in necessitous circumstances'. I only know what happened to a couple of hundred dollars because a young doctor contacted me and wanted to give me the money he had been given as a loan. 'All trace of the grant or scholarship has disappeared,' he told me. I said it was not my money. 'What about your son?' Evan felt as I did; I told him to keep it.

I don't know how it happened, but Evan turned 20. It was 1987. He decided to travel around Australia as he knew more about California than he did his own country. This was partly because I had taken him back to California to all the places he remembered playing with his dad. I suppose you could say it was the laying of the ghost.

I did not want Evan to go, but I knew that I'd had to leave home in order to grow up.

I missed him very much. Though we kept in touch it was never enough for me. Once he called to say he was in a pub and the customers had taken up a collection so he could call me and tell me not to give up. I had often wondered if he was embarrassed by my activities, so I was relieved by this message.

Then, in 1988 I heard an announcement by Suharto that the blockade of East Timor that had been in place since 1975 was going to be lifted. I called Evan, who was working in Alice Springs, and asked him how he would feel if I went into East

Timor. He replied, 'Well you always think things through, Shirl. Will it be dangerous?' I could not give assurances, but I promised not to take any silly chances. I mainly wanted to see East Timor for myself. I did not expect to be in touch with anyone of importance because I was so low on the scale of VIPs. I did expect to be frustrated – Pat Walsh from the Australian Council for Overseas Aid had gone with a group of religious people for one night. They went for a walk in the afternoon and saw Javanese soldiers mistreating one of their own. They were confined to their hotel except for that one little walk, and I was expecting much the same.

'Well,' said Evan, 'take lots to read and your knitting, Mum. If you want to go, I think you should.'

By then I was thoroughly fed up; nothing any of us had done had made the slightest difference to the lives of the Timorese. The Javanese were said to be as cruel as ever and I had made no progress in finding Brian Peters' family. Malcolm's mother Mina was too ill to be active. I kept in touch with Carmel Budiardjo and, each time I went to England, she arranged some radio interviews for me with the BBC. They were momentarily satisfying, but personal achievement was never part of my agenda. I wanted to know if the Jakarta Lobby was right when its members claimed life had improved for the Timorese in the past fourteen years. If there was evidence supporting this rosy view I might be able stop what so often appeared to be a waste of my life.

Then, a huge announcement was made: the pope was to hold a mass in Dili. With news of the papal visit came assurances from the Timorese Resistance Army that the Javanese would keep a very low profile during His Holiness' visit. There would never be a better time for me to visit. I was nervous. There was a danger from disease – rabies, typhoid, polio, hepatitis, cerebral malaria, leprosy, Japanese encephalitis, tuberculosis, yaws and

Clockwise from top left: At age three — I was determined to defend my baby brother Bruce to the death as I did not trust the photographer; Greg always adored this photo of him and Shonny; me over a hot stove, looking cool as a cucumber.

Clockwise from top left: On our wedding day, 7 May 1966; Evan, at age four, was delighted to be considered grown-up enough to use the telephone; the three Shackletons on our bicycles, opposite our first house.
Opposite page: The news about the Balibo Five made the front page of the *Australian* on 21 October 1975.

gastric disorders associated with contaminated drinking water. I began to have the same terrible nightmares I had suffered after Greg was murdered.

Evan remained supportive and this freed me in advance from guilt if anything went wrong. I almost decided not to go when the only flight available would take me via Bali, where troops destined for East Timor were trained. It may seem stupid but I did not want to support Udayana troops in any way. When I could not get a return flight I was initially relieved. I had dealt with the fact that I would be in uncharted territory, but I did not want to be stuck in Dili indefinitely. I began to think I should stay home: perhaps the Timorese in the diaspora exaggerated. When they heard of events from afar, perhaps their dread was magnified. Perhaps our Department of Foreign Affairs and Trade really did know better. It was hard to imagine anyone accepting Indonesian propaganda in view of the violence, but DFAT insisted on talking about improvements, and maybe it was true.

I knew of massacres in 1976 in Suai and Aileu, in 1977 at Bobonaro, and in 1978 at Quelicai. There were reports that the village of Lakluta had been surrounded at night and the houses machine-gunned, and that the victims were women and children. At Kraras in 1983 a party of Falantil guerrillas had surrendered with their women and their children. According to eyewitness accounts some of the women were taken away, but the rest were shot and their bodies covered with dry grass and set alight. Four hundred were said to have died. Any form of retaliation against Javanese troops initiated more raping and killing. Timorese could be burnt alive in their homes, and one of Indonesia's most notorious commanders, Prabowo, was said to have played a leading role in carrying out several massacres. No international response was launched to ask the Indonesian military to stop the killings. A common reaction to complaints by people like me from the Jakarta Lobby was that Falintil should stop provoking the Javanese military by resisting. Blame the victims was part of their lexicon.

With all of the above in mind, it was with some trepidation that I boarded the flight to Denpasar. A young Indonesian boy misbehaved en route; his grandmother and mother indulged him. When he shouted that he wanted to piss piss they shrieked with laughter. As he followed his mother down the aisle he took out his penis and wagged it. His grandmother burst into peals of adoring laughter. I was sitting next to a beautiful Balinese woman who had reacted sympathetically when I told her I was going to East Timor. I decided to take a chance.

'That's how it starts,' I said.

'And it ends with Suharto, Prabowo, Murdani, Kalbuadi and thousands of other spoiled brutes. They are indulged from the day they are born,' she whispered. 'That is how they took the lives of my family and my country. I hate them all.'

At the airport in Denpasar the attendant looked briefly at my passport then put it aside. I was told to wait while every other passenger boarded the flight to Dili. When they were safely on board he went to a room behind the desk and I could see him through a dark glass partition speaking on the telephone. The propeller of the plane started up but I tried to look unconcerned. After a while I approached the desk and beckoned the attendant. He exited the office.

'Tell them if they turn me away I will go straight back to Australia and get front page news. If you let me in I won't even get a sentence on the back page.'

Comoro airport in Dili teemed with restless men in combat uniform. An emaciated man watched me with half-closed eyes. Was he an informer or part of the Resistance Army? My fantasies of being brave collapsed in the presence of so many assault rifles. The air inside the building was stifling. I wondered again if this was the silliest thing I had ever done.

As I joined the queue waiting for our documentation to be scrutinised, someone walking behind spoke in clear, accented English. 'We knew you were coming.' Was he friend or foe? Was this a warning or a welcome? I nodded my head absentmindedly in the hope that this would telegraph acceptance of what I hoped was a welcome.

Outside I hailed a dilapidated car. A rusty, illegible sign dangled precariously from the back bumper bar. There were no Timor ponies, the main means of transportation before the invasion. The practice of selling hundreds of thousands of these delightful animals to Indonesia, apart from the underlying motive to restrict travel for Timorese, was designed to enable the army of occupation to make personal fortunes by creating a market for motor scooters.

Under-nourished, ill-clad, barefoot Timorese walked in the dust at the side of the road. They were passed by military jeeps occupied by well-groomed Indonesians of both genders. My heart sank and I worried anew: why would anyone trust me? I wanted to hear local people's perceptions and memories, not the official versions flooding the western press from ANTARA (Indonesian News Agency).

A huge crude painting of Suharto had been erected in a prominent position on the roundabout leading to Avenida Marginal, the promenade stretching along the seafront. As my taxi turned left I saw a painting of the pope in a lesser position. Policemen brandishing pistols stopped the traffic. A group of elderly Timorese women and young children alighted from a bus. A television crew smoked and joked together as a director in a safari suit instructed heavily armed assault troops to distribute red and white Indonesian hand flags. The director

The Circle of Silence

demonstrated how to wave the flags. The people held them stiffly and made awkward, jerky movements. The director ordered the soldiers to threaten them, but the same awkward movements were repeated.

'Are they resisting?' I asked the driver. He nodded for answer, after making a sound as if he was swearing and then spat out of the window before lapsing into brooding silence.

Having booked into the Hotel Turismo, I slung my case into my room and, feeling rather foolish, moved like lightning through the back of the hotel. My intention was to try to make contact before I could be followed. I hailed a taxi and gave an address. The driver's English was minimal, which suited my purpose. On the way I made sure he understood I was asking for directions to visit Dare, where Australian Commandos had established their observation post above Dili (Dili o pip) in World War II.

Just before we reached the turn-off I asked the driver to continue up the road to the left. When I could see my destination I paid him and took photographs of Dili. When he moved out of sight I walked the rest of the way, wondering if I had done the right thing. My contact was surprised to see me. I told him if the Javanese came I would say I had really wanted to visit Dili o pip but that the driver had misunderstood. I was carrying a lot of money for Falintil and I wanted to get rid of it in case I was searched. Abel Guterres had asked me to find out if money sent in regularly for Falintil was received. The answer was no. My contact was surprised that I was staying at the Turismo.

'I decided to go into the hornet's nest. That way I won't drop my guard.'

I did not stay more than two minutes, having handed over a bottle of whisky for Xanana or for anyone it might help. Before I left, I asked my contact what I should be doing while in Timor.

'Go out, look around,' he said. 'Take a bus, go anywhere. You will see enough.'

I woke next morning to the sound of the Muslim call to prayer from loudspeakers. Where I found it mysterious and calming in Iran I was uncomfortable hearing it in this beleaguered city. An incongruous pink lounge in the foyer of the hotel was occupied with staff watching Indonesian television. I stopped to watch the self-elected president-for-life Suharto as he told the world that East Timor was like a bird in a gilded cage. The twenty-seventh province of Indonesia was open for tourism and would soon have a reputation to rival Bali.

As I left the hotel the chess players chorused, 'Where are you going?'

'Out.'

Stallholders and farm animals at the local market were painfully skinny; small malnourished boys and old women scavenged in the dirt for scraps of food. Women wearing hand-woven *t'ais* sat on the ground behind modest pyramids of tiny tomatoes, mandarins and bunches of greens. One lady sold one segment of a mandarin at a time. Truncheon-swinging soldiers, armed as if for battle, strolled through the market taking goods without paying. The silence was noticeable. I had entered a closed world.

The beasts are in the garden
and the herb beds stink;
diseases spreads over
Lisbon lemon grove.

The lustful brood
growl, claw and

The Circle of Silence

*gnash their teeth
over human blood and bone.*

*Vapours rise from swollen pits,
the air reeks from a
never-ending funeral ...
the closed world is a catacomb.*

The situation in Dili was like that of the *Tonton Macoute* (a paramilitary force) in Haiti. Secret agents posing as chess-playing tourists wore Balinese shirts, military haircuts and military trousers. If you went for a walk down the beach after sundown you might be able to trace the secret agent assigned to follow you (or someone else) by the circular tip of the cigarette he was smoking. The fiery red tips stand out among billions of fireflies. In Australia I occasionally felt that something covert like this was going on, but there were no doubts in Timor. Men stood in doorways for hours on end, and the eyes of people walking in the streets were watchful, ever watchful. As they walked their eyes swivelled, trying to watch their backs.

Two days later, as I waited in a dusty street to hitch a ride out of Dili, a truck stopped for me and I recognised a man nearby who I had seen hanging around the hotel. He slunk out of a doorway and watched me with a wide-open mouth. I would not have noticed him if he had not reacted. As a youth pulled me on board I watched carefully to see if he noted down the registration, but he just looked surprised. So he was there to dupe me into thinking I had spotted the real spy. You might think I was paranoid; so be it.

The youth and the driver were brothers going to Gleno, a large and fertile district not far from Dili that had been 'requisitioned' for Indonesian immigrants. My hosts spoke

English very well, though they addressed me as 'senhora'. They seemed to be putting me through a test, which was comforting; if they were spies they would be more likely to have accepted me without question.

A succession of scenes flashed by. I saw wood smoke from ancient agricultural practices and Timorese carrying heavy bundles of firewood. Even the tiniest child, trailing slightly behind its mother, carried heavy loads of wood or water. Some areas were dry and sparse, others tropical. I was amazed at the number of military roadblocks. My hosts took my *surat jalan* (travel pass) and my passport to save me from standing in the hot sun when they were checked.

We had lunch together, a delicious vegetable stew served with rice. I noticed our leftovers were scraped back into the pot, which meant we had been eating someone else's leftovers. I did not want to drink the water they offered but it would have been rude to refuse so I drank it all. I told them I was worried they might be punished for helping me. They laughed. Their truck could not be identified because it was not registered. It used to belong to their father before 'They' came.

'*Our master*, the Corporal, owns it now. He fixes any trouble.' They mimicked shooting someone in the side of the head. And your father? They smiled proudly and mouthed, 'mountains'. I told them I was there to see how the New Order was treating them. They spat their disgust after answering each question intelligently, quietly . . . very, very quietly. Timorese had menial jobs – had I noticed there were two kitchens in the Turismo? I had not, so what they told me accounted for a great deal of confusion. I had overheard several complaints from guests who claimed they had paid cash to the 'Indonesian kitchen' for their meals when they were seated, yet when they checked out of their hotel they had to pay again. Food was delivered to the wrong table.

The Circle of Silence

There was always a long wait; the recipients were so hungry they just ate what they were given.

That led me to an understanding of another mystery. Messages went missing on an all-too-regular basis, which caused some guests to feel paranoid. They thought they were being investigated by Javanese agents. The hotel was divided. As with the two kitchens there were two sets of staff, one made up of Indonesians and the other consisting of Timorese. Since I was in the Timorese section if I left a message with the Indonesian receptionist it was never delivered and vice versa.

The young men still asked questions as if they were trying to decide whether to trust me. It was only after I objected to their chain-smoking that they relaxed.

'I don't mind Them smoking,' I said with an evil grin. 'I want Them to die of cancer, but not you. Why do their job for them? Don't smoke.'

We got pally after that and I told them about Aceh and West Papua. My hosts told me about the germ warfare that happened when They came. I told them that it must be hearsay since they would have been two years old at most when They invaded. 'But you are right,' I said. Many eyewitnesses have described green powder covering acres of vegetation. Widespread infestations of what were described to me by many survivors as maggots destroyed huge areas of bushland. Whether this was a deliberate scheme or the result of tens of thousands of dead bodies left unattended has never been investigated. My hosts insisted that precision airstrikes using satellite and sensor-based systems made Timorese easy targets. I said, 'They won't win unless They stop using Timor as an experimental laboratory and treating East Timor as if it is one big slave plantation.'

My hosts' father was a commander working with Xanana; he had been a teacher, which accounted for their command of English. Their mother and sisters had been taken away ten years before. The expressions on their faces made further questioning about the fate of their 'missing' family redundant. The father had been forced to add 'the Corporal's' name to the deeds of their house. If the boys failed to do their master's bidding their father's house could be sold without notice.

They were to take a journey in two days' time and I could go with them. 'This is something you must witness.' I had to wait in front of Bishop Belo's house on Jalan Merdeka at 4 a.m.

'Freedom Street, my eye,' I said. They smiled conspiratorially. If we were questioned I was to say I was a tourist waiting for Papa Pope. I found their irreverence charming.

As with resistance members they differentiated between Indonesian civilians and the military by naming them 'Javanese' and every time they referred to Javanese they spat. I had already noticed that even polite Timorese always spat when they referred to the Javanese.

They went off to buy produce, very pleased and amused that I had 'shouted' their lunch. I wandered around the village built for Indonesian workers. The houses were tiny with corrugated iron roofing that would make the occupants swelter in this heat. I left after a while as no one spoke English. Back on the road I hitched a ride on a small bus filled with Indonesian farmers, fresh vegetables and some roosters, all bound for the market in Dili.

At the first roadblock everyone climbed out. We waited to join the queue on the opposite side of the road. An old woman looking tired and ill drooped listlessly. A soldier barked an order without looking at her. She reared back as if she expected to be slapped. He moved on and without looking at me shouted at me. I began to ask what he wanted. Though he looked right at me, his eyes did not focus. He began to shout in my face, I shoved my passport right in his face and asked softly, 'Is this what you want?'

The Circle of Silence

He grabbed my passport.

'Why must these people wait here?' I spoke so quietly he had to move forward to hear my words. 'It's much cooler over there, and there is plenty of room.' He clicked his fingers in my face. I was quietly determined to oppose him. 'Stop treating us this way. President Suharto expects tourists to come here; you will be court-martialled if you treat tourists like this. Lots of trouble for you. Understand?'

His eyes narrowed and he shrugged his contempt. I fanned the old lady until we received permission to cross the road. The Javanese on duty were nasty to everyone. As soon as we returned to the bus the Sulawesi farmers heaped produce on my lap and one tried to give me a splendid bright yellow rooster – I was certain its feathers had been dyed. The older passengers smiled toothless smiles and congratulated me. At the next roadblock I was alarmed when one of the young passengers made a cheeky remark to the soldier on guard. She smiled triumphantly at me. She got away with it because she was pretty, but when we returned to the bus she was criticised by the elder in their group.

On that short trip I saw many instances where the Javanese treated their own people badly and it was clear that they were not free to object.

On my return to the Turismo the chess players chorused, 'Where have you been?'

'Out.'

I sat in the courtyard where Greg had dined with Tony and Gary under red and white Bintang beer umbrellas. The mozzies loved me. I made certain to order from the Timorese kitchen, but I was so sad thinking of the enthusiastic trio when we had discussed the possibility that they might be incarcerated in a third-world gaol that I lost my appetite. I kept seeing them alive and happy and I wondered again what had happened to Greg's notebooks? That voice in my head said don't worry about it, you will get them one day.

I set the alarm for 3 a.m. and it was just as well: the truck arrived promptly at four. My fellow passenger was an old man who did not speak. His head remained bowed over his clasped hands for the entire journey. I was very tired. The Javanese had partied in the front of the hotel until the small hours of the morning and the radio blared all night – they had the worst taste in music, poor things. I had assumed that no-one could tell them to shut up since they were armed and very drunk.

As I waited for the truck Timorese conscripts arrived and formed groups at regular intervals. They looked sleepy and bored until an army jeep accompanied by outriders on motorbikes swept through the deserted city. Then they snapped to attention and saluted the passing jeep in which the head of intelligence was riding to work. I later asked my hosts if they knew what that had been all about.

'It's about washing the brains. It's about forcing them to pay obeisance. It's about grinding them into the dust.' They were very angry. Their favourite cousin had been paid to inform for the Javanese. When he got to know too much the Javanese had killed him.

I slept on the floor of the truck for most of the way, opening my eyes occasionally and seeing lovely scenes that brought me joy, such as women bathing their babies in tubs in their front gardens, looking happy as they gazed adoringly into their little ones' eyes. The scenery was impressive. I was reminded of World War II veterans who had told me how various landscapes in East Timor were evocative of Australia. The tropical parts were no surprise, but I did see long stretches of black smoke that proved to be the traditional method of agriculture (swidden, or slash and burn), which afforded temporary enrichment of the soil but left the dreadful image of a bushfire. I had no idea where we were going or what to expect until we pulled up at the top of a cliff overlooking a deep valley.

The two youths helped the old man alight and all three knelt at the edge of the cliff and prayed. After a long time the old man made the sign of the cross and the youths followed suit. This place was notorious. It was where the old, the sick, and those who refused to cooperate were dispatched by the New Order.

*Do you see wildflowers
growing in this valley?
My children were alive
when they were sown,
at Bulico.*

*I would destroy all these flowers;
for I prefer to see their bones
bleached by the sun than have
tourists see only wildflowers,
at Bulico*

Those whom I have cherished springing into flower.

On my return to Dili, I walked the streets. Timorese were watchful, seemingly intrigued to see a white woman, but they did not speak and I did not ask as it might have caused them trouble. I was very aware that the set-up was artificial because numbers of Javanese soldiers had been reduced with the increased presence of foreigners. Many Timorese people had told me there were hundreds of thousands of Javanese in Dili.

Almost every child ducked if a Javanese soldier passed by and on two occasions I learned why. Officers carrying swagger sticks delivered sharp blows to the unsuspecting as a matter of course. If an Australian child like my son and his friends were treated that way, they would join the resistance as soon as they were able – and, of course, that was precisely what was happening.

It is hard to explain to an Australian audience what it is to experience a repressive regime. The sudden look of terror when a car backfires. The way people try to scan the way ahead while not daring to check behind because they might look as if they had done something wrong. The flash of panic when a squad of soldiers appeared. And of course betrayal was rampant. If the reports were true, rape was used as a weapon of war – many fathers complained to their priests of being forced to watch their wives and daughters being gang raped. If they objected they were beaten and could be shot, and so the daughters would beg their father not to intervene. One way to understand is to say 'we' and 'our' or 'you' and 'yours': How would you feel if your children were raped in your presence and you were unable to protect them?

I remembered Abel Guterres telling me what happened to East Timorese friends who lived in Australia when they were united with a relative and his 5-year-old son who had recently escaped from East Timor. While the friend and the son enjoyed afternoon tea with their long-lost family, someone knocked loudly on the front door. The visiting man leapt into a wardrobe while the friends removed the extra cutlery and crockery to the kitchen. The 5-year-old picked up his father's notebook, unzipped a flat cushion cover, slid the notebook in and sat on the cushion swinging his legs with an innocent expression on his face. It was a false alarm; the Australian-based family was amazed that the child knew what to do from his experiences in East Timor.

The Circle of Silence

* * *

The blockede and the curfew had been officially lifted for the papal visit but the streets remained deserted at night. That was when I learned of patrols of black-clad, masked soldiers roaming in packs, beating up Timorese civilians, calling themselves Ninjas. In the bar of the Turismo I shouted drinks for the Javanese and picked up a lot of information, especially about the fighting. According to the Jakarta Lobby, Falintil was a spent force, but I enjoyed knowing they were the same spent force that had resisted the enemy for fourteen years. Needless to say I did not express my views to my guests; I was wide-eyed with ignorance about Tim Tim.

The way to glean information is not to ask questions and you certainly must never appear to take notice of anything that is said. I sat quietly as they talked together and, although I did not speak their language, I learned a lot from the way they moved and from their facial expressions. Those poor young soldiers were very lonely and shocked by their recent losses – they had lost a lot of friends that week. A helicopter pilot whom I had met earlier added to the surreal quality of our encounter by introducing himself once again with the words, 'I am good man, but I cannot dance.' He had joined the air force because he could not stand the sight of blood.

I was shocked the next morning to be given short notice; my room had been let in advance for the period of the papal mass. I asked Bishop Belo if I could sleep at the Canossian Daughters of Charity across the road from his house. The bishop wore thick black socks. In that heat! He promised to arrange something but we could not speak for long as several people were waiting in line to see him.

He had written a letter to the UN describing Timor's plight: 'We are dying as a nation.' His letter caught everyone's attention and he had subsequently survived several assassination attempts. When I asked what his first thought was upon waking he replied, 'I wonder if I will die today.'

The Timorese staff seemed determined to display efficiency, gallantry and light-hearted gaiety with one exception – if anyone wished them *bom dia* they reacted in a terrified manner. It's a Portuguese word, they explained, and they could be shot for speaking Portuguese. There was a new Indonesian receptionist; her lips were painted into a scarlet heart and outside the courtyard the intelligence agents got drunk while the courtyard buzzed with conversation and mosquitoes. Television reports from Indonesia showed signs proclaiming 'Viva Papa, Viva Superstar'. A twenty-one-gun salute had greeted His Holiness in Jakarta and an air force Hercules had been placed at his disposal. Indonesian Catholics travelled miles just to see him pass by; some had waited twelve hours or more.

The government was using the papal visit as if the pope's presence condoned their activities in the 27th Province of East Timor. Roads and venues had been extensively renovated for His Holiness. President Suharto warned Indonesian Catholics to keep a low profile for fear that the numerically superior Muslims might whip up an anti-Catholic jihad against them. In Dili there was much speculation as to whether he would kiss the ground when he landed at the airport, thereby recognising Timor as a separate country and not a province of Indonesia.

I went to Taci-Tolu where the mass was to be held and watched soldiers hamming it up on the partly built dais. They addressed imaginary crowds, holding hammers and screwdrivers as if they were microphones. A couple of them crooned and their choice of song was evidently hilarious. By the time I had circumnavigated the perimeter the red carpet was being laid. I felt no anger at the shenanigans; it helped me see the killers as almost human.

I met my contact that night. He was worried about my safety if I failed to get a flight out. He also asked if I would be prepared to take a journey into the country by bus in order to meet someone important. It would be an ordinary bus and there would be no protection if anything went wrong. The driver would stop and give me a prearranged signal to alight. I would be met and if on my return intelligence asked what I had been doing, I would say I was merely continuing my practice of seeing as much of Tim Tim as possible and had become lost. With all the activity for the papal mass, they did not think I would be in any danger.

My room at the Turismo had a little private patio sheltered by a huge magnolia tree in full bloom. Day and night the view was spectacular and the perfume of magnolia was memorable. I sat on the patio that night with Paddy Kenneally, a staunch supporter of the Timorese, with whom I had attended many a protest in Sydney. He was incensed to report P.T. Denok was now called P.T. Bataran India Group and it controlled the coffee industry and ran a large department store in Dili. As the geckoes came out to serenade us with clicks, Paddy reminisced. He had fought here in World War II. We shared a beer or two, marvelling at the beauty of the fireflies while swatting mozzies. It was a most memorable night.

The next morning I joined the large crowd at Dili airport waiting for the pope to arrive. A soldier pushed me hard without looking and ordered me to move on. As we were standing outside a high metal fence I asked him to explain why we must move.

'You must not stand here.'

'I heard you the first time. Tell me, please, why can't we stand here?'

Another military policeman, brandishing a baton, pushed forward.

'Hi, there,' I said, as if exchanging pleasantries at a garden party. 'Perhaps you can explain why we can't stand here.'

He conferred with his colleague: 'His superior told him no one was to stand there. That is why.'

'Not acceptable,' I replied, planting my feet firmly. Their faces turned puce under their dark skin. 'We are a quarter of a mile from the tarmac, so we could hardly harm the pope.'

Before they could answer, the gates were opened and everyone ran through. There was a mad scramble towards the tarmac and a distressing lack of Christian charity when it came to finding a good position. Eventually the pushing and shoving ceased and all eyes searched the sky for the coming of God's representative on earth.

On the tarmac, arms folded, stood a man wearing a black t-shirt and a baseball cap turned the wrong way round. His name was whispered in horrified awe . . . General Murdani. Eventually a tiny speck appeared in the sky and the jostling began again. As soon as the papal jet touched down people fell to their knees and prayed. Their prayers were not answered. Instead of kissing the ground, Pope John Paul II crossed the tarmac and entered General Murdani's private jet. His aircraft was too long for the runway at Lombok or Flores, and all these years later I've forgotten where exactly he was going. One woman fell to her knees and sobbed 'garuda bird', and she was joined by many who wept inconsolably as they watched Murdani's garuda bird take flight.

That afternoon I was asked to take Peter Philp, the editor of the *Advocate,* to meet my contact. On the way I realised I had read his book, *Journey with the Poor*. He had worked in many countries under repressive regimes. He said he had never found it necessary to take as many precautions as he had in Timor.

'You only have to look at their eyes to recognise their dread,' I said, and I recommended that he should walk the streets as I had done in order to ascertain that a military cantonment was situated in every single street. When he realised I had nowhere to sleep for the next three nights, he offered to put me up in a flat he had been loaned while the occupant was away in Indonesia. We arranged to meet at the Turismo as I had been invited to dine with Tom Hyland, Graeme Dobell and Lindsay Murdoch.

On that walk I experienced a desire to confide in Peter Philp that I had a fair idea where Xanana was hiding. I could not understand at the time why I would even consider taking such an extraordinary chance. I had no reason not to trust Peter, but I have wondered ever since how many times the possessor of a secret has burned to share it, how many people have succumbed and been punished for their treachery. It might be a desire to share responsibility; it might be a matter of ego – the 'I know something you don't know' syndrome – but whatever prompts the madness, it is very frightening.

THIRTEEN

Dinner was to be served at 7.30 p.m. precisely. We entered the dining room on time. I was amazed at the splendour of fine bone china dinner settings and crystal glassware set on a long central table covered with a starched white linen tablecloth and ornate silver cutlery, accompanied by large white tureens and starched table napkins. Arsénio Ramos-Horta, José Ramos-Horta's brother, was in attendance, looking absurd in a white Portuguese shirt with fancy sleeves and a red cummerbund around his ample waist. He approached us and with a low bow and a theatrical movement of his arm indicated the courtyard. Someone asked who the feast in the dining room was for and Arsénio replied, 'The general.'

I had once met the owners of the Hotel Turismo in Perth and they were incandescent with rage because Arsénio Ramos-Horta was managing the hotel without their permission. Like many properties in East Timor it had been acquired by a high-ranking official. A Chinese Indonesian seemed to me to be the owner, but he was believed to be a front for an Indonesian general. Murdani was the hot favourite.

I made a horrified squeak at the thought of Murdani and was told curtly, by I don't know whom, not to be so silly. Thoroughly admonished, I wondered if he knew what that man meant to me. I would have to either leave or suffer his presence.

The contrasts between the dining room and the courtyard were interesting. We were seated on red plastic chairs matching the red and white theme of Indonesia's national colours, replicated by umbrellas over each table. The tables were rickety, there were no tablecloths, the cutlery was plastic and paper napkins were cut in half. After an hour, in swaggered Murdani surrounded by his coterie of hangers-on. I watched them through the windows laughing and toasting each other as they celebrated the spoils of war.

David Jenkins had published an article in the *Sydney Morning Herald* in 1986 listing details of the Suharto family's personal wealth. It was called 'After Marcos, now for the Suharto Billions' – in Indonesia they were known as the 'kleptocracy'. As a result, Australian journalists were immediately banned from Indonesia. Three years later, as his lavish dinner ended, Murdani stood and swaggered out of the dining room. I was in a position to see him and I thought from his body language he was going to turn right and enter the courtyard. I hurriedly told Peter if he approached us and was asked to sit down, I would have to leave, and that Peter need not follow as I would wait for him outside. Peter's eyes popped as he could not see what I could see.

As the general credited with planning the attack on Balibó and the invasion, Murdani would have given the orders for Team Susi to kill all five journalists. Looming out of the darkness, puffing on his big fat number 5 Havana cigar, he made straight for our table. The journalists tried to cover their amazement and I heard Tom (I think it was Tom) invite him to join them. As his bottom touched the seat I rose and walked quietly away. An hour or two later Peter came looking for me. I was waiting outside watching fireflies lighting up the stretch of beach leading to the wharf.

On this stretch of beath betwixt
 memory and a rotting wharf;
a cornucopia of shells replicating
 eyes gaze at troubled skies
or clam shut trying to ignore
indelible stains saturating the shore.

The soughing sea sighs,
 low murmurs lost in time ...
as breezes swirl to a
 slow waltz set to water music
where blood ran cold
into a wash of corrosive gold.

The beach will not bare its bones.
 Bound by pity and piety
each grain of sand
protests reality.
Did people lie in the sun
before the trouble had begun?

Thought sharpens the eye;
 memory burns clear beneath
gusts of fireflies illuminating the
 slick, sticky with decay —
are these those who passed away?
Is it fanciful to see fireflies as their souls?

* * *

According to Murdani, Dili was circled with seven sets of combat troops to prevent Xanana from entering. I had been told as I climbed to a meeting that he was very close by. We were way out in the open but my contact whispered as if we were surrounded by spies. I had complained that he must not trust anyone.

'If we can't trust you, we can't trust anyone.'

'That's precisely the point. If they had my son and were going to hurt him, I would tell them everything. No one knows if they are going to be brave or cowardly.'

Peter now told me that the general's answers to the journalists' questions had been carefully worded. Everyone knew that the important factor was simply that General Murdani had deigned to join them. For the record he began by drinking Tiger beer, but moved on to Swan lager. The journalists had asked what he would have said to me if I had stayed and questioned him about Balibó.

'I would say nothing.'

I was cast down. Seven circles of combat troops waiting to catch Xanana ended any possibility for me to leave Dili. I would not be taking that bus ride after all.

The digs where Peter was staying were near Balide church, at the Santa Cruz cemetery. If I remember correctly we were too weary to walk and, as we had been warned that military hoodlums dressed as Ninja were known to make murderous patrols at night, we took a taxi. Entering the house through a living room with a sparse kitchen annex, I looked at a collection of books that were all about war. The room was bare of anything that might give a clue to the personality of its usual occupant, the man who was away in Indonesia.

'This man is weird,' I said. 'It's as if he wants to remain anonymous. Look at the titles, there isn't a decent one among them.' I picked up several books and noted that different names were written on the flyleaves. I mentioned that they would make a suitable vehicle for an Arnold Schwarzenegger film.

'What does he do?' I asked. Peter told me that he worked for a voluntary organisation.

I did not sleep well. Partly angry and partly pleased to have had the discipline to leave, I wrestled all night with my problem: I had missed a golden opportunity to put Murdani on the spot. I decided I would have to approach him and ask a few salient questions. The next morning, Peter insisted on coming with me.

'I don't want you to get involved in any way,' I explained. 'I don't care what happens to me; I just need you to be a witness.'

Murdani might be having breakfast in his room; he might have been invited to some barracks or other. Whatever he was doing, I intended to hang around the Turismo until he appeared. I knew he was staying in the red brick extension that looked as if it had been designed by an Australian council architect. I could not believe my luck when I entered the dining room and he was there, eating breakfast. I stood just over a metre away and I introduced myself.

'General Murdani, my name is Shirley Shackleton. I would like to speak with you.' All activity ceased. The sudden silence was noticeable. He looked up and shook his head.

I said, 'No journalists.' He pouted, then shrugged and spoke imperiously.

'After breakfast.'

I sat down and Peter came and joined me at the table. We all entered a circle of silence until João, the head waiter, shot across the room carrying a large pot of coffee and whispered, 'Double strength for courage.'

The dining room emptied rather quickly. As I moved to sit at the general's table I became aware of his pectoral muscles, which he flexed repeatedly. This was a body sculpted in a gymnasium, a body, however, that was losing definition. He had puffy eyes, and flab bulged over his belt as he breathed. I studied his large, ugly hands, knowing he could reach forward and with a flick of his wrist break my neck. A succession of journalists strolled past the door taking sly peeks inside. It was very comforting.

I wanted to slap his grinning face so badly that I sat on my right hand. I asked him to tell me what had happened at Balibó – I appealed to him as a Christian. He denied any knowledge of the fate of the Balibo Five or of Roger East. I asked him to explain the battleships moored on the Timorese side of the border. He mumbled something along the lines of, 'Balibó is nowhere near the coast.' At that he stood to leave. I jumped up and bending my arm whacked my hand into his elbow. Surprised by my own action I heard my voice say, 'Sit down. I want to tell you what I have seen.' He sat down.

I spoke slowly, describing how badly his troops behaved towards their own people and how unnecessarily cruel they were to the Timorese. I asked if he knew how many young men who were being tortured had Indonesian fathers who had raped their Timorese mothers. 'When you allow your troops to commit atrocities you make sure that Timorese will never accept you and neither will these sons of rapists whose mothers care for the cuckoos in their nests.' His eyes drooped as he looked past me. In desperation I said, 'Timorese are not peasants, they are a refined people, a cultured people.'

'Oh, I agree with you,' he said, sounding terminally bored. He was so sure of himself. Time stretched as I stared at him. 'I've come full circle,' I said. He obviously lived by a geometry of his own making, unfettered by rules of decency. He stood abruptly, turned his back to me and sauntered away.

This was the man who had supervised the extinction of hundreds of thousands of Timorese, West Papuans and Indonesians. I should have been afraid of him. It was impossible not to compare him with a Nazi and yet I felt no fear. The stupidity and lack of imagination of men who sanction the murder of artists, doctors, scientists and babies renders them banal. Without the trappings of war there is nothing remarkable about them.

*The general has a Christian soul
and an almost kindly smile
so it's easy to forget his role
in the genocide of this Isle.*

*When I ask him for the simple truth
I can see by the look in his eyes
with all his power he can only tell
weak, pathetic lies.*

My contact called me at the Turismo; he wanted to show me something. As he rang off he said, 'The Whisky is in the Mountains.' Oh my goodness, I ran around in circles on the beach with my arms stretched out like wings. I have never been more pleased.

I had been repeatedly calling the Melbourne travel agency for information about my flight out. I had been warned not to hang around once the papal mass was over as the military curfew and all military personnel would be reinstated as soon as the press left. The woman in Melbourne who had arranged my flight was never there; it cost a fortune to call; and whoever answered asked if I was having a lovely time in Bali. Sometimes I just had to give up because they had never heard of East Timor. If all else failed, I had the bus routes that went through Western

Timor, which would mean I would then have to travel by ferry to Flores to Bali or to Lombok. I knew how to do this but I would stand out like the proverbial and it could be dangerous, so I had to keep calling Australia.

Arsénio Ramos-Horta's wife confronted me. 'Father Locatelli came looking for you yesterday,' she said. 'What would *he* want with *you*?' I had no idea. I knew who he was but I had never had any contact with him. It was said he had had contact with Xanana.

My contact wanted me to see where military tanks had been hidden for the time of the papal visit. You would have to know where to look in order to see them, as they were camouflaged – the Javanese denied the use of tanks. He drove me to a track behind Taci-Tolu, the place where the mass was to be held. It was too dangerous for us to drive along the track where there were enormous open pits. Several weeks before, the population of Dili had been made to walk past them after being warned that was where they would end up if they did not behave at the mass.

The great day was going to be a scorcher. We rose early expecting a long walk. Paddy Kenneally greeted me as I arrived at the Turismo for coffee: 'What did you think of His Holiness's disgraceful behaviour?'

'Next time he kisses the ground, someone should rub his nose in it!' I replied.

Paddy was a wonderful source of information. He had been travelling for several weeks trying to locate old friends and hitching all over Timor. He said the roads were worse than they had been in World War II. We decided against breakfast as there were only four makeshift dunnies at Taci-Tolu and it was going to be a mighty long day.

A Japanese journalist, Hiro, asked me for an interview. When he realised we were about to set off on foot, he offered us a lift as the authorities had provided him with his own means of transport. As we waited for the shiny black limousine to be brought around, we overheard two men dressed as scout masters discussing the mass. I recognised them both: they were regular chess players at the hotel.

Timorese stared in amazement at our limousine and at shiny new buses brought in for the mass. Hiro remarked, 'I expected joy, but these poor people are so drowned in sadness, even a pope cannot break through.'

Paddy responded, saying, 'With the billions of dollars of aid going to the Javanese for Timor, why are these people so thin, that's what I'd like to know!'

At the roundabout the position of the two huge billboards of President Suharto and Pope John Paul had been reversed to give the pope temporary top billing. The way was lined with woven palms attached to semi-circular hoops. Thousands upon thousands of red and white Indonesian flags fluttered next to them.

'I thought this was supposed to be a religious occasion,' said our host.

'The Timorese were issued with orders to make the decorations,' said Paddy with a contemptuous sniff.

Our Press Only limousine was allowed to cruise through all the roadblocks. The old and the very young walked in blasting heat. It was then that Paddy remarked, 'Have you noticed, there are two generations of men missing?' We three stared at each other; I felt sick. The Japanese journalist looked at the crowd with horrified interest while Paddy explained that Taci-Tolu was where the population had been sent to be 'educated' to accept Indonesian rule by being beaten into the ground. Many died of their wounds. His voice broke. 'This is

The Circle of Silence

Cactus Flats where we staged our raid [in World War II] in a forlorn attempt to rescue Merv Ryan.'

When a Timorese cultural group entered the arena, people stared as if they were reincarnations of an ancient race. Though somewhat dilapidated their decorative traditional clothing and headdresses featured brightly coloured feathers, but their celestial ornamentation of silver half-moons flanked by vibrating stars previously wrought in solid silver were made of cardboard covered with silver tin-foil. Their full suns or *belaks*, formerly made of solid gold, were fashioned from painted cardboard circles suspended on pieces of string. Paddy enlightened us. Enemy soldiers had collected the original ornamentation from the dead and dying warriors for war trophies or they had them melted down for cash.

Upon entering the arena many made the sign of the cross, and as they whispered they looked around so see if anyone was watching.

'They are saying,' said Paddy, 'we are standing on the bones of our loved ones.'

Many wept, some fell to their knees and kissed the ground, some spoke in hushed tones to the earth. My mind flipped back to the Yazdī plain and the Zoroastrian shrine: the similarities were unmistakable. The killing field of Taci-Tolu formed a huge circle, but the skeletons in this ossuary were hidden away beneath a thick crust of salt earth. Tears sprang from my eyes. I crouched down and patted the soil as if it was alive. This was an unconscious reaction, but I was fully aware of my intentions when I scraped some of the earth into the palm of my hand and let it run through my fingers. The residue looked like ash ... *ashes to ashes and dust to dust*. I did not then and do not now find anything sacrilegious in my conviction that the proceedings that day were not just for Catholics. I saw the papal mass as part of human history, albeit a terrible part of human misery. I was at a *hağğ*, and Taci-Tolu was a sacred site in the universe – a silent circle.

The sun was halfway up the sky. A lone eagle pivoted slowly. Two huge billboards faced the high altar. Proud as Lucifer, President Suharto had equal billing with Pope John Paul II. Cordoned sections bore the names of towns and villages. People waited under umbrellas and makeshift paper hats to conserve their energy for the long wait and the long walk home. Some had travelled for days. I thought the Indonesians had organised it well, until Paddy pointed out the reality. The sections were designed to control the people: if a protest was launched, the military would be able to identify the protestor's village – after the pope and the press had quit the country, the people knew a slaughter would begin.

Shaded shelters with seats flanked the dais and portable ice-chests were filled with soft drinks and ice. We decided to rest in the shade for a while but we were turned away by a scout master. Those seats were reserved for Indonesian Catholics and foreign journalists. A suspicious bulge under the so-called scout master's left armpit had me wondering about a gun.

Four hundred thousand red and white hand flags had been distributed with orders for them to be waved enthusiastically throughout the mass. No one would be admitted without a flag. Xanana had predicted between one hundred and one hundred and fifty thousand would attend, which amounted to a boycott. The government had predicted a crowd of three hundred and fifty to four hundred thousand. An unofficial census was taken the night before, and the numbers of campers assembled in the closed city suggested Xanana's estimate was correct. Since the government couldn't afford to lose anyone, when people came empty-handed they were admitted, flags or no flags.

The eagle continued to circle overhead with slow deliberation. 'Scout masters' raised their arms and pulled imaginary triggers, like small boys playing bang, bang you're dead. The eagle hovered for at least an hour then flew away towards the east. I felt a mystical empathy with that eagle, which I cannot explain other than it was another connection with my visit to the Zoroastrian sacred site. We waited in the stupefying heat sipping water, warm as blood.

Throughout the morning a choir sang, as nuns and priests wearing white, grey or yellow robes arrived to take their places. Rows of solid gold chalices stood on long tables covered with starched white tablecloths. The sound of drums and buffalo horns began an ancient ritual of welcome. The dancers, looking tired and dispirited, formed groups. The leader blew into a buffalo horn and my skin began to prickle as the ancient sound vibrated around us. In the excitement several pious worshippers forgot themselves. 'There is no other God but God,' they chanted, 'and Mohammed is His prophet.' Paddy and I laughed until it hurt.

The pope arrived, surrounded by men with huge biceps wearing superbly tailored suits and suspicious bulges under their left armpits. As the pope entered the newly erected imitation of a traditional Los Palos house, a priest approached the microphone. The people fell silent when the drums ceased.

'Salute for Pope John Paul the second!' he cried.

'Viva!'

'Salute for the Roma Catolica Church.'

'Viva!'

His voice rising with excitement, the priest shouted: 'Salute East Timor.'

The response was deafening. 'Viva! Viva! Viva! Viva Timor! Timor Leste.'

Three times the priest repeated the three phrases and three times the crowd responded; shivers ran up and down my spine as the voices of the dead and the living rose together in a mighty crescendo.

To a tremendous ovation Pope John Paul II walked along the red carpet in his 'Over the Rainbow' ruby red slippers. He was followed by Bishop Carlos Filipe Ximenes Belo – I could not see if he was wearing his thick black woollen socks. The cheers were deafening. Bishop Belo walked forward and opened a green folder waiting for him on a lectern. The pope had elected to speak English for the press. After each paragraph, Bishop Belo was to translate in *Tetuñ*. When Pope John Paul raised his hand, an expectant hush fell across the worshippers. Bishop Belo opened the green folder but instead of reading the translation, his face registered shock and disbelief. He raised his eyes and looked accusingly at the faces of each priest on the dais.

The pope then spoke at length to the crowd: 'In your great suffering you are the salt of the earth.' The crowd cheered wildly. Later, when the pope said that the people must be prepared for reconciliation, there was total silence. Paddy grabbed my hand as prickles ran up and down my spine. This was extraordinary. The Timorese were certainly not agreeing with any suggestion of reconciliation. Priests in gorgeously embroidered cassocks came forward holding the gold chalices towards heaven for the papal blessing and the chosen few began to stand in line. In the queue of Christians chosen to take the sacrament from the pope's own hands was General Leonardus Benyamin Murdani.

Michele Turner had seen a photograph of the young Benny Murdani and she described him as luminously beautiful. By the time we met he was the opposite of Dorian Gray, and this can be clearly seen in a close-up of Murdani at the pope's mass in John Pilger's ground-breaking documentary *Death of the Nation*.

After hours of waiting the ceremony was over in a flash. When Pope John Paul II began to wave farewell, several youths moved uncertainly towards the altar, raising banners attached to long poles. Somehow they managed to form a straight line as they moved from a canter to a gallop. In fact they ran like well-trained infantry braving enemy guns. Waving frantically a priest ran forward. Paddy said he screamed to the choristers: 'Don't get involved, run, run away.' The batik-shirted brigade moved in, hitting the youths with truncheons. Scout masters wielding metal chairs rushed to beat protestors into the ground. One young man clutched at his jaw in agony when a scout master wearing army boots began to kick him about the head.

The pope walked down the red carpet to the front of the dais and witnessed the proceedings in silence. I wanted him to protest since everyone knows silence is acceptance. When a group of Timorese standing behind the demonstrators saw what was happening, they found the courage to raise their fists; cameras appeared as if by magic and they were photographed. Uniformed police appeared and began to hurl chairs at anyone in the vicinity. Dust began to rise as if the Taci-Tolu massacres were being repeated. When a hundred or so Timorese found the courage to try to help the protesters, they were beaten with riot sticks and chairs. A Filipino journalist's camera was torn from his hands; the film was ripped out and the camera was thrown to the ground. An iron grip held me fast.

'I'm getting you out of here,' said Paddy. I went quietly.

A bus drew up beside us and an Indonesian journalist called to us to jump in. As we pulled away we looked back over the site; the earth at Taci-Tolu was rising like a desert storm and a great bloom of red dust hung above the bogus Los Palos house. The driver said he was going to our hotel via the airport. All the journalists on board were flying out immediately. The Indonesian journalist called to me, 'The government spent so much money for this fiasco; it's like a football team that wins every match until the day of the finals, but doesn't kick a goal.'

We grinned at him and gave him the thumbs-up.

* * *

Rodney Hughes, a reporter from Darwin, told us when the protest began that he had asked his Indonesian press minder what was written on the banners. While looking straight at them, he replied, 'What banners?'

'Maubere people welcomes Pappa. Long live Fretilin. Viva Fretilin. Pope save East Timor,' said Paddy sourly.

As the bulk of international journalists quit the country, having reported the manufactured story, the real story began. Men hunted down choirboys, and intelligence agents made routine arrests while waiting for incriminating film to be developed that would allow them to embark upon many more arrests based on the photographic evidence. This would be done in secret, and the families, like those whose loved ones resided underground in the sacred site of Taci-Tolu, would disappear.

At the Turismo the Filipino photographer limped towards us. The priest who had warned the choirboys not to get involved had been arrested along with numerous eyewitnesses. Forty youths had taken refuge in Bishop Belo's house, which was surrounded by troops. The priest who had told the choirboys to run away was accused of being a Falintil spy; his accusers claimed they had proof he had directed the protest.

Arsénio Ramos-Horta arrived and boasted that he had film of the protest. We all crowded into a small room to watch it. Later Arsénio was frogmarched out of the hotel by uniformed soldiers. I suggested we should do something to help him, but was warned not to get involved. He turned up later shrugging his arrest away.

Reports that Bishop Belo was going to be murdered were rife; it was said that he alleged his translation of the papal homily into *Tetuñ* had been substituted. That would explain why he hesitated and had stared at each priest on the dais before proceeding. We walked to the bishop's house, which was surrounded by soldiers. Guns were drawn. A dog began to bark. Soldiers broke ranks and fought viciously to gain a position at the front.

Amazing claims were made about Xanana. When I watched that eagle hovering over Taci-Tolu it had made a powerful impression. It seemed to signify something mystical, but of course that eagle was merely a raptor looking at a banquet – us! Xanana was admired by many Indonesian soldiers because they were animists. He was said to have escaped capture many times in seemingly miraculous circumstances, so the Javanese animists believed he possessed supernatural powers. He was now supposed to be hiding at the Bishop's house. During the search for him a stray dog had been arrested, tied up and placed in the back of a small truck. The word went round: Xanana had been captured and had changed into a dog. There was great excitement until the dog leapt from the vehicle and escaped.

In fact, the demonstration at Taci-Tolu resulted in the beating and torture of the participants, but I do not believe this outrage reached the Western press.

That afternoon three boys who said they were 13 years old entered the courtyard of the hotel. Walking boldly past prying eyes they said they had come to speak to me. They addressed me as 'senhora'. I begged them to leave at once and tell everyone to stay away for their own safety. I assured them that they didn't need to tell me what was going on: I knew more than enough. I told them about people like the Americans Noam Chomsky and Rear Admiral Gene La Rocque. The retired admiral's report for the Centre for Defence Information entitled *A World at War – 1983* had established that casualties in East Timor were the second highest in all wars currently raging at that time. 'There can be no doubt that the 200,000 estimated death toll will soon have to be revised upwards.' I wanted them to know that there were people outside who cared. 'Yes,' I said, 'and everyone knows that another fact should be included in the research. Most of the dead are non-combatants.'

'Where is America? Why are *they* still here? Where is the land our fathers owned? Where are our relatives? And where is this admiral with his meaningless words and numbers?'

One with a broken nose said, 'They are going to kill us anyway; we want to be certain you really understand,' and they launched into the following, all whispering at cross-purposes so I could only make the sketchiest of notes: their teachers were from Lombok and other islands in the Indonesian archipelago. 'They say our fathers are common street criminals. *They* say we have just come down from the trees. We are instructed to remember President Suharto in our prayers and we must beseech Allah to reward the butcher Suharto for all the good he has done in Tim Tim. Brave Javanese soldiers died to free us from our Portuguese slave owners. *They* talk as if they are making political broadcasts and we dare not tell the truth to our young brothers and sisters. We have to lie to them to save them and when they understand what we have done they don't trust us.'

Conscious to avoid trite advice I ventured to say they could try to beat Them by studying.

'Yes,' they said, 'we used to think like you before *they* raped our mothers and little sisters and forced us to watch.'

As I said goodbye, the smallest showed me his scars from beatings. 'I do nothing wrong,' he said, 'this you must understand. I get this from *them* because I am Timorese.'

The one with the broken nose told me his father still believed they could win if the UN or the pope would take up their cause and, glancing repeatedly over his shoulder, he whispered, 'We still fight against superior powers. Are we not worthy of help?'

Those boys were exceptional. They wanted to study and lead useful lives. But their only option as they saw it then was to join their fathers in the mountains. I agreed to meet with them the following morning to hear schoolchildren singing the Indonesian national anthem. As we waited, one of them informed me that their Indonesian teachers repeatedly told them to leave the country, saying, 'We don't want you; we only want your land.'

The next day when I arrived at the school, the sweet perfume from the cananga trees mingled with an overpowering stench emanating from cracked open drains. Angelic voices sang 'Indonesia Raya', or 'Great Indonesia' – the longest national anthem in the world. The children failed to pronounce the words correctly and sang out of time and out of tune until it came to the words, 'Indonesia *Tanah Ku,* my country'. This they shouted with all their might with perfect diction and rhythm, pronouncing *ku* in the Portuguese way, meaning 'anus', as in 'Indonesia is an arse-hole country'.

These young birds in their gilded cage
are strong and courageous
to the point of no return.
They might as well be abandoned luggage.

This is no oasis!
The bars of their cages
imprinted on their burned flesh
lock them in with greedy vultures.

Behind their tarnished bars
they burn for freedom while
Ozymandius, king of kings,
clips their budding wings.

* * *

There is really no way to be sure who to trust in an occupied country. The tropical setting, the general air of optimism – Timorese are very optimistic – street stalls selling *t'ais*, fruit vendors with their little wooden hand carts and colourful produce had appeared as if by magic giving a feeling of carnival at the seaside. An uncouth Australian, who boasted he had been fed three times that night by different Timorese families, questioned me in a way that allowed him to deduce where I lived. I tried not to smile as I informed him if he had simply asked me straight up I would have told him my address.

'According to a report I read before coming here, there are many more hospital beds and ninety-six doctors,' he said, meaning an improvement under Indonesian rule.

'I know that report,' I replied. 'The Indonesian doctors spoke for the military, not the Timorese! Did you notice the inconsistencies? If the ratio of hospital beds per population is correct, then there must have been a misprint earlier in the same report because the population was given as 618,000, yet the ratio given later in the same report would make the population 672,000. Anyway it's water under the proverbial because that report was compiled in 1983.' I then quoted to him a report by an American, Dr Willard A. Hanna, who had toured East Timor before the invasion, called *Medical Facilities in Portuguese Timor*. In Hanna's opinion an update on medical services was due. But he also reported the indigenous healers had a profound knowledge of natural medicines and treatments; for those patients who required modern medical attention the hospital in Dili performed major surgery and provided other services including X-rays and blood tests. I began to tell him what had happened to the X-ray machines, but he interrupted.

'You have to admit there are a lot more schools?'

The Circle of Silence

'According to official Portuguese sources there were a total of 522 schools in 1975, and that figure did not take into account all the schools Fretilin started with their literacy program. According to the Indonesian figures, there were only forty-nine Timorese schools in 1975. It depends who you trust. If the Indonesian figures are correct, and there are more schools now, how do you explain that in 1986 only nine East Timorese had completed tertiary education?'

I could tell from the resentment in his voice that he was determined to dismiss whatever I said, and I was unable to discover who he was.

A retired hairdresser from Adelaide and her husband, Ken, befriended me. They assumed I was a Catholic who had come to Timor for the mass. They were celebrating their retirement by sailing the Pacific and having encountered difficulties had been saved by the Indonesian navy who 'could not do enough for them'.

They had sailed into Dili in the bad-old-days, when the Portuguese ruled with an iron fist. Everything was so much better now. 'These marvellous Indonesians are the best thing that has happened here for four centuries.' Since they wanted to see the real Timor before they set sail on the morrow, I took them to Passer Senegal Biden Decidere – or maybe it was Lecidere, my notes are smudged – a desperately sad place with pitifully small amounts of produce for sale, and where half-naked children and dejected women sat listlessly in the dusty street. We were offered young boys and girls for sex; a variety of drugs were available; and Ken was badgered to attend a cockfight. These destitute Indonesians lived a scratch-dirt existence. I had been there before – one beautiful young girl had told me she was taken from Surabaya without warning and packed in with many people like cattle on a ship bound for East Timor.

Those insensitive brutes from Adelaide took photographs as if they were in the tourist section of Honolulu. 'Smile,' they cried. 'Come on, smile. Bakshi, bakshi.'

Upon our return Ken wanted to buy a souvenir, so he bounded across the boulevard to inspect some *t'ais*.

'You don't want those,' I said. 'They are not authentic.'

'And how would you know, little lady?' was his response.

'The threads are machine-spun and the dyes do not come from local sources. The patterns do not invert; in other words each half of the design should form a mirror image of the other to be traditional Timorese designs. These are made in a factory in Jakarta.'

'Who cares?' said Ken. 'No-one will know.' With that he gathered up his treasures with a smile as bogus as his keepsakes.

FOURTEEN

Louise Williams, correspondent for the Melbourne *Age*, was heading east and she invited me along. Roy, also a journalist, was our surly travelling companion, and found fault with everything. As I waited in the kitchen with Arsénio Ramos-Horta, who was to drive us, he complained of too much coconut in his breakfast dish – an ox heart oozing blood. Arsénio was a bronco-bucking driver if ever there was one. Thank goodness Louise had insisted I sit inside the car, leaving her and Roy outside. That proved to be a disaster for them, because, as they bounced around, they choked on dust. When we stopped and I suggested it was their turn to sit inside, Louise demurred. Roy pushed me aside and fairly vaulted into the cabin. At this point, I didn't care about anything – dust, jarred bones and anything else fate cared to fling at me was worth it if I got to see Matebian and the forest of Lore.

We stopped to drink our water and Arsénio made it clear that he had expected everything to be provided for him, including his water. He had brought none. They ignored him. I handed over my water bottle. He took it without thanks and moved to put it in the cabin. I asked for it back as it was all I had. He returned it with poor grace. Two surly males – oh well, that was their problem.

Arsénio was anxious to tell us his story. After the invasion he had been hiding by a stream and was starving. Javanese soldiers gave him milk. He got a job selling meat, but when I asked where he got it he prevaricated. He claimed to have sold his produce to a woman who was related to the Indonesian-appointed Timorese governor, Mário Carrascalão, and they had married.

We took the spectacular coast road. The country resembled northern Australia, with grassland and gum trees. If I hadn't known about the military posts disguised as grass huts I would never have suspected their purpose. They were positioned within sight of each other along the 130 kilometre stretch between Dili and Baucau. They housed ten to twelve fully armed Indonesian troops who kept watch on the traffic and patrolled surrounding villages at night.

Everyone we interviewed was uncomfortable in Arsénio's presence, so I made a habit of asking him to escort me to the toilet to give Louise a chance to get honest answers. At our first interview, as soon as we left the room, the priests hastened to explain that anything they said should be reversed. 'If we say yes we mean no.' You could tell what people thought by the way they referred to Javanese with exaggerated politeness. They referred to the Javanese as 'our masters' or 'the authorities'.

Arsénio was not keen to take us to Matebian and the forest of Lore, but we persuaded him to drive into guerrilla territory. He would not stop, but I had plenty of time to observe the harshness of the terrain and to imagine the difficulties in climbing those rugged precipices.

As I tried to take in the enormity of Matebian, Arsénio stopped to smoke a cigarette. I walked away to be by myself in the presence of this shrine of shrines to heroes of the resistance. The silence was overwhelming, profound. Hidden in caves were the remains of children and their parents killed by American and British attack aircraft. Survivors were doomed to eventually die from the bullets lodged in their wasted bodies, spreading lead poisoning and causing kidney failure, seizures and coma.

The countryside changed around Los Palos; it was more like cattle country. Arsénio boasted of his father-in-law's herds and at the same time he praised his new leather boots. This reminded me of the response my contact had given when I asked what had been done with the money I had brought in and was told walkie-talkie radios and medicines had been purchased. 'Everything is available here. We just do not have money to buy.'

In Los Palos we asked directions from a very old Portuguese priest who was so frail a mere puff of wind could have blown him over. He offered us the use of a shower, which was gratefully accepted, although I found it unnerving to be naked with only the thinnest of partitions separating me from some elderly priests practising a Gregorian chant. Louise asked if we might be able to sleep there.

'No, no. People will be thinking terrible naughty things,' came the reply, which thrust me into a paroxysm of stifled laughter.

We visited a school in Fatumaca built by Father Locatelli of the Salesian order. Father Locatelli had been looking for me in Dili, and now I met the most impressive human being I was ever likely to know.

The man who now slid from behind the steering wheel looked more like a labourer than a priest. Children came from every direction to greet him. He patted their heads fondly and I saw the kindness in his smile and the energy in his stride.

He said that when he came to Timor twenty years before there were only stones. He set to and built some buildings from those very stones. He had successfully rescued the Spanish priest who had been arrested for allegedly orchestrating the protest at the mass, by demanding to see the 'evidence'. The Spanish priest had told his choristers to run away – Father Locatelli was proud of the children as they had been very brave. He passed many of them on the way to INTEL; they did not weep or ask for help despite being on their own in the big city for the first time and despite the fact they were terrified of the Javanese.

'Arsénio provided a video recording that established the truth and so INTEL had to let most of the detainees go,' Father Locatelli told us. He had spent that day negotiating to prevent a blood drinking ceremony, at which Timorese would be forced to swear allegiance to General Suharto. Since all the priests present at the meeting spoke against the proposition, he was hopeful that the orders would eventually be withdrawn.

'They said it was dishonest for the Catholic Church to object to the drinking of blood since the mass celebrates the drinking of blood.' He mopped his forehead. 'Today shows what the church could achieve if we were always in agreement. Do you know they tried to force us to agree for the papal mass to be spoken in Indonesian?' I mentioned that the Jakarta Lobby claimed Portuguese and *Tetuñ* were not banned.

'No. You will not find it written down; our masters are too wily to record such damning evidence. Just don't try it or you will be dead.'

We were told in Los Palos that Falintil had burned down a newly built village. Father Locatelli disabused us. Javanese builders set fire on completion of their own work on a regular basis, and then blamed Falintil: 'They'll just build another village. Arson keeps them employed and your government will probably pay for it.' I asked why he had come to see me

The Circle of Silence

at the Turismo. 'I came to pay my respects.' He spoke without affectation; I was awed by this and must have shown it. 'We know what you do and we are happy to have you here.'

When he left to attend to urgent business his priests explained to us that he had accepted orphans when their parents died on Matebian. 'When the soldiers come to kill them he stands in front of the children and tells them to kill him first. He has been beaten many times. They will come again.'

The Spanish priest exclaimed in a despairing voice. 'If this was Europe it would be front page news every day!'

The day before our arrival, Father Locatelli had been asked to intercede with the authorities for permission to search for a missing girl. Any Timorese searching for bush food or honey who strayed past unmarked military boundaries could be shot by nervous soldiers mistaking them for resistance fighters. The invisible boundaries changed daily and only appeared on military maps. Originally designed to prevent Timorese from joining the resistance, they also prevented the gathering of food, which contributed to the severity of the famines that had followed the invasion.

But it was not all grim. When Canossian nuns working in Los Palos had driven to Dili for the mass, unused to car travel, they all suffered travel sickness. As they drove through an intersection into the city, the mother superior handed a large vomit-filled bag to the military policeman on traffic duty and asked him to throw it away. He couldn't have heard correctly, for as the bus moved forward they saw him opening the bag with an expression on his face that showed he thought it was a gift. We all got a fit of the giggles at this story and ended up shrieking with laughter.

The college taught printing, wood- and metal-working, computers and auto mechanics, in addition to sewing for girls. All the students worked in the fields to produce food: the school at Fatumaca had its own farm, where an abundance of vegetables and black and red rice were grown, and where chickens, small pigs and huge buffalo thrived. I suggested the girls should all be taught plumbing, considering the state of the pipes and lack of deep drainage throughout East Timor.

A brass band started up and a group of boys forced tortured sounds from an assortment of battered brass instruments while a priest blew into a dented trumpet with more enthusiasm than musical ability. They played a tortured version of 'Que Sera Sera'. The musicians stole shy glances at us. When we clapped the teacher's smile became an exultation of joy. The students, however, looked disbelievingly at each other and it was obvious that they thought we were mad. Some time elapsed before they could be coaxed to smile dutifully. I learned later that some students had been tortured, even when they worked at tilling the land they kept their shirts on – they were ashamed of their scars. One of the priests whispered to me, 'Our masters force entrance to the people at night with fierce dogs, they shoot weapons and drag away perceived suspects. We live in terror. Our students cannot sleep for fear.' I could do nothing except hold his hand in a weak attempt to give solace.

I asked Father Locatelli to tell me something about Xanana. His eyes lit up as he whispered, 'We priests survive by discipline, I live with extremely disciplined men, but he is the most disciplined human being I have ever encountered.' He also said Xanana told youthful volunteers to study and be better than the Javanese. I noted that he also made the distinction between Indonesians (civilians) and Javanese (soldiers).

I did not learn until much later that after we left Fatumaca, the college was searched, and the children and teachers bullied and threatened in a cruel attempt to incriminate Father Locatelli in the papal mass protest.

The Circle of Silence

We had to get permission to stay the night in the village from police at the Los Palos gaol. As Louise talked to the officer I stepped through a doorway into a dark, silent world. Men behind bars stared at me from bare cells. They were clothed in rags. I saw no sign of torture. I wondered if they realised they were in a gaol within a gaol – the whole country was a prison. When I handed over my documentation I asked the officer if any of the inmates were resistance fighters. He smiled and drew his forefinger across his throat, which I took to mean they did not live long enough to be sent to gaol.

The following morning, after a disturbed night in a sleep-out where the builders who had burned down the village smoked, drank and made a lot of noise, we started early for Dili. We had been told that several Javanese had been killed in a battle the night before. Colonel Edmun D Bimo Prakoso (known as Colonel Bimo), head of intelligence, arrived in his helicopter as we were having breakfast.

Driving along the road to Baucau a Land Rover passed us. I was sitting in the front seat. Arsénio casually remarked that it was carrying the corpses of the Indonesian soldiers killed in the fighting to the cemetery. I asked where that was. 'Back there,' he responded, pointing to a site nearby.

'Quick, turn around,' I said. He shook his head and increased speed. I banged on the back window to get Louise's and Roy's attention – they took no notice, so I hung out the side window and pointing back to the truck yelled as loudly as I could. When they realised what I was saying they ordered Arsénio to stop and, after a few heated words, he turned our car around and pulled up at the Indonesian Heroes cemetery.

I had never seen Arsénio move faster than a snailpace before, but now he was electric. He leapt out and threw up the engine cover. His hands shook as he begged Roy not to take photographs. To make things worse a truck carrying a company of very tired looking troops wearing full battle dress passed us. I tried to feel sorry for them and failed.

Roy made a furtive attempt to take photographs while Arsénio objected. I watched to see if we were being observed. Arsénio was clearly distressed and we could hardly expect to stay; Captain Bimo, the head of INTEL, was on his way to officiate.

As we drove out of Los Palos we were followed by the builders. We never understood why. They stayed on our tail for some distance. We passed what would have been a gracious building but was now a deserted ruin.

'Bombs,' said Arsénio. 'La Bomba. Sounds like a dance.' Dozens of empty cartridges were scattered over the ground.

Back in Dili Louise asked Captain Bimo how many soldiers from Los Palos had been killed the night before. She was assured that no Indonesians had died, the dead were Timorese bandits.

'So why were they buried in an Indonesian Heroes graveyard?'

Later, in Australia, Louise told me that she was approached at the airport by military personnel who showed her numerous photographs they had taken of us on our trip.

Despite my phone calls I still did not have a plane ticket out. One morning, after watching the sun rise, I saw the date on the reception desk, 14 October. I realised with shock that the anniversary of the murders at Balibó would fall in two days time. I had been so preoccupied I'd lost track of time. I instantly knew I must get to Balibó. Perhaps I could plant a tree to commemorate Greg, Tony, Malcolm, Brian and Gary. The only person with a suitable vehicle was Arsénio Ramos-Horta. He agreed to drive me if I could get permission. I had to ask a Mark Forster for a tree. I arranged to hire Arsénio's four-wheel drive and pay all of his expenses.

Mark Forster agreed to get a eucalyptus tree for me to plant and he introduced me to a very pretty young woman who had been appointed the minister for women's affairs. I asked several basic questions to which she had no answers. I stared at her – her pretty little dress was a mass of frills, tiny bows and puffed sleeves. With each question she hunched her shoulders and retracted her head while smiling like a little child. As Mark Forster escorted me out of the building he answered each question. He spoke angrily: 'The women have their babies on dirt floors; most of them die. If the mothers cannot produce milk the baby dies anyway; Indonesian doctors give the women injections. I can't discover what they are really for. Some pregnant women are afraid to get them and many women tell me that they have lost a baby after an injection. Some claim that after their baby was manipulated in the womb it had died. I'm beginning to believe that their stories are true. There is no health system for the Timorese; the Green Cross centres are a farce.'

Getting the permit to visit Balibó was not quite so easy. Arsénio sent me to the chief of police. The policeman on duty said there was no need to speak to Mr Rudini as there was no ban on Balibó. Colonel Bimo was the man to see. I went to intelligence headquarters in Farol. Colonel Bimo was not there, and he would not be back until 2 p.m. I was told I must get a pass from Mr Rudini, the minister for home affairs. I trudged off to see Mr Rudini who had just left – he had 'tummy troubles'. 'You must speak to Colonel Bimo,' I was told. Colonel Bimo had 'a stomach upset' and would not be back.

Thoroughly dejected and paranoid I set off for the hotel. I wasn't even sure if I was walking in the right direction when I approached a set of huge metal gates with a sign: Seventh of December Park. It was too much. I collapsed on the nearest seat and wept. I expect all invading armies are insensitive to the people they have vanquished. In the park live deer were tethered at intervals and a sculpture of giant frogs appeared to be doing to each other what the Indonesian armed forces were doing to the Timorese. I wondered about the nationality of the sculptors and if the grotesque statues were a protest, an unconscious admission of guilt or deep-seated sexual perversion.

I hailed a young officer walking up the path towards me. Was I anywhere near the seafront? He stopped and saluted. Yes, it was at the bottom of the path. He asked what was an Australian lady doing in Dili.

'You lot murdered my husband,' I said, too tired and sweaty to care. He wanted to know more so I told him. He invited me to sit down and as we talked I suddenly knew he had been to Australia. When I told him this he asked how I could possibly know. 'You're giving me straight answers.'

'Yes,' he said with feeling, 'I like this way very much.' He said Australians were not interested in anything to do with Indonesia, neither their art nor history. Everyone wanted to know about the journalists who died at Balibó.

'They did not die,' I said. 'They were murdered by Yunus Yosfiah and Team Susi.' Since he seemed a decent sort of chap and, unlike Murdani, was prepared to answer questions, I took a lot of chances by making critical comments and questions, like why is your army so cruel? This elicited the answer, 'We have our share of thugs in uniform.' Though it was honest it was also disarming since it is applicable to all armies. I worked up to asking about the actual murders. He protested: surely I did not want to know. I explained 'I am not responsible for my imagination. Fear makes one illogical – dreadful images form of their own accord. No matter how bad the reality is, once you know the truth you can heal. That is why truth is essential.'

He said the men murdered in Balibó did not die immediately. After being shot they had been beaten and those not already dead were stabbed. He believed some were sexually mutilated. As I tried to take this new horror in, I studied him carefully and decided from the look on his face that he would hardly be likely to lie about something so dreadful, and of which he obviously disapproved. I also felt if he had to kill, he would do it quickly.

We walked down the path together in silence. He called to the driver of a military jeep to take me wherever I wanted to go. I asked what he had been doing when I stopped him. There was a party for Prabowo that night and he was helping with the arrangements. He saluted and wished me well. I felt very strongly that I should offer to put him up if he ever came to Melbourne but, of course, this could never happen. I think he would have been about Greg's age and I have regretted ever since not asking his name and giving him my address. I wanted to know both sides of the story, which would have been the motive of both news teams as they waited for the Javanese advance into the deserted village of Balibó.

Before I left East Timor I asked three separate people I trusted what they thought about the possibility that the murderers had tortured and sexually mutilated my husband and his colleagues. All three gave similar answers. It was not uncommon for a family to find a son or father strung upside-down outside their house. The cause of death was loss of blood or asphyxiation. Sexual mutilation was part of the revolting practice.

The University of New South Wales at the Australian Defence Force Academy has the following information on their website on torture used in Indonesia.

From the invasion of 1975 till the end of the occupation in 1999 the Indonesian military committed widespread and systematic torture against the people of East Timor.

The following acts of torture were common:
- beating with fists or with implements such as a wooden club or a branch, an iron bar, a rifle butt, chains, a hammer, a belt or electric cables
- kicking, usually while wearing military or police boots, including around the head and face
- punching and slapping
- whipping
- cutting with a knife
- cutting with a razor blade
- placing the victim's toes under the leg of a chair or table and then having one or more people sit on it
- burning the victim's flesh, including the victim's genitalia with cigarettes or a gas lighter
- applying electric shocks to different parts of the victim's body, including the victim's genitalia
- firmly tying someone's hands and feet or tying the victim and hanging him or her from a tree or roof
- using water in various ways, including holding a person's head under water; keeping a victim in a water tank for a prolonged period, sometimes up to three days; soaking and softening a victim's skin in water before beating the victim; placing the victim in a drum filled with water and rolling it; pouring very hot or very cold water over the victim; pouring very dirty water or sewage over the victim
- sexual harassment, sexual forms of torture and ill-treatment or rape
- cutting off a victim's ear to mark the victim

- tying the victim behind a car and forcing him or her to run behind it or be dragged across the ground
- placing lizards with sharp teeth and claws (*lafaek rai maran*) in the water tank with the victim and then goading it to bite the softened skin on different parts of the victim's body including the victim's genitalia
- pulling out of fingernails and toenails with pliers
- running over a victim with a motorbike
- forcing a victim to drink a soldier's urine or eat non-food items such as live small lizards or a pair of socks
- leaving the victim in the hot sun for extended periods
- humiliating detainees in front of their communities, for example by making them stand or walk through the town naked
- threatening the victim or the victim's family with death or harming a member of the victim's family in front of them.

The report goes on to say: 'It should be noted that the prohibition against torture has long been contained in Indonesia's own Criminal Code, KUHP (*Kitab Undang-undang Hukum Pidana*). Indonesian military personnel who committed torture and other crimes against humanity remain at large in Indonesia where they constitute an ongoing threat to Indonesia's own democratic transition.'

I had plenty of time to think about Arsénio. Everyone we met believed he was a collaborator. I thought about writing a play based on his family. Dona Natalina loses three children to the enemy, one son leads the resistance in the diaspora and the other could be accused of collaboration. This was going to be Timor's greatest problem when they won their freedom. How could anyone function, and especially run a business, without appearing to be collaborating? After World War II had ended people accused of collaborating were abused and murdered. Some of them had been loyally reporting vital information to the resistance in their individual countries. One way to escape was to attach oneself to a wealthy relative who could provide freedom from persecution, but what would happen to a poor man or woman?

Arsénio told me he was going to a big party on the foreshore for a VIP, Prabowo Subianto, that night. He offered to ask for permission to take me to Balibó. 'You could come to the party with me,' he said.

'I would prefer to stare at the wall until I leave rather than tolerate that terrible man for one second.' Married to Suharto's daughter, Prabowo Subianto was the most hated man in East Timor because of his ruthlessness.

Late that afternoon I managed to speak to the original tourist agent who had my ticket on her desk all the time. I was to fly via Denpasar in seven days. I felt so relieved. When I arrived back at the hotel a new set of chess players chorused:

'Where has you been?'

'I has been out.'

Arsénio had a hangover the next day, but I was in luck. A French journalist told me where Colonel Bimo was dining. I went to the restaurant and stood a few feet from his table. That was when I realised I was not scared of anyone or anything. Whether confronting Murdani was responsible I do not know, but I had become fatalistic and it was wonderful.

All the diners fell silent. Colonel Bimo looked up and started in surprise. I apologised for interrupting his dinner and asked if he had recovered his health. I then asked if he would let me go to Balibó. He said he would see to it.

'Thank you, Colonel Bimo,' I said, resisting an impulse to bow ingratiatingly. 'Please don't let me down.'

I was woken at 4 a.m. the next day by a policeman who demanded my passport. Arsénio had said we should leave by 7 a.m. I waited in the garden but Arsénio did not appear until 10 a.m. I went to collect the tree and my passport while he had breakfast. Mark Forster was no longer friendly. He said he had been unable to get my eucalyptus tree because they did not survive in that climate.

We finally left at 1.30 p.m. At last I might stand where Greg stood and see what he saw in the last hours of his life. I would walk where he had walked when he was alive and looking forward to his very rosy future.

We passed a bus that had fallen down a gully. A man lying by the side of the road said the injured and the dead had been taken away. Arsénio said, 'That is the bus you would have been on if you had gone without me.'

After a gruelling four-hour drive, we reached Maliana. Arsénio wanted a rest before tackling the next 45-minute drive over crude roads and two huge dried-up riverbeds. After constantly pointing out healthy eucalypts on the way, I asked for one when I met the *liurai* of Maliana and he promised to get me a eucalypt sapling. When Arsénio was finally ready to move, a tree was brought to me – not a eucalypt as I had wanted, but a cocoa tree. Arsénio insisted a eucalypt would most certainly die. This was ridiculous but I assumed an Australian tree was too much of a political statement. I nursed the sapling on my lap and concentrated upon its bright green leaves, so perky and so alive. The sun was setting by the time we drove into Balibó.

As soon as we arrived, I could see that there would be nowhere to plant the tree – the earth was hard-baked and the town centre was taken up with a gigantic statue of a Timorese warrior whose Portuguese bonds of slavery had been broken after being 'liberated' by the Javanese. The statue looked as if the warrior had been shot in the back! Maybe the man who sculpted the frogs and this statue were one and the same.

The policeman in charge did not want me to plant the tree. We discussed this for an hour. Arsénio wanted me to abandon the tree; he wanted to go somewhere and eat. While Arsénio and the policeman talked, I listened to the doleful clicks of geckoes. Somewhere here, Greg had died. Somewhere here in the dust of this town something of him existed. I thought of Tony, his youth, his enthusiasm, and Gary with his larger-than-life appetites and his laughter. The other men were still shadows to me, but they were there, waiting in the wings to be discovered, to be remembered. The darkness softened the horror and I began to lose the sense of urgency that had been driving me all day. Arsénio kept complaining that he was hungry. Calm entered me. I said I was prepared to sit there all night and all next day if necessary, patiently waiting for permission to plant a tree.

The mosquitoes continued their malaria-laden dive-bombing attacks. My sunburn itched. I was sticky with sweat, covered with dust, and hungry and thirsty. The sun was going down on the anniversary of my husband's last day of life and I was getting nowhere. Overwhelmed by loss and regret I fought back tears.

After another interminable discussion, which seemed to be about the captain's preference for flowers rather than trees, I

The Circle of Silence

looked him straight in the eyes and whispered, 'Why can't you just tell me what is worrying you?'

He hesitated, coughed and spoke: 'An American lost his watch in an earthquake in Irian Jaya and the Western press reported it was stolen.' I studied his face for a clue to the meaning of this anecdote and seeing none smiled and leaned forward to touch his arm and encourage him to continue. He took a deep breath and spoke hesitantly, 'What will happen if the tree dies?'

After a stunned silence I said, 'Now I understand. Do you think I will blame you if the tree dies?'

'Yes.'

I assured him I would not.

'Ah well,' he said, 'in that case you can plant it anywhere you like.'

Geckoes clicked; bells rang; and choirs sang the Hallelujah chorus.

Arsénio was keen to get it over and done with, grab some food and leave. We were to sleep back at Maliana. I reflected on all the cover-ups.

'Look here,' I said. 'I'll be damned if I will plant this tree in the dark. I'm going to plant it in full sunlight and I'll sleep in the car.' Arsénio was appalled, but when he saw how determined I was he drove me to the local priest who said I could plant the tree in his garden the next day. We returned to the police station and asked for permission to come back tomorrow and then took the long drive back to Maliana.

The next morning as we crossed the two riverbeds and negotiated the appalling roads Arsénio informed me that in another week the wet season would start and we wouldn't have been able to get to Balibó at all. I gave thanks for the miraculous timing of the papal visit.

As I loosened the tree from its container, a policeman rode up on a motorcycle with instructions for me to go yet again to the local police station. The man I had seen before was no longer on duty, so I had to go through the whole rigmarole once more. Having learned something of the way an Indonesian official thinks it didn't take as long this time.

From the site, I could look into West Timor. I walked between the two houses where the journalists had rested, but I did not ask to go in. They were sacred shrines. I did not want to see the neglect, or go into the dark. I was determined to do everything in full sun. I did not care how long it took. I was going to plant the tree in full blazing sunlight. The Portuguese fort Greg had described was still there. It might have offered protection in times past, but a single shot from an American-supplied cannon would have demolished it, so I was in no doubt as to why they chose not to shelter there. The priest had already dug the hole for the tree and he gave us a tour of the new church of Santo Antonius. I thought of the *liurai* of Maliana's offer to place a white marble headstone by the tree if I could send money from Australia, or if I would ever be able to afford or be allowed to install a leadlight window in the church – St George and the komodo dragon came to mind. I was told that the whole town wanted to watch.

'Everyone is welcome,' I said. No, we were told, it was not allowed. As I loosened the roots of the tree soldiers and police laughed and told jokes. I felt sorry that they were the only witnesses.

Greg's favourite perfume of mine was Essence of Rose. I held my flacon to my nose and took a deep breath, then sprinkled the roots with the delicate scent. As I lowered the tree into the hole a children's choir began to sing in *Tetuñ*. I stayed on my knees, listening in wonder. The purity of their voices was a benediction. 'In your great suffering you are the salt of the earth,' the pope had said. As I concentrated on the singing the sound of crude laughter melted away. I was in a beautiful bubble floating on pure sound.

Overcome with emotion I spoke aloud the names of my husband and each of his colleagues – Brian, Malcolm, Tony, Gary and Greg. I told them their deaths had not been in vain, they had drawn attention to Timor as nothing else had. I spoke to Roger East and sprinkled the tree with the perfume. The salt of my tears mingled with Essence of Rose as I backfilled the tree. My hands were covered with soil, water, Essence of Rose and perhaps their remains comingling with all those who had died in that border town over the years since the invasion. Perhaps the soil on my hands was enriched with their blood, tears and ashes from the pyre that had destroyed the evidence of their terrible wounds.

When the singing ceased I asked who the choristers were and was told it was just some children practising the mass. The singing had come from behind a dilapidated shed. It was so incongruous I wanted to cross the road and speak to the choristers, but something told me not to go there.

It was so late when we returned to Maliana that we had to stay another night. I woke around midnight and sat straight up in bed – suddenly understanding the significance of the choir. It was a deliberate attempt to support me, born of determination to have a presence at what was for the people of Balibó a sacred rite. Prickles ran up and down my spine – they are going to win, I thought. People who go to those lengths *have to win*. I had witnessed their determination to outwit their implacable enemy. I dare not talk about their courage for fear of retribution for them. I was reminded of my feelings when I surveyed the vast emptiness of the desert outside Yazd. I was both frightened and exhilarated and that was how those children must feel, trapped as they were in their totalitarian world.

I slept fitfully, floating in my bubble, trying to see the dilemma as a transcendental victory on the part of the children of a little border town, east of nowhere as far as the army of occupation cared.

'When it comes to understanding Indonesians, you Australians are incredibly thick.' I was exhausted by conflicting emotions. As soon as we returned to Dili I had showered and gone to bed. At 10.30 p.m. Mark Forster had knocked on my door and told me to get dressed and meet him in the courtyard and buy him dinner. This was so extraordinary, I did as I was ordered. We had to sit in a particular spot in the courtyard, so I took it for granted that our conversation was going to be recorded in some way, especially after his opening words.

'Go on, then, Mark Forster, or whoever-the-hell-you-say-you-are,' I said. 'Get it off your chest.'

'By every word and gesture, they treated you with consideration. Yet from the day you arrived you have continued to grossly insult them by your actions. Worse, you compromised every single one who tried to help you to go to Balibó.' I didn't understand and said so. 'Oh, come on, you systematically and deliberately rubbed their noses in the whole Balibó botch-up. They know it was a huge tactical error. You thought up the tree planting just to embarrass them.'

I appreciated his attempt to educate me, but I would not be told what I thought. I suggested he might want to consider the little matter of who had committed the murders. So why spit venom at me?

'By telling the police you compromised them, yet they still said you could go. By telling Bimo you involved two departments.

They had to protect their backs. If Bimo and Rudini had consented to see you, they would have been forced to refuse you. You should have just gone and done it on the quiet.'

'What, go behind their backs? What are you talking about? That would be dishonest and would have given them the right to arrest me. I have done everything by the book; by *their* book.' The image of the bus in the gulch flashed into my mind. He countered with a truly silly statement.

'If you wanted to plant a tree in a public place in Australia you would just go ahead and do it.'

I enlightened him regarding the bureaucratic power held by local councils. 'I don't know who is pulling your strings,' I said, 'but you are a pig in a poke.' I was so angry by then I didn't care if I mixed my metaphors and made as little sense as he had. All the same, the fact that he just sat there convinced me he was acting under instruction, otherwise he would have walked out. A tiny memory surfaced, one I had forgotten. I had the same intuition with Murdani when I realised I had a moment, or maybe just a flash, when I could dare to take a chance and say what I wanted. I had forgotten this until now. I knew Murdani would not retaliate with all those journalists walking past the dining room and this was a reprise of that situation.

'Who are you really? CIA or are you a member of *Operasi Komodo*? Oh dear, let us hope the wind doesn't change; are those scales on your hands?' I grinned evilly, which made him laugh. 'And by the way, you have an atrocious taste in books. Not a decent one among 'em and all about war. All about violence; no true insights. War isn't cops and robbers as you should know living here of all places.' This clearly stung, but his expression and manner changed from an autocratic bully to one of interest.

'Do you understand why I wanted to go to Balibó in such a hurry? And, by the way, if I had intended to rub their noses in it why would I have left the arrangements to the last minute?' Neither he nor whoever was pulling his strings had realised the significance of the date.

'Oh, course not,' I complained. 'What are five lives to the likes of you? How many Timorese have died?' I then followed the rule that silence can speak volumes and let my body language indicate my feelings. We discussed books eventually and I offered to send him one I thought he would love which might set him on the road to some absorbing reading. He hadn't read *Slaughterhouse Five*, *The Naked and the Dead* or *The Red Badge of Courage*.

He ordered some wine and we drank together. By the end of the meal I felt free to tell him that since he thought like an Indonesian it made me very suspicious of him. 'You are certainly not an American,' I said. 'That's all too obvious.'

'How would you know?'

'Every American schoolboy reads *The Red Badge of Courage*. They take it in with their mother's milk. It's the one classic that makes sense to every one of them. *The American Civil War* is a perfect book for this conflict; the resentment still flares in America as it will here for eons to come. And by the way, in case you are interested, Stephen Crane's protagonist is a coward – he lacks the courage to stand up for his beliefs until the end – when he is redeemed. It's okay to be scared; it's not okay to assist bully boys and murderers.'

He took it very well, ordered another bottle of wine and ended by telling me what he believed had happened to the Australian journalists in Balibó: 'They were shot, cut to pieces and their bodies were eventually burned.'

I was asked to meet my contact for the last time and though I always felt ridiculous going through the motions to avoid being followed I took no chances for fear of putting others in danger. My contact asked if I would be prepared to take out handwritten letters by Xanana. They were addressed to His Holiness the pope, the Australian, British, Irish and New Zealand prime ministers, and the Portuguese and American presidents.

Handwritten letters! 'Are they signed?' They were. I must say I felt very strange about it, indeed. There would be no way of pretending innocence; talk about being caught red-handed.

'I wouldn't want to collect them until the last moment, since I could be searched at any time.' I knew my room was searched on a regular basis by the way certain articles were moved. I had tested a single wet hair placed across a door or at the side of a case, which is supposed to stay in place unless the article is opened. It is a favourite of crime novelists, and it actually works. Something else had been happening to me since my arrival. Someone walking towards me would stare almost maniacally. I would then realise I had seen that same person a few moments earlier. When I saw them a third time I would nod and take the letter they handed me. It was always stamped with the correct postage from Denpasar and correctly addressed. I had in my possession one hundred and ninety-eight letters, which I carried on me all the time. They bore addresses to Australia, Portugal and France.

I had learned quite early that it was dangerous to make calls from the telephone exchange. They went through a Jakarta switchboard, as some poor souls had discovered to their loss. I had been advised never to post letters from there either. Someone else had already taken photocopies of letters out and he was to have telephoned when he arrived home safely. Although the Resistance had him watched and therefore knew he had not been apprehended at either Dili or Denpasar airports, he had failed to make the call.

On the day I collected Xanana's letters I was appalled to find that they were handwritten on large sheets of stiff photocopy paper. I had planned to carry them in my shoulder bag to Dili airport, then go to the toilet and stuff them down the front of my trousers. A promise is a promise, so I took them without comment. I felt emotional as I said goodbye. My contact was exceptionally brave and had been warned that he was taking too many risks by being seen with me. I have to add a few words here about being followed.

My experiences in East Timor convinced me that you simply cannot avoid being followed unless you can change your appearance en route and have extensive knowledge of every street, lane, corridor and exit. It is not difficult to identify someone who is following you. Stop in front of a series of shop windows, for example, or use your pocket mirror to put on your lipstick and look behind, but you may as well not bother as the person you are able to identify is a mere decoy. The real espionage agent is not so easily identified and is replaced on a regular basis. My contact was horrified when I observed that I could not tell the difference between Timorese and Indonesians, apart from their hair, which in any case was not foolproof. If I was close enough I might be able to identify a straight-haired Indonesian wearing a curly wig, but I wouldn't want to risk my life on it. And what if the Indonesian spy has naturally curly hair? I'll never forget the look of horror on his face when I admitted this; he said every nerve in his body bristled when he was anywhere near an Indonesian. But what if you are in the presence of a Timorese traitor? This upset him even more.

After our meeting, I walked down a long dark corridor towards the open door thinking I would never see my contact again. The glare outside shimmered. A strange feeling came over me. I closed my eyes and turned back, intending to ask for a glass of water. I heard my voice coming from a long way

The Circle of Silence

away: 'We're going to meet again soon and we'll be able to have coffee and eat together in public without fear of being arrested.' His face registered shock; after all, he had just given me incriminating documents that could get him tortured or killed.

'I don't know why I said that, I feel stupid,' I said, but my mind wanted to insist that it *was* going to happen. What was happening to me? It was time to get out of the damned country with its spooks in every nook and cranny, and its petrified population.

My flight was delayed by a day so I returned to the Turismo. Having slid the letters inside the lining of my jacket I stayed locked in my room. In the morning I sat for the last time in the courtyard making notes. There was so much to remember and some of the most important events had occurred in an instant and took time to coalesce in the mind, like the singing in Balibó. Looking back I could not understand why I had not realised what really had been happening outside that exquisite, translucent, circular bubble.

A very old man, surely the most deracinated human being I have ever seen, entered the courtyard. His clothing was threadbare; his ribcage actually looked like the rungs of a bird cage. He bowed. I invited him to sit and share a cup of tea, but he remained standing. He held his hands together as if in prayer. His voice, a trembling whisper, said. 'Before, Portugal bad. Now, Indonesia bad, bad, bad.' He shuddered and stood there listening to the birds as if lost in memory.

I don't remember what I said, something useless I expect. He just kept bowing and repeating the word bad.

When I checked out, Arsénio told me Mark Forster had gone to the airport to see me off the previous day. 'He was running everywhere looking for you.'

* * *

I had learned in my teens to pretend I was having a good time. This initiated an amazing transformation in me: I would stop feeling shy and would actually have a good time. Just put one foot in front of the other might be a cliché, but it works. From the time I was deliberately delayed at Denpasar airport in Bali on the way into East Timor I had found the whole experience inspiring, despite the way my heart beat when danger threatened. *I am not in danger. There is no danger. Just put one foot in front of the other.* I also applied the philosophy that had helped me since Greg was murdered: *No matter how shattered you feel, don't be dramatic. This is Greg's tragedy, not yours.*

As I entered Dili airport footsteps followed me. *You cannot watch your back, stay calm.* To the left an Indonesian soldier idly pointed an M-16 towards me. He looked bored. *He is only doing his job.* I wandered across the cement floor, remembering how upon my arrival a voice behind had murmured in clear English, 'We knew you were coming.' It was obviously a welcome or I would have been arrested there and then. I knew my progress was being observed by friends, so if I was apprehended and the letters found, news would reach sympathetic journalists in Sydney, Melbourne and London within the hour. Cold comfort.

I went through customs without a hitch, but had a dreadful fright when I realised I was to sit next to a Javanese officer for the first leg of the flight to Kupang. When I sat down, the incriminating papers stuffed into my jeans crackled loudly. My heart beat so furiously I thought I was having a heart attack. I made a lot of noise coughing and I was far too nervous to move, so I sat straight up in my seat as if I was laced into an old-fashioned whalebone corset.

As the plane rose above Dili I felt guilty to be leaving. By then I had been taken secretly to mass graves by survivors too frightened of consequences to make a public report or to allow me to make a drawing of the locations. As John Pilger would note, 'I had no idea that much of the country is a mass grave, marked by paths that end abruptly, and fields inexplicably bulldozed, and earth inexplicably covered with tarmac.'

One aspect of the opportunities given me during my time in Timor was that I came away knowing that, though Portuguese colonialism had been less than perfect, since individual Portuguese had believed themselves superior to the indigenous people, the Indonesian government's repressive occupation was infinitely more intrusive, having resulted in dislocation, massive loss of life and suffering to the extent that widespread nostalgia for the return of the Portuguese was now endemic.

From the air, which is how Gough Whitlam had viewed the twenty-seventh province of Indonesia, the country looked like paradise and the landscape appeared to be in league with liars and opportunists. I remembered the tortured eyes of the people who took such risks for me and marvelled that anyone had trusted me in such repressive circumstances. They were extraordinarily brave. The coastline, edged with golden sands beneath azure skies, presented a peaceful vista – apart from the rusting landing barges that had brought death in the form of soldiers there was little to show of the repression. As our plane moved inland, Aussie ghost gums reared above Jurassic grasses almost as tall as the trees. I saw a couple of heat-boxes passing for houses with tin roofs – part of Whitlam's propaganda.

I held a different view, a view from the salt of the earth, a *vaqt-e vaqt* ('time-of-all-times').

FIFTEEN

On my return to Melbourne I handed the precious letters to Pat Walsh of the Australian Council for Overseas Aid, and he never said another word about them. My meeting with Murdani had made the front pages here. After due diligence I decided I would also talk about my meeting with the officer in the Seventh of December Park. His account of what happened in Balibó was horribly similar to information that had circulated in 1975 and had put Shonny into hospital. I strongly believed, since that form of torture was common in East Timor, the practice should be exposed. I made it clear I did not necessarily believe it any more than all the other versions of the atrocity at Balibó, but a deciding factor was that the officer certainly believed it. Besides, I felt it was not my place to withhold information.

In going to East Timor I had hoped to find that the Indonesian military were not as bad as painted by ex-patriate Timorese. In going to Balibó I hoped to find peace. Neither happened. Indonesian civilians are kind and considerate, and the Javanese army did not consist entirely of rabble. However, they would never have dared to kill journalists (especially five all at once) without orders from the top, and only a blind man would not be able to see the dread affecting all Timorese living under Javanese rule – the Timorese have an appropriate saying: 'If you cannot see with clear eyes you cannot see at all.'

I sent Mark Forster *All Quiet on the Western Front* and *Empire of the Sun*, and he sent me a copy of *The Good War* by Studs Terkel. Some years later I was told at a conference in Sydney by a known Timorese collaborator that Mark Forster had tragically blown his brains out. I still wake up at night wondering who he was and what really happened to him.

I made an appointment to see long-time admirer of Indonesia, Herb Feith – humanitarian and political scientist, as well as an expert on Indonesia and Indonesian politics – who favoured a plan for East Timor called 'the third way'. I thought it was nonsense, but I respected him and felt a duty to tell him something of what I had seen for myself. On arrival at his house he asked if I would like a dressing-gown to wear. He had no heating and was wearing one. I accepted the offer gladly. We sat around in our dressing-gowns discussing East Timor. He was appalled to hear my eyewitness accounts. I knew if he were to go there and publish his findings they would be taken seriously. He was encouraging, but his distress was great. He loved Indonesia. He first went to the country as a graduate in the 1950s and it had captivated him. I understood how he felt because my experience regarding East Timor was identical. As I told him some of the fascinating history and about the unique flora and fauna his eyes gleamed and I dared to think for a tiny moment that he would travel there to see for himself. But later, after lunch, he said he was afraid to go; if he saw what I had seen he would have a heart attack and die.

The fall of the Berlin Wall on 9 November 1989 worked wonders for weary and flagging activists all over the world. I woke to hear that East Germans were streaming through

Checkpoint Charlie and the infamous wall separating East and West was being demolished in a brave and united effort by citizens from either side. It was impossible then, as excited Germans went and cheered, to understand how such a miracle had occurred. As I walked downstairs all the energy drained from my legs and I had to sit down for fear of falling. Various terrible facts about life under Communist control were all too similar to East Timor. Stazi (the secret police) used dogs against escaping civilians; the Javanese didn't need dogs, they trained Timorese mercenaries to kill their own people.

East Timorese in and out of Timor celebrated as if they had been liberated. We sang the National anthem Foho Ramalau. This began a campaign in East Timor to speak disarmingly and politely to Javanese while asking, 'Kapan Pulang, When are you going home?'

I will never forget the evening in 1990 when Mark Aarons, then a producer for the ABC program 'Background Briefing', called and said, 'Something will appear in the *Sunday Age* tomorrow, Shirley. You will be very, very happy.' Naturally I tried to persuade him to give me a hint. 'It has to be something about you-know-who,' I said. He would not say a word. I tried again. 'Numero Uno.'

'Just get the *Sunday Age*,' he replied.

Filled with excitement I caught the tram and waited in the outdoor area where the first edition of the *Age* was dispatched around midnight. When it did arrive, I was too excited to wait, so I read the news by the light from a street lamp.

Robert Domm, an Australian lawyer, and former merchant seaman who had been to East Timor several times before the invasion, had gone into the country undercover. His mission was to make contact with Xanana and record a wide-ranging

The Circle of Silence

interview. He was guided by hundreds of volunteers, mostly civilians. His guides were unarmed as the route took them through villages and towns as well as through jungle and up and down moutnain ranges. Had he been detected they would not have been able to defend him. Ten thousand Javanese troops were operating in the country at that time. Resistance fighters were easily identified because they had taken a vow not to cut their hair until the Javanese were chased out of East Timor. After a gruelling journey Robert met Xanana in his mountain headquarters, situated at the top of rugged mountains somewhere in East Timor. Robert described the location as a mini Matterhorn surrounded by seemingly impenetrable jungle.

I met Robert soon after his marathon journey and he told me after arriving at the secret camp he was looking for a way to steady the microphone when Xanana appeared and with one glance produced a roll of sticky tape from his shoulder bag and proceeded to fasten the microphone in place. Robert spoke with a chuckle. 'Imagine it, Shirley. I, who came from the world of plenty, felt useless and he, who existed despite crippling ill-health and deprivation, had the solution.' Robert's eyes shone when I told him Father Locatelli had said that Xanana was the most disciplined person he had ever met.

A year after my visit to East Timor I was able by pure luck to initiate a series of events that would result in something of a miracle. This would take place over two years of concentrated activity and involved a lot of extraordinary people.

After returning from East Timor I published several accounts of my visit in Australian newspapers and these led to an invitation from a historian specialising in East Timor, Dr Peter Carey, of Trinity College, Oxford to give a paper at the first conference to be held on East Timor in the world. The proceedings were to start on the evening of Friday, 7 December

1990 – the fifteenth anniversary of the invasion – through the auspices of St Anthony's College. It was thought at that time I would be the only speaker who could give an eyewitness report, which is partly why I went. In fact, two Timorese youths and the Bishop of New York attended at the last minute. It was as well that I did not know the bishop had spent three days in Dili during the mass as I would have not felt such a pressing need to attend.

No sooner had I arrived in London than I heard that London-based journalist John Pilger was in Melbourne searching for me! I presumed he wanted to talk to me about the murders at Balibó and I was thrilled at the possibilities for exposure of any documentary Pilger might make. But I would have to meet up with him another time.

In London, I was to be interviewed by the BBC on the morning I was to leave for Oxford, and was booked to fly home on the Monday after the conference, so I took my luggage to the BBC. This was my third BBC interview that week. Carmel Budiardjo, the editor of the *Tapol Bulletin*, had arranged the interviews for me, but we could not know how important this last interview was destined to be.

The program was running late. As there would be no refund for my booked seat if I missed the train I was very nervous. The interviewer asked excellent questions, so we covered a lot of ground. As I left Broadcasting House with sufficient time to catch the train, it started to rain. I was approaching the underground when a thought struck me. What if someone responded? Would they be likely to go to the trouble of contacting me in Australia and were they likely to be able to find my digs at Oxford? I stopped walking and dithered, oblivious of the rain, cursing that I should have left a contact phone number at the reception desk. But then, how likely was it that anyone would call?

I ran back to the BBC and as I burst through the doors I heard my name being called. The concierge smiled when he saw me. He held the phone towards me. 'A call for you, Mrs Shackleton.' It was Peter Gordon, who worked for Yorkshire Television. He had heard the interview but had never heard of East Timor and did not even know where it was.

'There is a very good reason for that,' I said. 'Millions of rupiah have been spent to make sure no one believes activists like me.'

'Since you have brought it up,' he said, 'are you sure you haven't imagined it?'

I told him I was not deranged and I did not blame him for being cautious, as I found it so hard to believe what I knew to be happening in East Timor because it was all so terrible. He asked if I would meet him the following Thursday with a view to briefing him. In order to meet, I would have to cancel my flight, and cancelling my flight that close to Christmas would almost certainly mean being stuck in London. There wasn't even time to think about it. But here was an opportunity too good to miss. I decided to take a chance.

Fortunately, I knew Geraldine Brooks' house in London was available to me. She was on the Saudi border reporting on the First Gulf War for the *Wall Street Journal*. She offered her house with the words, 'After all, Shirley, if it wasn't for you I wouldn't have a house in London.' So I gave Peter Gordon Geraldine's address in Hampstead and raced to catch the train to Oxford.

I was to be met at the station when I arrived in Oxford by someone I did not know. I saw an interesting young chap and wished he could be my minder. He wore a beautiful black fedora and a raincoat tied at the waist with a hank of string. Film directors and stars like Humphrey Bogart wore them, and Indiana Jones. The young man smiled at me and introduced himself. His name was George Monbiot. He now has a regular column in the British newspaper the *Guardian* and he had also written a bestseller called *Poisoned Arrows*, set in West Papua. He was a delight and I had a lovely time with him – including a memorable snow fight through the streets of Oxford. He has a marvellous sense of humour and is a wonderful companion.

I learned a lot during the conference, especially from two Timorese youths who described the torture they had endured after the papal mass. The heated exchanges were thrilling, especially those between Dr Roger S Clark, a New Zealander, and a distinguished professor of law at Rutgers University, and pro-Indonesia academics from Oxford. Not for the first time, I wished I had studied Law. Roger Clark exposed those pro-Indonesia academics with stunning, accurate logic. His paper exposing the faults in the infamous Australian government Timor Gap Treaty (11 December 1989) had established that it was 'a blatant manifestation of exploitation of this exploration because nowhere in the treaty was there any mention of the rights and interests of the East Timorese people themselves'.

Donaciano Gomes had been one of the standard bearers at the protest at Taci-Tolu. He described his treatment by Kopassus Red Beret commandos. Having hidden in the hills after the mass, he finally went to Bishop Belo for help. The bishop was assured that Gomes would be released after he and others were taken to four different military headquarters. Donaciano was subjected to cigarette burns and electric shocks. A dagger was stuck in his back and he received blows to his head. Gun muzzles were pointed at his chest and head, and shoved in his mouth. The torment continued for fifteen days because the torturers wanted him to accuse a particular priest of having instigated the demonstration at the papal mass.

At the time of the conference in 1990, the terror in East Timor was at its height, as the brutality had increased after the pope had failed to recognise East Timor as a separate country. When the pro-Indonesian professors did not believe Donaciano's claims that he had been tortured he promptly offered to expose the scars on his body. They demurred, but when he pulled up his shirt I distinctly saw them.

Dr Peter Carey of Trinity College gave a very disturbing account of a meeting with the Indonesian attaché in London on 3 August 1990, who said to him, 'Now this is off the record, elder sister to younger brother. A friendly piece of advice if you don't mind?' She told him how disappointed she was to have read Peter's foreword to John Taylor's *The Indonesian Occupation of East Timor, 1974–1989*, where the destruction wrought in East Timor was compared to Pol Pot's reign of terror in Cambodia. 'How can you, a friend of Indonesia, say these terrible things about our army? You know they are not true. I hope you will remember that you are married to an Indonesian. What would your Indonesian relatives – your father-in-law in particular – think if you fell into disrepute?'

After my talk I was greeted by gatherings of people in corridors, some speaking Portuguese, some *Tetuñ*, most in English. We might live on opposite sides of the globe but they all had a common purpose: the need to know more from someone who had walked the dusty streets and had *seen* for themselves what the country was like after being 'liberated' by Indonesia.

Back in London I castigated myself for being such a fool for cancelling my flight. A combination of the First Gulf War and Christmas made it impossible to get a plane home for another two and a half months. Fancy hanging around London on the promise of a phone call from a stranger! Geraldine was due to return to England in another week, and I wondered where I would go then. I was determined not to overstay my welcome.

Peter Gordon arrived on time, having just missed meeting my neighbour, Dame Judy Dench. I did make one attempt to interest the great actress in East Timor's plight, but as she had sprained her ankle she declined. Poor Peter; I was very painstaking and my briefing took several hours. As I did not know how to turn on the heating, it was freezing. He spoke as if he *was* definitely going to make a documentary, though I hardly dared believe it. I had learned early on not to use the word 'if' as it can be counterproductive.

As well as educating Peter with the historical facts, I gave verifiable details about the immense wall of propaganda concerning every aspect of Indonesia's invasion and its bloody aftermath. I told him how to conduct himself in East Timor (by posing as a dumb tourist and filming secretly) and cautioned him to call East Timor 'Tim Tim', and not to mention Portugal or use any Portuguese words. I told him how to contact Kirsty Sword — a friend who was sympathetic to Timor — without endangering her safety and I recommended that he take her to East Timor with him. She was above suspicion back then as she was working legitimately in Indonesia teaching English as a second language.

I gave Peter all my trusted contacts in England, America, East Timor and Australia. He was surprised how readily I gave him these details. He said most people want to hold the reins. That, as far as I am concerned, smacks of ego and a desire to gain credit as well as power, which must never be the point of the exercise. It's also inefficient. For me, to initiate a system where he would have to keep contact with me in Australia might mean his enthusiasm could fizzle out.

I had gone to England for three weeks; I would not get home for three months. My friend Di Gameson had volunteered to water my garden back home, but I couldn't help think what a nuisance it would be for her. I also wondered how likely it

The Circle of Silence

would be that Yorkshire Television would allow Peter to go on such a dangerous assignment. I was deeply depressed until I decided to take a bus to Barcelona where my nephew Darren Venn was teaching English. I asked Carmel Budiardjo if she would lend me some money. She took me to the bank and withdrew all her savings. She refused to accept an IOU, which is typical of this wonderful woman.

I found a place to stay with a friend's friend, who would be away over the festive season. Unfortunately, my hostess insisted I was not to cook onions in her immaculate white kitchen and I was not to eat or drink in front of TV while sitting on her white leather couch. She went off to the country while I spent Christmas Day sitting on her white carpet watching dreadful TV but eating delicious little Christmas snacks bought with some of wonderful Carmel's money.

A day later I received a message to call someone in Brussels. I knew no one in that city – my hostess thought it was a spy luring me to my death. The call was from my contact in Dili, the one I had prophesied would soon be free to meet me in a public place where we could have coffee together! He had been sent out of East Timor for safekeeping and he said to me, 'From now on, everything you say I believe.'

I immediately made arrangements to meet him in Brussels and go from there to Barcelona. What happened in Brussels is instructive of two people's different reactions to something one cannot explain: the one who lives in freedom and the one who has lived under repression. We went to a pleasant-looking restaurant, and I was so very thrilled to be making my prediction come true. We toasted each other with coffee and said 'Viva Timor' rather often; we were drunk with hope. We ordered lunch and he offered to tell me everything he had been unable to tell me in Dili, but his facial expression changed suddenly.

Didn't he like the food? What was wrong? He was suspicious of a man sitting behind us. Had he seen him before? No, but he was acting strangely. Speaking loudly enough for this man to hear I announced I was going to the toilet at the back of the restaurant. I did not enter the toilet; I went to see if there was a way out through the kitchen. I watched the large dark brooding man as I returned to my seat. A medium-sized black box sat on his table. The lid was open and though his hands were inside I could not see what he was doing. As I walked past him he closed the lid, placed his hands in his lap and looked at the ceiling like an innocent child. The box could have been a recording device; it could have been something else. As soon as I sat down he opened the lid and placed his hands inside again.

He seemed to be fiddling with an apparatus of some kind. I didn't want to spoil this occasion by being paranoid and I didn't want to belittle my friend's concern, but I could not believe that the long arm of Indonesia might be operating in Brussels. To an Australian it was absurd, but not to my friend. If this man fiddling inside a black box was spying on us I would put my friend in danger by not taking it seriously. I used signals to indicate that he should leave through the kitchen. As soon as it became apparent that he was not coming back the stranger went to the telephone and made a call. He whispered a few words, returned to his seat, packed up and, after paying the bill, left.

If my friend had not pointed him out I wouldn't have even noticed him. That's the difference between someone who has been subjected to constant surveillance and one who has not. We met later in my room so we could talk about all the things we had not dared to voice in Dili, but we did not meet publicly again. I was angered by the incident and my failure to grasp the nettle – as soon as my friend left I should have confronted that man and demanded to know what was in the box.

The Circle of Silence

On my return from Barcelona Carmel told me John Pilger was back in London so I went to see him and his marvellous producer David Munro. I was very impressed with their up-to-date information about East Timor. Their questions were so perceptive I felt any documentary they might make would put East Timor on the map. They assured me a time would come when they would go and see for themselves: 'We have to get the timing right and that means patience.'

Back in Melbourne I found Di had paid all my bills and my garden looked splendid. But I spent the whole next year feeling miserable. In retrospect, the idea of a documentary seemed a figment of my imagination. Some people wanted to believe I was permanently transfixed with grief over Greg. I won't claim this was a deliberate attempt to undermine me, but it certainly felt like it. At one radio station I was asked off-air to make a statement on air explaining why I had not remarried. I told the interviewer, 'You won't like my answer,' which was, 'My husband promised me a gold-plated wheelchair. He believed marriage is not equitable for women and I didn't come down in the last shower.' The interviewer was offended, but his wife was delighted.

A little under a year later I attended a breakfast for José Ramos-Horta. I had never told anyone about my meeting with Peter Gordon for obvious reasons. Pat Walsh, who was at the breakfast, had to leave early. I overheard him saying he had to return to his office to receive a call from someone who had just been to Timor with Kirsty Sword. 'What's his name?' I asked. He did not remember. 'Could it be Peter Gordon?'

'Ah, that might be it.'

I tracked Peter down that night. He was in Darwin viewing the footage that he'd taken.

'It's just as bad as you said,' he told me. 'I still can't believe how terrible it is there. Everything you told me is true.' He was hoping for dramatic footage of a proposed visit by a Portuguese parliamentary delegation. I told him the Portuguese would cancel their visit because people like me warned them that they would be shot as soon as they set foot on Timorese soil. He did not believe this as he had found no hatred for the Portuguese among the Timorese.

'They will be murdered by Indonesian soldiers disguised as Timorese or by paid assassins,' I explained.

He had met a British documentary maker who had been 'sniffing around'. Since he did not want to be gazumped he had offered to put him on salary. The man was waiting in Dili. This was Max Stahl, famous in England for having hosted a popular children's TV show called *Blue Peter* in his youth, and respected for his reports from El Salvador, Lebanon and Vietnam. I met Peter in Melbourne and we had dinner together with Kirsty and her parents. By then the failure of the Portuguese to visit their lost colony had put a damper on proceedings.

Peter returned to England with his footage and Max intended to follow him a week or so later. I reflected on the pointlessness of work like mine when the forces of evil hold all the cards. Though I never expected to achieve anything of note, I would have liked some evidence that my work had purpose.

On 28 October 1991, at the Motael church, Sebastião Gomes was shot in the stomach by a Javanese soldier in front of dozens of stunned parishioners. Timorese hold what they call the Ceremony of the Bitter Flowers when a loved one dies. Later, when they have come to terms with their grief, they hold the Ceremony of the Sweet Flowers. In some Western cultures this is known as 'the laying of the ghost'. The laying of the sweet flowers was to occur on 12 November in the Santa Cruz cemetery where Sebastião had been buried. Max Stahl was due to leave East Timor the following day.

He wrote some letters in the morning half-thinking he would give the ceremony a miss. However, once a newshound always a newshound. When the time came he tossed his letters aside, picked up his money, camera and ID and went to the Motael Church to witness the memorial mass. Luckily he had hidden his air ticket in his room.

A large number of mourners were in attendance, and on the walk to the cemetery a banner was unfurled and Fretilin flags were raised in protest. Major Gerhan Lantara was stabbed – Max said Lantana had attacked a young girl for carrying a Fretilin flag. As Sebastião's family placed the sweet flowers on his grave they were shocked to see squads of Javanese marching into the cemetery. Without any warning they shot at the unarmed mourners.

This was the first time a massacre in Timor had been captured on film and the first time Westerners were present. Two American reporters were threatened: Amy Goodman was about to be clubbed by the butt of an assault rifle when she glimpsed the maker's name – 'Colts. West Hartford U.S.A.' Fellow journalist Allan Nairn threw himself over her and took the blow. His skull was fractured.

Max took shelter at the entrance of a crypt with a British photographer, Steve Cox. They shielded children from bullets ricocheting around them. Steve's close-up of a young girl's blood-spattered face became an icon – Max told me the side of her face was a bloody mess. He managed to hide his film in a grave before being arrested. As he waited to meet his fate he witnessed hundreds being driven away in trucks never to be seen again. He was searched; his possessions were stolen; and an unexposed film he had cleverly loaded before capture was destroyed. Eventually allowed to leave, he returned to the hotel and then braved the death squads by going back to the cemetery in pitch-black darkness to retrieve the incriminating film. Though the streets still swarmed with death squads he managed to evade them. The morning after the massacre he recognised Saskia Kouwenberg, a Dutch girl he had met in Darwin, having breakfast in the dining room and he asked her to smuggle out the film as he was certain to be searched at Dili airport. She was flying home to Holland on KLM via Jakarta that morning. Max was flying to Darwin.

Saskia later told me, 'I wear those big bloomers so I cut the crutch open, slipped in the films and sewed them in place. On the way to Jakarta I told the flight attendants what I was doing. They agreed to help me. They said to go to a toilet near the exit for re-entry to their flight and wait there. On no account was I to allow myself to be taken away by the Javanese who were waiting to interview the passengers. They were waiting for me at the end of the corridor.' Then she told me something, which I'll never forget.

'You know how when you were a kid we used to pick our noses, Shirley, and make them bleed?'

'What?'

Evidently she was very good at this. She made her nose bleed profusely and smeared the blood over the crutch in her bloomers in case she was searched. After what seemed an interminable wait the flight attendants returned and when the waiting soldiers' attention was momentarily diverted they beckoned to Saskia to make a run for it. They rushed her on board through their own entrance. It must have been terrible waiting for the plane to take off. On arrival in Holland she posted the film to Peter Gordon and he got the scoop of his life. *In Cold Blood* was broadcast all over the world. Peter Gordon is now a top executive for Yorkshire Television.

My Timorese friends told me the families of the victims of the Santa Cruz massacre refused to grieve publicly for the deaths of their family members; unlike the hundreds of thousands of deaths in all the massacres since the Indonesian invasion, they felt that their loved ones had not died in vain.

British photographer Steve Cox was the only passenger on a flight from Timor to be body searched by Australian customs officials in Darwin. 'It was perfectly obvious that they were looking for my films.' He had given them to another passenger, who hid them in her clothing.

The Indonesian government claimed *only* nineteen were killed, as though that made the murders okay. Gareth Evans defended his previous position that 'on balance the best evidence suggested that the Santa Cruz massacre was an aberration, not systematic, that not so many were killed'. Later he claimed that the missing hundreds 'could have run away and were hiding in the bush'.

In Max Stahl's estimation the number killed exceeded four hundred. Late in 1998 Mário Carrascalão, then the governor of East Timor, spoke in Jakarta of ongoing killings at various places in Dili following the massacre at the Santa Cruz cemetery. Hundreds of brave deeds by Timorese who will never be credited occurred during and after the massacre. Some took risks for others, such as the Red Cross ambulance driver who tried to save New Zealander Kamal Bamadhaj.

Eyewitnesses saw 21-year-old Kamal – a New Zealand student-activist and a visitor to East Timor – walking away from the scene of carnage nursing a wounded arm. In the documentary *Punitive Damage* (1999), José Verdial, a Timorese who took part in the demonstration, said he saw Kamal outside the cemetery. When a military truck following him pulled up, Kamal was shot in his chest by an intelligence officer. He was left lying on the roadside, but managed to flag down the passing

Red Cross ambulance. 'When he was picked up by the driver, he was still talking,' recounted Verdial. 'Every time he spoke, blood gushed out from his wound.'

Indonesian police forced the ambulance driver to turn away at several checkpoints. Kamal knew he was dying. They were finally directed into a police station compound where demands were made for the ambulance driver to dump Kamal. He refused. When he was finally given permission to leave he managed to get Kamal to hospital. He died 20 minutes after admission.

Helen Todd, Kamal's mother, was prevented by Indonesian authorities from going to Dili to collect her son's body. Delayed in Jakarta for three days she was told he had been buried immediately and then exhumed, which meant he was unrecognisable – Kamal's uncle recognised him by his hair. José Ramos-Horta said, 'He was totally, totally innocent and his death was an absolutely unforgivable murder.'[1]

In contrast to José's statement, General Try Sutrisno, the Indonesian commander-in-chief, said, 'The army cannot be underestimated. Finally we had to shoot them. Delinquents like these agitators must be shot, and they will be shot.'[2]

East Timorese living in Canberra placed white crosses to commemorate each victim outside the Indonesian embassy in Canberra. A wonderful barrister, Bernard Collaery, received a tip-off just before an announcement was made on the ABC News that the minister for foreign affairs, Gareth Evans, had ordered the federal police to seize the crosses. He drove to the embassy and retrieved the crosses, with help from the police, who disapproved of Evans' orders.

---

1 Cited in Ong Ju Lin, 'Death of an Activist', *Star Malaysia*, 8 May 2000, quoted on www.etan.org
2 Cited in Rodney Tiffin, *Deplomatic Deceits: Government, Media and East Timor*, University of New South Wales Press, Sydney, 2001.

Bernard Collaery represented the East Timor Independence Committee in the first Melbourne court case, as the law required evidence that there had been a massacre in the Santa Cruz cemetery before a determination could be made to reinstate the crosses. Max Stahl sent uncut film and the people in the gallery were horrified by the scenes of violence that had been cut from the television reports. When Collaery's success was reported, Gareth Evans passed another regulation. Subsequently, each time Collaery won, Evans passed another regulation. I must report here that Colleary's services were pro bono; every time Evan's acted, Australian tax payers footed the bill.

At the last court proceedings, five High Court judges supported Collaery's arguments. Bernard remembers: 'We planted the crosses at 3 p.m., the hour of the crucifixion on Good Friday. The bishops of Canberra and the head of the Uniting Church re-blessed the crosses and we installed a lantern. I insisted that only Timorese walk up the road to the Indonesian Embassy saying the rosary and singing, each carrying a white cross. I saw veteran newsmen weep and I cried too – it was the defining moment of my legal life.'

A certain amount of vandalism followed, so Bernard collected the crosses again and he placed them in his back garden where to this day they gleam eerily in the moonlight.

In response to international outrage over Kamal's death, the Indonesian government sent their military commander in East Timor, Sintong Panjaitan, along with another commander, to Harvard University in Boston to study English, presumably as a 'punishment'. In 1994, aided by the US Center for Constitutional Rights and 'using a little-known 200-year-old US law that allowed human rights violators to be tried wherever they were found, Helen Todd sued for compensatory and punitive damages. Panjaitan, upon receiving his summons, immediately fled back to Indonesia ... The US court eventually awarded Todd and Kamal's estate a total of US$22 million ... Panjaitan refused to acknowledge the court's jurisdiction, calling the suit a "joke".[3]

Sintong Panjaitan joined the Indonesian public service and rose to become an adviser to President B.J. Habibie. Soon after his return to Indonesia, I received two phone calls early one morning asking, 'Did I know General Sintong Panjaitan was a guest of the Australian government? He was touring Australia in a chauffeur-driven government limousine with all expenses paid.' The first caller wanted me to arrange a protest.

'Would I what? Who are you?' She worked for the defence industries in Maribyrnong in Victoria. He was arriving there in an hour. I was very sorry to have to tell these passionate Aussies that such short notice made it impossible. Timorese in Australia worked two jobs to get money to bring out their family members and most of them started early in factories so they would not be available. I did not have access to a car, nor did I have a secretary to call the media. The second caller got very irate with me and said, 'We make the best bullets in the world, they probably killed your husband.'

It should be noted that there were many massacres in Dili during the Indonesian occupation. The first occurred on 7 December 1975 when thousands of Chinese and Timorese were murdered. A second massacre took place the day after the Indonesian invasion when Roger East was murdered. The organisation *A Paz e Possivel em Timor Leste* (Peace Is Possible in Timor-Leste) published a list of their findings

---

3 Ong Ju Lin, 'Death of an Activist', op. cit.

into the number of massacre victims at Santa Cruz in leading Portuguese newspapers in November 1992. José Ramos-Horta described how the data was obtained: '[It] has been compiled by 12 teams of East Timorese students, school teachers, priests, nuns, nurses, paramedics, hospital staff, workers at the morgues, totalling 72 researchers, working round the clock for three months, interviewing household members in each barrio, immediately after 12 November 1991.' The preliminary report reached Lisbon in February and was handed over to two specialist groups in Portugal that had been investigating human rights abuses in East Timor for more than ten years. A copy was channelled to Amnesty International for independent verification.

Max Stahl's film footage and subsequent reporting by Americans Amy Goodman and Alan Nairn broke the backs of the Jakarta Lobby's compromised assurances that Timorese fared well under Indonesian rule. According to José Ramos-Horta, it took six months for the mass of detailed information about the Santa Cruz massacre to be processed and analysed. The researchers took extreme care in double-checking each piece of information. They listed:

271 killed
278 wounded
103 hospitalised
270 disappeared

The day after the massacre at Santa Cruz a group of young Timorese students living in Melbourne telephoned the Indonesian consulate for an appointment with the consul general to discuss their concerns for their student counterparts in East Timor. This was granted and I was asked to attend at the South Melbourne consulate at 10 a.m. the following day.

I always used my appearance and dress for protection during demonstrations. While others were arrested I led a charmed life. It was very hot that day so I wore a lilac dress and my beautiful lilac hat, which made me look as if I was going to a garden party. I arrived at five minutes to ten to find a line of policemen barring entrance to the consulate. Having been told that the students were being held upstairs, I walked straight through the police lines smiling and asking if this was the right place for the Indonesian consulate.

The office was on the top floor and the way up was by a steep circular staircase. A police officer stood on guard in the foyer and about a dozen young people were sitting quietly on the floor. I smiled at them and walked right past the officer as if I owned the place before sitting and ruffling in my handbag for my book, which I proceeded to read. From time to time I sneaked glances at the students. They were scared. After a while I asked what they were waiting for? The police officer answered for them – they had smashed the very thick glass panels leading into the foyer.

'Good heavens,' I said. 'Why did you do that?' The answer came from one and all – it had been like that when they arrived. I asked the police officer if he had caught them in the act. He had not. 'So you are working on supposition. Why don't you believe them and how did you get here?' The consul general had made a complaint about the violence. 'What makes you believe him and not them; they don't look violent to me.' He did not have an answer.

I encouraged the students to tell me why they were there and that police officer got an earful. I told him I believed it was obvious that they had a legitimate grievance; would he please ask the consul general why he was refusing to keep his promise. 'He's an adult; they are only kids, and scared kids at that.'

The Circle of Silence

At that moment we heard the wailing of police sirens. The police officer advised me to leave as the students were going to be arrested. I said, 'Shame on you.'

I touched each of the students as I left while mouthing 'don't resist'. As I walked down the stairs I watched through a window as a bevy of police armed with riot sticks leapt from cars and ran full-pelt at the building. They entered and rushed past me. They pulled some of the boys down the stairs backwards so that their heads repeatedly hit the steps. I asked them to stop. Everyone was screaming in fear as they were being so roughly handled. I ran to where I had parked my car and drove to the South Melbourne police station. If they had not arrived within five minutes I would have gone on to the St Kilda police station.

Several vans pulled in. Students packed into the vans sweated profusely – the cooling systems had been switched off. I stood where they would pass me on the way into the station. As each of them drew near I said, 'Viva.' Every one of them smiled with relief. I entered the station. Their names were recorded and they were told to go. I made a show of inspecting their backs and shoulders, which were bright red from their violent handling, and I asked if this evidence had been noted. I got a surly, noncommittal response. I made an appointment for the following day to make a complaint.

The next day the senior detective was conciliatory. They had received an official complaint alleging violence; the police were only youngsters and they were prepared for a riot. I insisted on making a sworn statement that there was no excuse for the police to harm the young Timorese when all they were doing was waiting peacefully for an official to keep his appointment.

Timorese students had told me that they didn't dare demonstrate at Monash University when Gareth Evans was due to attend a dinner there. Indonesians regularly took their photographs and they expected the visit to Monash would be no different. They feared reprisals against their relatives back in Timor.

Ignorance about events in East Timor was not confined to the media and government, or the Australian people. I mentioned the head of the Timorese Resistance Army to a group of Timorese youths in Perth after a commemoration service for the victims of Santa Cruz and they had never even heard about Lobato or Xanana. We were standing outside the church when I was asked to tell them more. The sound of four hundred motorbikes drowned me out. Local motorcycle gangs were on the way to present Christmas toys to the children's hospital. I was surprised by my audience's reaction, for they did not seem to hear the cacophony approaching us. I did not want to lose them so I soldiered on against a backdrop of huge, hairy blokes covered in tattoos carrying teddy bears, winged fairies, dollies whose rag arms were 'Doin' the Lambeth Walk' with Superman and Elvis Presley facsimiles. Yet again I felt I had wandered into a film set where everyone knew the plot except me.

These young Timorese were unaware of the history of their own country, so I offered to meet any one of them for further discussion. 'In a park, in a coffee bar, anywhere.' They hired a small hall and forty-three showed up. I explained that I was not asking to be believed in everything I was going to tell them, and I gave them a list of books and suggested they might make a small library by buying one each and passing them around. Having read the available literature they would then be in a position to make up their own minds. They knew so little I had to take the chance of insulting them.

'Could members of your family have belonged to either the Apodeti or UDT political parties?' I quickly added that I did not need replies; I just wanted them to acknowledge the question privately for their own edification. I then explained the historical realities. Timorese culture demands that family members pay respect to the views of their elders and as the families are huge – some extending to five hundred or more – the process of autonomy in 1975 was doomed to be lengthy. I then asked my audience, 'Do you believe that the Fretilin political party started a civil war?' When most answered 'yes', I quailed at the task before me.

'Please think carefully about this,' I said. 'Could it be that your family members were and are anti-Fretilin?' Almost everyone in the hall put their hands up. 'Wouldn't you like to know what really happened?' I asked. They stared with surprised, wide-open eyes as I told them the bare bones of the attempted coup plus some additional information that I had come to understand by then. Though some UDT officials had welcomed the opportunity to rule, other more moral men refused to take part in the illegal proceedings because it swept away all hope of democracy. I was defensive about the way the coup was called a civil war since it was masterminded from Jakarta. Ambushes, skirmishes and murders had occurred when the coup was launched and many of these deaths were the result of long-standing internal feuds – more to do with payback than politics. The violence divided families and damaged traditional ties. As events spiralled, families split in their allegiances and relationships were fractured.

The Portuguese governor and other officials made no attempt to intervene; they claimed to be waiting for Portuguese emissaries to arrive from Lisbon. The first envoy was detained in Indonesia and was returned to Portugal. All other emissaries were conspicuous by their absence. In the meantime, Falintil, the fighting arm of Fretilin, gained public support and the coup was put down in eleven days, although sporadic fighting continued along the border for another ten days.

'No prizes for guessing who was involved,' I said, to my shocked audience. Around one and a half thousand soldiers and civilians were killed or wounded, and Indonesia claimed this was a bloody civil war, accusing Fretilin of seizing power from the rightful Portuguese government. Many Portuguese officials and members of UDT panicked and left the country. Indonesian-controlled radio stations and the Western media reported the failed coup as a civil war. The killings from the left were more harshly judged than the killings by the right. UDT members were presented as aristocrats defending themselves and their rightful possessions against a communist-inspired insurrection. Few Timorese had any clear idea of what had really happened and when they listened to shortwave radios tuned to Radio Australia and BBC World Service they heard Fretilin being blamed for a civil war and described as communists, they believed it. The Catholic church did little to stem hatred and suspicion. Some priests openly supported UDT, because they also believed the propaganda that Fretilin was a front for communists.

All this information was received in stunned silence, which encouraged me to continue. 'To this day many Timorese do not know what I have just told you. They left the country with hatred and bitterness in their hearts. They went to Portugal and Australia blaming Fretilin for the civil war. They remain locked in a dead past and at times are so divisive that they might just as well be agents provocateurs working for the Indonesian dictator.'

The fact that UDT had launched the coup was scarcely mentioned. Western government lackeys and pro-Jakarta journalists and academics accused Western activists of being anti-Indonesian when they insisted on calling the proceedings a coup. Jakarta claimed that forty-five thousand Timorese had fled to West Timor after the civil war and these exaggerated reports were widely publicised. In fact, Timorese who went to Western Timor were badly treated by their Indonesian hosts and some were forced into slave labour.

One of the students accused Portugal of complete and utter neglect. He was understandably defensive but I had to disagree with him. It was clear to me that Portugal was the whipping boy of Gough Whitlam, the Australian prime minister and that he had to blame someone for his own perfidy. Portugal certainly had neglected Timor but many, including José Ramos-Horta, had described Portuguese rule to me as 'benign neglect'. Most people living under colonial rule feel inferior to their masters. Australians swear allegiance to the queen of England and some try to affect an English accent. To climb to the top in Timor, you had to be able to speak Portuguese, to deny your animistic beliefs and become a Catholic.

This last observation caused wry smiles of recognition. 'So maybe I know a thing or two,' I said. One young man said his father was told by an Indonesian working in Dili as a fabric importer that he was terrified of Fretilin because they were communists. I pointed out that the number of Indonesians listed as communists in Indonesia was larger than Timor's entire population and that that was the same cover story Yunus Yosfiah had used in Dili before he led Team Susi to kill Greg and his colleagues.

I told them what little I knew about Xanana. He had been put in command of a platoon of archers at the time of the failed coup.

Before the meeting broke up I asked them to consider the guilt their relatives might be feeling. UDT members had been kept ignorant of their leader's bid to seize power. 'If shooting breaks out I don't suppose you care if it's called a coup or civil war. It would have been terrifying, so don't expect logic from anyone. Even if they were not in the know or did not take part they are likely to feel responsible.' In sucking-up to Suharto the leaders of the coup had provided Indonesia with the perfect excuse to launch an invasion. The Indonesian dictator claimed he had to invade East Timor to stop the stupid natives from killing each other. But what really scared him was that a free East Timor might start the domino effect in Indonesian provinces.

I offered to answer any subsequent questions they had by mail or phone. A young woman offered me a lift home. She told me her grandfather was a *liurai*.

'Which circumspection?' I asked

'Atsabe.'

'The *liurai* of Atsabe, Guilherme Gonçalves?' He and his sons had committed treason. José and Thomas had led Indonesian battalions into East Timor via Balibó.

'Well, your grandfather is a very bad man,' I said.

We shared a short-lived burst of hysterical laughter.

'He says he is very sorry; he never dreamed the Indonesians could be so cruel.'

I corrected her. 'The Indonesian army; the Javanese. I made her awre of the distinction that Falintil uses to differentiate between the barbarous army and Indonesian civilians.' I was touchy about this. Many attempts had been made to coerce me into expressing hatred for Indonesia and, by implication, the Indonesian people. I felt I had earned the right to be pedantic. I would not want to be judged by the actions of my own heads of government and so I refused to judge the Indonesian people by the Suharto regime.

She said just to know that a Timorese was fighting back made her feel proud. She placed her hand over her heart; I was certain the gesture was unconscious. I told her about

Nicolau dos Reis Lobato the original great leader, though I left out gruesome details about his murder at the hands of Yunus Yosfiah. I could see she was really frightened at the thought of the Indonesian army.

'Hell, no,' I said. 'They're only good at fighting unarmed civilians' – which wasn't entirely true. As I discovered several years later when I met White Bat, an Australian who had fought against elite Javanese troops alongside elite Timorese troops on a regular basis. His is yet another amazing episode in the saga of East Timor.

SIXTEEN

When I was asked in 1992 to join a Peace Mission to East Timor on a Portuguese car ferry destined for East Timor called the *Lusitania* I said, 'Are you kidding? I wouldn't go sailing on the Albert Park Lake in a ship with that name!' If this *Lusitania* repeated its World War I performance by being sunk by an enemy warship I would drown. I had already faced death by drowning in Tonga with fellow activist Neva Finch, and it was a very nasty experience. On reflection I realised that the Portuguese plan for a Peace Mission to sail to East Timor was quite brilliant. Student organisers in Portugal intended to land at the Dili wharf and proceed to the Santa Cruz cemetery carrying flowers, keepsakes and wreaths on the anniversary of the Santa Cruz massacre. However, this could cause a repeat performance of what would have happened had the Portuguese parliamentary delegation carried out their plan to visit Dili. But any killings by the Indonesian navy could not be passed off as having been committed by disaffected Timorese, so there might be some safety there. Nevertheless, I found it difficult not to imagine the headlines LUSITANIA SINKS AGAIN, even though the enterprise was called The Lusitania Expresso Timor Peace Mission.

My phone stated to ring a day or two later – politicians and journalists wanted to know if I was going. I approved of the idea, of course; anything that would remind people with the power to make changes for the Timorese was worth doing. Official Indonesian and Australian reports still misrepresented not only facts about the massacre, they also suppressed bona fide information about the occupation by misrepresenting the bloody invasion as 'when Timor was incorporated into the territory of the Republic of Indonesia', Timorese were presented as 'them' or 'they', and as the ungrateful recipients of all the riches bestowed upon 'them' by the beneficent Suharto regime.

Various suggestions about taking flotation devices were made half-jokingly. I brushed them aside. I had serious concerns: would the Indonesian navy be as unprofessional as the army? Western public relations advisers would, of course, make the obvious excuse if the car ferry was sunk, claiming that the maritime boundaries had been breached. No matter how professional an Indonesian navy captain might be he would have to obey his admiral, who took his orders from Suharto. Before his murder Greg had reported a training action in Perth when the police were told to consider the target to be students. He was horrified and rightly so. So when I was told that students were volunteering from all over the world, it only strengthened my resolve not to go down with the ship.

I received a telephone call from Portugal promising to provide a cabin on board. When I asked what the overriding political aim was, I was told it would remind the world that East Timor was not an integral part of Indonesia.

'But if you fail the Indonesian press will use it to confirm the opposite of your intention,' I said.

On reflection I realised that Suharto would continue to assert his domination over his unwilling subjects no matter what happened on the high seas, but as the UN did not recognise Indonesia's rights to East Timor, a case could be made that the people on the ferry had not invaded Indonesian territory. From then on I stated in every interview, 'Timor was never Indonesian territory. It is not Indonesian territory now and it will never be Indonesian territory.' I was quite pleased with myself until a Melbourne priest criticised the statement on the grounds that Timor was indeed Indonesian territory. This acted as a spur: with friends like him Timor needed every bit of help on offer. I wrote to Evan and received his permission to go.

Australia's ambassador to Indonesia, Philip Flood, was reported on 2 March as saying that 'Australia will not sacrifice good relations with Jakarta' and threatened to take 'appropriate measures' if 'they [the peace mission members] act illegally'. It didn't occur to the stalwart of diplomatic relations to suggest to Suharto that it would be unwise from a public relations point of view to sink a civilian ship.

In Darwin, before setting sail, the Portuguese captain of the *Lusitania Expresso* warned us, if we were confronted by the Indonesian navy, to make no movements that could be misunderstood. In fact, not only were we to remain stationary, we were not to call out or even smile. If he could rely on us we could rely on him to do nothing that would endanger our safety. I spent my days in Darwin at the Mirrambeena Resort in a room filled with telephones and fax machines doing interviews, and I spent my evenings with long-term activists Andrew Alcock, Rob Wesley-Smith, ex-serviceman Jack Boardman and Timor archivist Kevin Sherlock.

Youthful volunteers came from France, Guinea-Bissau in Africa, Japan, Germany, Canada, Cape Verde, China, Indonesia, Holland, Austria, Vietnam, Italy, Brazil, India, Sweden, the United

The Circle of Silence

States, Britain, Australia and Portugal. Some of the volunteers on board had not been born when Indonesia invaded East Timor.

I was thrilled to be able to talk to the Portuguese reporter Adelino Gomes, who had brought out Greg's last, iconic, report. He was suffering the guilt of the survivor.

Australian, British and Canadian governments issued warnings to their citizens, and some girls were persuaded by this to leave. Never, at any stage, did these governments publicly issue warnings to the Indonesian government against taking offensive action against the peace ship.

The UDT political party held a dinner. The members' daughters performed a classical Spanish dance that had everyone, including the Portuguese, wondering what it all meant. One of the Portuguese organisers said it was typical of UDT: they had no understanding of real Timorese. I have never seen so much food thrown away as I did that night. Women in Portuguese mantillas came to the tables and scraped sweets, cheeses, fruit, custards, tarts, whole chickens, salads, and casseroles into dozens of huge garbage bags – a right mess of pottage.

Fretilin held a gathering in the bar of a pub and we bought our own food and drinks. The difference between the lavish waste on the one hand and the poverty on the other imparted a sense of shame in me. I decided to show a poster I had commissioned of Xanana to cheer them up. The next day a US student criticised me for showing the poster as 'a deliberate provocation'. I suggested that even if I had shown the poster at the UDT dinner it should not have been provocative. 'Xanana is fighting for all Timorese.' He did not seem convinced.

I fought back. 'Why do you want to punish me for being loyal to the head of the Resistance Army? What do you think you are here for? Do you realise what you are saying?' Self-destructive perversity was understandable in Timorese after all they had suffered, but I found it unforgivable in an American.

I am still puzzling over something from that night, which was typical of Timorese. At any function, if the UDT flag was raised outside a venue, Fretilin would turn their cars around and go home. If the position was reversed UDT went home. I got into trouble when I suggested at a meeting that all the flags should fly, saying, 'You are all in this together; divided you fall.' The objection came from an Australian who said I must allow for differences in Timorese culture. What baloney.

Xanana announced a ceasefire during the Peace Mission in order to protect us from retaliation. On the day we sailed I was asked to carry the official wreath aboard. White carnations were thrown into the sea and hundreds of white pigeons were released while five hundred Timorese sang the Peace Mission's anthem, 'To Free East Timor'. That night the Portuguese were embarrassed to confess that a politician had taken possession of my allotted cabin and refused to move. I had no sleeping gear as I had been told I wouldn't need any. I decided this was a test I must pass. Using my backpack stuffed with make-up and shoes as a pillow and with only my cardigan for warmth I lay on the floor and willed myself to sleep.

I made friends with a delightful Portuguese priest. Father Jaime Coelho (Jimmy Rabbit) had taught in Japan for thirty years and Professor Antonio Barbedo de Magalhaes taught me how to pronounce *saudades*, a beautiful Portuguese word for which there is no single English equivalent but as close as I can get to its meaning is 'disillusionment', 'regret', 'remembrance' and 'sorrow'. Perfect for East Timor.

On Tuesday 10 March 1992, Dili had to be blockaded by Javanese troops as thousands of East Timorese converged on the capital to welcome the Peace Mission. As far as I was concerned this fact alone made the enterprise worthwhile, because it established that the Timorese wanted the Portuguese to return. Information was also broadcast about threats to sink us by twelve warships lying in wait. If we actually landed, the Javanese promised we would be incarcerated at Atauro – the prison island surrounded by one of the largest reefs in the Pacific and known for its enormous sharks.

After a splendid breakfast of sardines and toast, the passengers lazed about in the sun, despite warnings of severe sunburn. At 11 a.m. a RAAF plane flew over us. At 2.40 p.m. an Indonesian Caribou aircraft swooped us twice. At 5 p.m. two Indonesian military aircraft made two sweeps. These activities were unsettling, but they were also exciting.

That night I could not find anywhere to sleep so I walked to the stern for some fresh air. A body swathed in a white sheet looking like a corpse lay at one end of a very long pew. I made a calculation and thought there was room at the other end for me, so I lay down and closed my eyes. Furious mutterings emanated from the corpse; I studiously pretended sleep. An hour or so later I was woken by excited exclamations – lights were following us. Lewis Carroll came to mind: *There's a porpoise close behind us, and he's treading on my tail.* It was too dark to see clearly but chattering passengers were certain it was the Australian navy watching over us. I could not believe how naive they were not to realise it was an Indonesian warship. It turned out to be an Australian warship, which had been supplied to Indonesia years before.

Next morning, 11 March, I woke at 4 a.m. to see the outline of eight warships following in our wake and soon afterwards a frigate began to shadow our port bow. It was still quite dark so I drifted back to sleep. At 6 a.m. I glimpsed through the morning mist the mountains of East Timor. This was thrilling. I imagined Xanana watching our progress – fanciful, I suppose, but the mind plays tricks like that. A young Englishman with a dreadful case of sunburn sat up rubbing his eyes, and when he saw all the warships and a helicopter buzzing our decks he exclaimed that he had never seen a more exciting sunrise.

People were very happy when I was able to point out some locations: Betano Beach where the 2/4th Independent Company landed in 1942 and the *Voyager*, the destroyer carrying them, ran aground; Jaco Island – it was famous for mouse deer and before the invasion thousands of the magnificent creatures used to swim to the mainland at night to forage for food and then return to their sanctuary at dawn – now everyone was struck with sadness as it had been regularly bombed and Timorese were thrown out of helicopters to their deaths there.

Battleships tagging us carried out anti-submarine manoeuvres and then they were joined by a corvette and all the ships shadowed us. We were soon only twenty-one kilometres from Dili. Word went round that an Indonesian reporter had been told by the editor of *Tempo* that the Indonesian captain had orders to fire a blank shot over our bow, to be immediately followed by a live shell if our captain did not obey orders to turn the ship around. As she had told me this the night before, I knew it was not a rumour.

At 7.30 a.m., while everyone was behaving impeccably, we silently witnessed their strategy. The Indonesian commander radioed Captain Luis dos Rios with orders to turn the ship around. After several exchanges our ship turned. During and after the manoeuvre the decks of our ship were continually buzzed by three Indonesian helicopters. Later, all six radio messages from the Indonesian commander were translated and this revealed that they had become increasingly threatening, and the Indonesian commander had displayed great anger. I thought that indicated fear on his part as he had to follow his orders. There were also several reports of fourteen Indonesian warships in the area, which I think was an exaggeration.

The *Lusitania* was held up for a couple of hours in a ruse to try to encourage the Indonesian commander to pay us a visit. During this time our captain attempted to contact the UN general secretary for permission to proceed into East Timor waters. The warships moved closer and closer to us; we all felt menaced as they closed in to two hundred metres. Some passengers reported seeing guns pointed our way.

We were told to assemble at the stern where a brief service was held and messages were voiced in eight different languages. Many wept openly. Wreaths were tossed overboard. As mine hit the water it appeared to be rushing towards East Timor in the swell. I was moved to tears and will always remember the flowers and wreaths rushing to East Timor as we sailed in the opposite direction. I have a special fondness for one conversation I overheard after we were on the way home. A Japanese girl and a German boy promised each other to dedicate their lives to working for the freedom of the Timorese.

The gallant car ferry was closely followed until 10.30 p.m. Though we failed to place our wreaths in the Santa Cruz cemetery the mission exceeded our wildest dreams. We attracted worldwide publicity over a period of two weeks and the Peace Mission was a stark reminder of how the oppressive Indonesian regime reacted to a very simple desire – to place wreaths in a cemetery in memory of the dead. American students from Brown University were thrilled that the confrontation was reported by CNN. Attention was focused on the arrogance of Indonesian claims of maritime ownership of the Timor Sea and, finally, the bravery of the Timorese was established once again when they had tried to greet the *Lusitania*. In the event every street in Dili had to be blocked by the Javanese.

In 1996 Richard Woolcott, former ambassador to Indonesia, and Greg Sheridan, foreign editor of the *Australian*, continued their campaign to denigrate the validity of Australian activists' right to publicise human rights violations in East Timor. At a conference entitled Indonesia Update, chaired by Woolcott, an Indonesian parliamentarian returned late from lunch and cracked a joke about the delay being due to a chef's cut finger. Sabam Siagian, the Indonesian ambassador to Australia, assured his audience that it had nothing to do with human rights abuses. Sycophantic guests laughed heartily. My poem, printed in the *Australian National University Reporter* on 28 October 1992, sums up my feelings:

> *Eager, wall-eyed*
> *pupiled with loculus memory*
> *you laugh with shocking ease*
> *at professional jokers:*
> *Jurassic Javanese.*
> *Komodo dragons trapped in time.*
> *Saurian jaws grind flesh*
> *into living clay.*
> *Go on, laugh at that if you may.*
> *Your hearts are plastic bags*
> *your souls are withered leaves*
> *your heads are hollow caves.*
> *Stacks on the mill more on still.*
> *When I lick my wounds I taste the salt of tears*
> *when you lick their boots you swallow lies of years.*

At another conference in Canberra arranged by Australian academic Dr Harold Crouch, political analyst on Indonesian politics, I had been given a lunch voucher. I saw a group of prominent Indonesian academics eating a rather sparse meal, so I ordered a platter of chips, eggs and hunks of corn and invited them to share. They showed surprise but accepted the food. Our conversation went well; they were taciturn and I was tactful. When we rose to return to the lecture hall the tall, grey-haired professor suddenly said, 'The roads have improved in East Timor.' I pondered the problem; how could I state my case without upsetting them? Timor was not of their doing. I shrugged, and replied in a passive tone that roads served the generals who had illegally acquired Timorese businesses.

'You have no idea how much money has been spent in East Timor,' he said. I replied that money was unimportant when the population was terrified.

I thought his defensiveness showed he knew the true situation but was not free to say so. This is the weakness of placing reliance on reports written by bureaucrats lacking any consideration for the throbbing reality of the suffering of humanity. 'I know what I am talking about, roads and buildings have been built.' Well, I was free to state the obvious and I could not ignore the reality because of politeness. I shook his hand and said, 'Who asked you to build anything?'

He understood perfectly.

That was the day Miles Kupa, senior adviser to Gareth Evans, opened the conference by reading from a prepared speech. I thought someone should object as it was all Indonesian propaganda. Someone did object. I heard a voice say, 'No, sorry. Can't allow that.' A thunderous applause filled the auditorium. When I realised the dissenting voice was mine, I went hot and cold. I was about to stammer an apology when I heard a catty remark, something along the lines of 'Trust her to draw attention to herself.' So judgmental! It shook me out of my embarrassment. I had not come to Canberra to hear Indonesian propaganda, especially parroted by a member of DFAT.

Harold Crouch hurried on stage and, while wringing his hands, said, 'We cannot have interruptions from the floor.'

'And we cannot have Indonesian propaganda either,' I said. Another round of thunderous applause broke out.

Miles Kupa continued reading his script until he said something about East Timor that I did not hear properly. Herb Feith leap to his feet and shouted angrily, 'Without the auspices of the UN.' He turned to me and smiled. I was vindicated; no one would complain about anything Herb said.

In June 1995 poor Miles Kupa got his comeuppance over the Mantiri Affair. Lieutenant General Herman Mantiri, Indonesia's armed forces chief, had made a highly offensive statement about the Santa Cruz massacre, in which he had been involved. He was also implicated in the Fence of Legs atrocities when, as a major general, he had control of all East Timor. In June 1992 he was quoted in the magazine *De Tick* as saying in reference to the Santa Cruz massacre, 'We don't regret anything. What happened was quite proper.' He was accused of bribery with British arms dealers before being nominated as the Indonesian ambassador to Australia.

The Australian public protested and his nomination was withdrawn. When Miles Kupa was nominated for ambassador to Indonesia positions were reversed – the Indonesian public played tit for tat and poor Miles Kupa was rejected.

In 1993 Tom Hyland, the convenor or the East Timor Ireland Solidarity Campaign (ETISC), invited me to pay a visit to Dublin, just as Prime Minister Paul Keating was about to embark on a much-publicised return to his ancestral home. I knew of Tom's wonderful group and readily agreed, as Ireland is the perfect metaphor for East Timor.

Tom had earned his living as a bus driver until he was pushed sideways to make room for new trainees who did not have to be paid the full wage. One night, as his friends played cards in his living room, the TV showed *In Cold Blood*, Peter Gordon's documentary on the Santa Cruz massacre. The group stopped what they were doing to watch. Like most people, Tom had never heard of East Timor. The following day he called Dublin newspapers and demanded to know why they did not carry reports of East Timor. He went to his local MP and asked for help to start an Irish support group. They gave him an electric typewriter, which he had to carry home in the bus to Ballyfermot, a working class district of Dublin, and he fully expected to be accused of having stolen the typewriter.

On the way to Ireland I had to spend a day at Frankfurt airport, where German passengers, cleaners and most of the staff sat under huge No Smoking signs and puffed away like old-style steam engines. The stench was horrible. I asked the airport manager if I could wait the eight hours out in his office as he loathed smoking as much as I did. Unfortunately there were rules preventing this, so after a pleasant chat I returned to hell. He was very sympathetic and said people had had enough of rules under Hitler; Nazis would never happen in Germany again.

'Yes, they will,' I said. 'Every country in the world will follow someone like Mr Hitler if he tells them they are the master race – what do you think the Olympics are about?' He ageed and he shouted me a gin and tonic.

I landed at Shannon airport late in the afternoon and was not encouraged by my welcoming committee. They seemed surprised by my appearance. I realised they must have seen photographs published eighteen years before and I had not slept on the long journey. I mentioned these facts in defence of my appearance and was told by one of the men, 'Oh, I know what's it like, when I fly home to Brazil it takes eight hours. It's dreadful.'

'That wouldn't get you to Singapore.' My comment fell on deaf ears. 'I'll be all right in the morning,' I said, trying to smile, though my face felt as if it was going to crack. By then I could only think about climbing into bed.

'We are taking you straight to Radio Dublin,' said Tom. 'This is the most popular show in Ireland. If you don't do well no one will touch you.'

It took some persuading to be taken to my lodgings so I could at least freshen up. My digs were at Jurys, a top hotel. When I asked why I was in such an expensive hotel I was told, 'Because to us you are a queen.' I swallowed my reaction, which was a little less of the blarney and some sleep would be nice. I wasted at least five seconds staring longingly at the bed.

Gerry Ryan knew everything about East Timor, which gave me ample opportunities, so I was quite pleased with the interview. I could see my minders through the huge glass partition in the viewing room and I knew from their reactions I had their full approval, until I voiced disappointment in Paul Keating for his neglect of the Timorese in favour of their oppressors.

'Oh, I don't know, your prime minister seems a very nice man to me,' said Ryan. In the viewing room everyone stiffened.

'They are all nice men,' I answered. 'They just do terrible things.'

I was so lucky. My minders leapt to their feet laughing and clapping. Later we were told that the phones had started ringing with offers to join ETISC right away.

I fell asleep in the car afterwards and then they woke me and said, 'Welcome to Dublin, this is a Portuguese restaurant and you are the guest of honour.' To this day I don't know how I did not fall asleep in the soup.

For two weeks before Keating's visit I did an immense number of radio interviews – TV was not so big there – and we travelled all over the country. On the morning of Keating's arrival in Dublin a full-page advertisement appeared in the newspaper. The heading acknowledged the Australian prime minister's achievements, but then asked why, since his relatives had been forced to leave their home in terrible circumstances, did he lack compassion for the Timorese? I was constantly surprised by Tom's inventiveness and passion and I count myself to have been lucky to be with his group. The advertisement invited people to attend a demonstration to be held outside Dublin Castle that night on the occasion of a state dinner in Keating's honour. I was asked to be early as the BBC wanted to interview me on the spot.

On the way the car broke down so I had to get out and run. As I turned the corner I was amazed to see four hundred people assembled in front of the castle. The policeman in charge of security was speaking to a woman holding a microphone. I moved towards them and as I drew close I heard the interviewer asking a question about Timor. The police officer was very well informed and gave the answers I would have given. She saw me and beckoned. I grinned madly and said he was doing such a fine job she should continue interviewing him. Only in Ireland could that happen – the policeman in charge of security doing the job of the activist brilliantly. He gave me a very warm welcome and shook my hand before departing to take up his duties.

While I did what was left of the interview candles and boxes of matches were distributed. We were told there would be ample warning to light the candles as someone would send a signal. We did not need a signal because we heard the motorcade's approach. As the limousine carrying Mr and Mrs Keating tore around the corner flanked by outriders tooting and revving their engines I saw their excited faces. It must be so very thrilling to streak through 'Dublin's fair city, where the girls are so pretty' at such a great speed. The Australian prime minister's facial expression darkened as the car sped forward and he read the signs and banners. People laughed as his eyes flared angrily. There was no rehearsal, yet everyone holding a lighted candle moved in a synchronised manner that was graceful and memorable. It really was remarkable.

That wonderful barrister Bernard Collaery told me he saw me standing in front of the crowd at Dublin castle in a photograph taken half an hour before Keating arrived for a state dinner with the *Taoiseach*, the Irish prime minister, and damn near burst into tears. I have to say I became tearful when I thought of my drunken great-grandmother's terrible life in Ireland.

The next day Paul Keating went to a big soccer match. As his state limousine drove through the gates, a man standing on them called out, 'What about East Timor?' Mr Keating was to hear that again and again on his visit to Ireland.

I was invited to morning coffee with the mayor of Dublin. He told me he had asked Keating about East Timor.

'Excuse me interrupting,' I said, 'but I can guess his reply. It was, "Surely you don't think we should have gone to war over East Timor?"'

'Well now,' came the surprised reaction, 'do you know, you're perfectly right?'

'What a shame I was not there.'

'And what would you be saying?'

'No-one ever asked you to go to war over East Timor, Prime Minister. All they wanted was a little bit of decency.'

Tom took me on a pub-crawl one Sunday night and we had a very jolly time. It was such a lovely night I elected to walk to my palatial quarters. We had only taken a few steps when a taxi pulled up.

'Is that Mrs Shackleton you've got there, Mr Hyland?' asked the driver. 'Father Cleary wants to give her the whole program.' Before I could take a breath Tom catapulted me into the back seat.

'All Ireland listens to Father Cleary's radio program,' he said, and so we set off at breakneck speed. We tried to pay

The Circle of Silence

the fare but the driver said he was honoured to be of service to East Timor. I thanked him publicly during the program. The switchboard immediately lit up with all the taxi drivers in Dublin saying, 'We were all looking for her.'

Father Michael Cleary was a delight. He was dying of cancer and shared his feelings and treatments with his audience. We were there for maybe three hours. Tom was in great form and I told the audience how lucky they were to have him. He didn't need me at all.

My last radio interview in Ireland followed a two-hour journey across country in a stuffy train in extremely hot weather. The interview took place in a studio the size of a broom cupboard and not only did the announcer smoke incessantly, an electric fan blew his cigarette smoke straight into my face. I couldn't stand the stench and, though I thought of objecting, I decided if this was the worst I would have to suffer for Timor I would be very lucky indeed. So I sweltered and suffocated for the cause. Tom was sympathetic; it was too much even for him, though he was not in the direct line of fire and he was a dedicated smoker.

The questions were well prepared (you can only be as good as the questions unless you take over, which is not a good idea as it insults the interviewer and can make you look like a bully). After the initial interview, the program was thrown open to the public. The first question came for a very irate woman. 'As a member of Amnesty International, I am utterly repulsed by the inappropriate spectacle of Mrs Shackleton's attack upon the Indonesians.'

Tom stiffened and chain-smoking Charlie suddenly announced that we would be back after a break. While they stared at me in suspense I gave thanks for all the years I had spent doing interviews. Chain-smoking Charlie made a gesture signalling, do you want to continue?

I spoke very deliberately. 'Yes, and I'm going to come out fighting.'

Tom gasped and looked worried. We three stared at each other silently until the break was over. The suspense was tangible. Chain-smoking Charlie introduced me again and Mrs Amnesty International repeated her accusation with knobs on. It was a nerve-wracking business. Assailed with smoke and brimstone, I crossed my fingers and toes, and plunged in: 'I will accept all responsibility for the undoubted attempted genocide inflicted on the Aboriginal Nation if that makes you feel any better, madame.' I spoke quietly and deliberately, giving myself time to think as I went along. 'Both sides of my family had nothing to do with the cruelty you speak about and I deny you the right to try to excuse the Javanese military for their brutal occupation of East Timor.'

After Timor voted for independence in 1999 Tom was nominated Man of the Year in Ireland. A former foreign minister, David Andrews, paid tribute to the work of ETISC in the *Irish Times*: 'Our involvement in the affairs of East Timor did not begin around the Cabinet table, or in Government Buildings, it all began in a Ballyfermot living room, with a wonderful individual, a bus driver named Tom Hyland.' Like the secret radio-link still operating, Tom is an ordinary person who does extraordinary things.

In 1996 the Irish foreign minister, Dick Spring, confronted Ali Alatas about Indonesian military violence in East Timor. Alatas declared that Ireland's position was tantamount to a declaration of war on Indonesia.

Tom has been living in East Timor since liberation. He teaches English, so get ready for Timorese who speak with the lilt of the Irish and some of the blarney.

The Circle of Silence

*　*　*

One of the most faithful supporters for justice in East Timor is Peter Cronau, now a producer of the ABC television program *Four Corners*. I can say this without fear or favour because when anything worthwhile regarding media coverage of East Timor appears Peter must be acknowledged for his unstinting and generous support with reliable, attributable information. In October 1995 he was teaching journalism and was director of the Centre for Independent Journalism (ACIJ) at the University of Technology Sydney. He invited me to Sydney to give a lecture at a seminar on the twentieth anniversary of the murders at Balibó. The seminar was called The Death of Truth in East Timor, and it was designed to study the official inaction over the deaths of the five journalists at Balibó and Roger East in Dili. Included in the program were members of the journalists' families, representatives of Fretilin and the Timorese community, lawyers, students and many Sydney journalists.

Peter arranged for a newspaper photographer to meet my flight. I remember feeling quite annoyed as I trailed around the airport for an hour and a half while the photographer tried to get the desired shot. When he asked me to find something less dull in colour to wear, he did not endear himself to me in the least little way.

The following morning, 16 October, the anniversary of the murders at Balibó, the photograph, featuring my old violet jacket against a background of bright green tropical ferns, did the trick. It set the scene for one of the most amazing episodes in my activist life. The photo was on the front page of the *Australian* under a banner headline WE'LL NEVER KNOW THE TRUTH ON TIMOR NEWSMEN: EVANS. A detailed article by Gabrielle Chan and Michelle Gunn featured the photographs of Greg and his colleagues that I had taken such trouble to copy and had sent to newspapers all over Australia and the world. The one of Tony Stewart was missing, so upon my return to Melbourne I sent them yet another copy. The article was supported by an editorial on page 8, 'NEW BALIBO CLAIMS NEED TO BE TESTED', and on page 11, 'CANBERRA IGNORES SPIRIT OF UN'.

Press releases had gone out for the seminar. With Peter as the lynchpin answering incoming phone calls, I did seventeen interviews that day. There was a lot of running as I tried to keep up with the demand. When I returned to my lodgings there were three more requests for interviews on the answering machine – from London, Japan and Portugal. The seminar attracted even more media coverage. Peter and I had a discussion late that night and wondered if we could use this public attention and ask foreign affairs minister Gareth Evans for a full judicial inquiry into the six deaths. We wrote him a letter and then decided that if the letter was made public how could he refuse? Later we invited Paul Stewart (Tony's brother) to add his signature.

Peter mentioned that the Australian Journalists Association (AJA) was holding a breakfast meeting the following morning. He thought I would be too exhausted to attend. I thought I would be too, but thank goodness for my powers of recuperation; I promised to go anyway. As it happened the speaker was Goenawan Mohamad, the editor of *Tempo*, an outspoken Indonesian magazine that had been banned by the Suharto government. Talk was almost inaudible in that sunny Redfern courtyard with overhead flights, general traffic noise and the clinking of cutlery. I sat there thinking how ironic it was that an Indonesian was the guest of honour on the anniversary of Greg's death. I also felt very sorry for him because it didn't seem to me that he was getting the right responses to his tale of woe.

At the end of his speech the AJA general secretary Chris Warren asked if I would like to say a few words. Would I what! I always try not to give answers or speeches that the audience might expect – so I opened with support for 'our Indonesian guest'.

'If you were members of his staff you would all have been sacked, blacklisted and would more than likely never work again as a journalist for the term of your natural life.' The change in that courtyard was instantaneous, which encouraged me to expand. *Tempo* had criticised the purchase of second-hand warships from Germany. 'That's all it took,' I said, 'for one of the best sources of uncensored information in Indonesia to be closed down.'

As I spoke briefly about the need for a full judicial inquiry into the murders at Balibó I noticed a TV team standing in the wings and a thought flew into my mind – *Oh, if only they would give me the chance I knew what I should say* – but even as the thought blossomed I doubted if I had the courage to express myself in the way I wanted.

Some of the audience seemed a little puzzled by my remarks about Balibó. Once again I was reminded that to young people Balibó was as remote to them as the Battle of Naseby, or the Crimean War. However, the TV team sent a runner to ask me for an interview. I can't remember the questions; I can only remember my blue funk as I tried to work up courage, and then I heard my voice as I stared into the lens and waggled my forefinger, 'No more bull-shitting, Gareth, it's time to hold a full judicial enquiry.' I pronounced Gareth in the Welsh way.

The interview appeared on the news that night. The first person to call me was my son. He was jubilant. He laughed and said the whole of Australia was laughing with me. I was thrilled with his reaction. Of course, the naysayers came out in force and some even said I had no right to speak, as Lord Avebury was trying to drum up support for an inquiry in London. Lord

Avebury had been very gracious in his support for my initiative when he offered to take me for afternoon tea at the House of Lords and invited me to his home for dinner.

Our letter was faxed to Evans on 25 October 1995, along with a copy of the Australian Centre for Independent Journalism press release for the next day, announcing the new call for the inquiry. Interviews with new witnesses to the murders were appearing on the ABC's *7.30 Report*, so the pressure on Evans was enormous. And this all came at a time when Paul Keating was discussing his new secret security pact with dictator Suharto. As a result, on 29 November 1995 Evans announced an inquiry would be conducted into the five deaths.

Four Corners producer Peter Cronau was incredibly generous when he wrote to me many years later and gave me credit for a lot of his own initiative and unflagging attention to detail.

> *Dear Shirley,*
> *It may not have been that call alone that resulted in the inquiry, but with your prominent demands in interviews ... pressure mounted and Evans announced the Sherman Inquiry on 29 November. From this flowed the Sherman report; the ICJ colloquium that demolished the Sherman Report; the interest leading to the ABC doing the* Foreign Correspondent *story; the second Sherman report; and all the other things that resulted from the renewed public interest —* the Death in Balibo, Lies in Canberra *book, even the NSW Coroner's Hearing, the Police request to former-general Sutiyoso to give evidence, and this year's film* Balibo *— all stemmed from your work.*
>
> *My notes from the time indicate that there were 30 media interviews resulting from the 1995 AICJ seminar,*

The Circle of Silence

by far the majority of them were with you!!!! Again, showing that it was YOU who was central to the whole progress of the search for the truth. And again, well done!

Based on experience, I have come to believe that governments hold inquiries to provide their spokespersons with a way to avoid perceptive questions. This is how it goes:

Unusually alert questioner: 'Mr Government Spokesperson, Please explain da da da da da?' Government Spokesperson: 'We held a very thorough investigation into the matter. I refer you to that.'

Journalists around the traps are beginners. They have to ask questions off-the-cuff on a wide-ranging set of topics. They cannot possibly know enough not to be stumped by these tactics, and so vital questions remain unanswered precisely because an inquiry has been held.

In the end the Sherman inquiry was severely limited by having no power to compel evidence or cross examine witnesses, and it was be run by a former government lawyer, Tom Sherman. It set in train a new chapter in the efforts of activists to unearth the truth and for the governments of Australia and Indonesia, and others, to keep the truth buried.

I was in Sydney in 1996 when the Sherman preliminary investigation was about to be tabled and decided I really should be in Canberra. Just before I left to catch the bus I had a stroke of luck. The *Sydney Morning Herald* asked me to write a piece for them, so I arranged to write it in their office in Parliament House. Once in the office, I was approached by many journos, who arranged for me to hold a press conference, which was widely attended and reported. I typed up the notes I had written on the bus journey and my piece appeared in the *Sydney*

Morning Herald the following day. I gave damning details of the history – and because when I boarded the bus to Canberra I had seen some extraordinary black flowers growing to an enormous height – I ended my article by likening these flowers to the Canberra politicians who had black hearts. Little did I realise they were Gymea lilies, the flowers Whitlam had used as an excuse for his inaction on 16 October 1975, when he claimed to be out of communication with Canberra because he was at a Gymea Lily Festival.

Gareth Evans renamed the Sherman document – it was no longer to be regarded as a preliminary investigation to determine if sufficient prima facie evidence had been established to warrant a full judicial inquiry. It was now The Sherman Report, game set and match. Fortunately I managed to procure a copy half an hour before it was to be tabled. I had it copied and I handed copies out to politicians and journalists so they were able to read it and understand what a farce it was.

In 2001 in the *Quarterly Essay*, John Birmingham was to write that the 'Balibó situation serves to remind us how prone to festering irritation the Australian–Indonesian relationship can be. Such are the lessons of recent history, and the not-to-be-ignored role of feeling on the street.'

The Jakarta Lobby worked hard to disguise the nature of Suharto's rule, the illegitimacy of his grisly rise to power and the behaviour of his armed forces in East Timor. In one extreme example, Suharto – whose bloody record, according to the CIA, bore comparison with Stalin, Hitler and Mao – was defended by Greg Sheridan in the *Australian* on 20 May 1998 as 'a monster of the Left's imagination'.

As John Pilger said in *Hidden Agendas* (1998), 'It is not enough for journalists to see themselves as mere messengers without understanding the hidden messages and myths that surround it.'

The International Commission of Jurists (ICJC) held a colloquium in Sydney in 1997. Their findings raised so many questions that Gareth Evans was forced to appoint Sherman to conduct an equally compromised repeat performance at the cost of another one hundred thousand dollars. I attended with Malcolm Rennie's mother, Mina and it was terrible to see her suffering. She was having trouble swallowing and this continued until she died.

SEVENTEEN

I was horrified when John Pilger and producer David Munro told me they were going into East Timor in 1993. They were both tall men, making it impossible for them to disappear in a crowd. I argued that they already knew more than enough to make a documentary, but being perfectionists they were determined to go to the scene of the crimes. I was very afraid John would be recognised and so I offered to accept a reverse-charge call from anyone in East Timor and, depending on the password they gave, I would immediately alert the press in England and Australia if they were missing, in danger or worse.

My only useful suggestion to them was that they should present themselves in a way that would appeal to the greed of the Javanese generals and their cohorts. They were way ahead of me. They intended to pose as travel consultants of a flourishing travel agency, their point-of-sale material making future travel in Tim Tim seem like a visit to Paradise. I thought John had missed his calling (thank heavens) when I read his brochure: 'Adventure Tours offers a new concept in developing third-world tourism that promises hard currency of the kind only tourism brings.' I laughed like mad at their chutzpah.

The plan was for three teams to go in separately. Team members went in under their pseudonyms. They reckoned at least one of the teams would make it out with luck. David Munro designed a bag with a concealed compartment in which their Hi8 video cameras could operate through a gauze screen.

I invited documentary maker David Bradbury to give John directions, as he intended to go through Kupang, where he would hire a four-wheel drive and enter East Timor from Indonesian-occupied West Timor, which David had done before. Their main guide was an old, incomplete aeronautical map. After crossing the border they came upon an unexpected hitch. Their driver was so frightened that he made a mistake and they somehow ended up back in Western Timor. This time John told the driver to gun the four-wheel drive through the checkpoint while the duty police were in their cabin. He accelerated and got them through. They told me later that as they drove through the guerrilla terrain bordering Matebian they noticed the same silence I had.

Timorese admired them for coming, but when they saw John careering around the country on the back of a motorbike their respect knew no bounds. To prevent being identified as a white man he covered his face with a scarf and his hands with black gloves. Interviews were conducted and they managed to establish details of the advancement of P.T. Denok, whose monopolies now included trade in Timorese marble, sandalwood, cumin, copra, coffee and cloves.

For safekeeping, David pinned their unused films into the pleats at the top of the curtains in his room; when he checked out he left the empty boxes in situ minus the pins for the spies who regularly searched the room. John told me much later, 'We got the film out by strapping the small cassettes to our inner thighs.

Those were the days before security and scans, but I must admit my heart almost stopped as we checked in and we were eyed with suspicion. When I sat down in the aircraft the sharp edge of one of the cassettes almost caused me an unfortunate injury. I let out a muffled "Oww!"

After their safe return John said he could not believe David's acting skills. When they met with their Indonesian partners-in-crime to explain their intentions to increase all their wealth, David waxed lyrical about their highly expensive plans to 'develop' tourism in Tim Tim. John said, 'I could hardly speak for amazement at David's inventiveness. My jaw would drop as he outlined his audacious plans. He won *me* over.'

The documentary, *Death of a Nation*, was a blinder. What I loved most was the way John led his interviewees on and then clobbered them with a killer question. The Indonesian Ambassador to the UN, Nugroho Wisnumurti, didn't stand a chance when John stated some of Amnesty International's findings. Poor little Nugroho gave an answer totally lacking in credibility, so John then asked, 'Are you saying Amnesty International is lying?' And in an attempt to discount the Santa Cruz massacre Nugroho called it 'the incident'. Under Pilger's disarming charm Richard Woolcott also lost the plot by stating, 'Journalists caused trouble after the massacre.'

Ben was the pseudonym for a British doctor who John had assigned to report on claims of 'tetanus' injections being given to Timorese females, including schoolgirls, that were in fact Depo-Provera, which rendered them sterile. Ben found large quantities of Depo-Provera in clinics that lacked all other medicinal preparations.

Death of a Nation went into detail about the 1983 massacre in the village of Kraras. Villagers were forced into their huts, which were then set alight. As they tried to escape the flames they were shot. A priest had made a detailed list of the names of three hundred murdered civilians, some of them children. Whole families were burned alive, or gunned down and buried in mass graves. Female survivors were resettled in the place that became known as the Village of the Widows, Kraras.

Gripping interviews with British politicians involved in selling Hawk fighter jets to Indonesia in 1978 seesawed between assertions that guarantees had been given by Indonesian politicians that the Hawk ground-attack jets would not be used to attack East Timorese, to shrugs and admissions that no such guarantees had been sought 'because the Hawks were merely trainers'. Carmel Budiardjo, founder of Tapol, had told me in 1978 how easy it was to convert a Hawk – you load the guns with bullets and slot the machine guns into position. Other deadly hardware used in East Timor included missiles, frigates and armoured vehicles, which the British sold to Indonesia. And following the Santa Cruz massacre, the British government had also made a grant of eighty-one million pounds to Indonesia. The minister for overseas development, Baroness Chalker, offered assurances that the sale of war hardware 'helps the poor of Indonesia'.

British Foreign Secretary David Owen dismissed estimates of East Timorese dead as 'exaggerated' and he proceeded to sell the Indonesian generals eight Hawk aircraft. Britain sold, or agreed to sell, a further forty Hawks. That was in addition to Wasp helicopters, Sea Wolf and Rapier missiles, Tribal class frigates, battlefield communications systems, seabed mine disposal equipment, Saladin, Saracen and Ferret armoured vehicles, and a fully equipped institute of technology for the Indonesian army, plus training for Indonesian officers in Britain. In 1992 Margaret Thatcher received an Indonesian award for 'helping technology'. She said of Indonesia, 'I am proud to be one of you.'

The faces of the apologists in the documentary initially appeared sure of themselves, in fact smugly so. As the questioning became acute a slight expression of surprise appeared and their eyes became ever so slightly hooded. Wary now, a look of alarm suggested that no one had ever asked them such perceptive questions before. John Pilger led the British Conservative MP Alan Clark up the garden path into the realm of grim satire by innocently inquiring if he was a vegetarian after they discussed the sale of ground-attack Hawks to Indonesia. 'Yes,' replied Clark, who admitted that the methods used to kill animals for their meat was of great concern to him.

'I ask you that question because I wonder if you hold similar concerns for human beings.'

'No, curiously not.'

The callous remarks of officialdom in *Death of a Nation* was a clear indication of how their minds work in order to normalise the unthinkable.

I had formed a very bad habit of not being able to sleep until after the 1 a.m. ABC radio newscast. For some reason, I was convinced if Xanana was captured I would hear it on that program. Once I knew he was still free I could sleep. As I listened on the fateful night of 20 November 1992, the first item had me jumping out of bed and running downstairs to telephone Carmel in London and then everyone in the diaspora who was connected to the fight.

'Xanana has been captured.'

'Not possible!' Carmel declared.

'It was broadcast two minutes ago on the ABC.'

'Nothing's come though here.'

'It will,' I insisted. 'Everyone must start calling the Indonesian government. The sooner we make a fuss the better for him – you know they'll torture him. We have to work fast to stop them killing him.'

The Circle of Silence

Some Australian activists were initially annoyed at having been woken up. Like Carmel, they also had trouble believing me – it was such a devastating blow that their reluctance was understandable. I then rang everyone else in my contact book. Making the phone calls took most of the night, and I slept only after I had completed my self-appointed task.

Over the next day I congratulated myself for ignoring my critics. I had commissioned a poster that showed a drawing of Xanana's face (based on a photograph by Robert Domm) and in capital letters: XANANA. EAST TIMOR. It featured in many news reports in Australia. After film was shown of him in captivity, author Michele Turner called to say she thought he looked beautiful. I realised I had been so distracted with worry about his stupefied appearance that I had been robbed of any vestige of commonsense, which had also denied me the relief of weeping. When I met him years later, he said he had given himself permission to cry when the torture got too great to stand. I remembered Father Locatelli telling me that Xanana was the most disciplined human being he had ever known.

As a result of his capture Xanana's wife, Emilia, requested a meeting with Gareth Evans. She asked me to accompany her, and I agreed as long as she understood that she must speak for herself – as was my custom, I preferred to bear witness. Surprised to see Emilia and her party of three Timorese shivering on the steps outside the foreign minister's Melbourne office, I asked. 'Surely you're not waiting for me?' They had not wanted to enter the building until the time of the appointment. Oh dear, I thought, *this is how you lost your country*, by being too polite and self-effacing. I led them inside and we were shown to a lovely warm waiting room.

Emilia stopped shivering, but the responsibility of her husband's life weighed heavily. Soon after her parents had paid all the bribes to enable her and the two children to quit Timor,

I had interviewed the family in their Melbourne home. When I put my arms around her she wept in a way that I knew well. Her emotion, though initially visceral, surged up through her tiny frame as she trembled and gritted her teeth. Crying at such a level of intensity is damaging; I remembered my ribs feeling as if they had been thumped with a mallet and yet I was never maltreated as Emilia was.

In 1975 she had been placed under house arrest and forced to live with Indonesian officers because her husband had gained some respect for letters he had published in the local paper under the nom de plume Xanana. She was frequently questioned late at night and she had to wake her sleeping children and take them with her. I can't go into details about her maltreatment as I do not want to cause her further humiliation, but she was abused, which was bad enough, but, worse, it was done in front of her children. Her abuse always ended with threats to take her children away and bring them up as Indonesian Muslims.

She had not seen her husband since the invasion. Surely, I thought, Gareth Evans will want to help her and he will be gentle with her. He must have been informed about her mistreatment by ASIO, which I had talked about in the article published in the *Age*. In an attempt to bolster her I reminded her of the day she left Dili. On the way to the airport hundreds of schoolchildren ostensibly engaged in field excursions stopped their work to stand with heads bowed as her taxi drove past – a silent and most moving tribute to their recognition of her great suffering.

Senator Evans stood in the doorway of his plush office as we approached. He merely nodded at the Timorese. 'Mrs Shackleton,' he said, as I passed him. I wished him good morning. The Timorese asked for permission to tape the proceedings. They were assured that this was not necessary as the meeting was being taped and copies would be made available. The atmosphere turned electric around us as Emilia pleaded for intervention.

As she talked about her fears for her husband's safety, I studied Gareth Evans. The expression on his face contained no hint of the charming smile you see in public. His impatient gestures dredged up a frightening reality – he did not want to be there and he did not want to grant her request. His eyes remained hooded as he insisted that everything was being done. Others in the group tried to support her, but they quailed under his intense gaze.

As Emilia began to plead, I reflected that this was a man who prided himself on his abilities, a man with all the advantages a democracy has to offer. Emilia's posture clearly indicated her state of mind. Anger surged through me – any fool could see how deeply she had been harmed and how desperate she was. This quivering human being's voice sank to a whisper as she too watched the expression on his face.

All my muscles ached as I restrained my desire to leap up and strike him. A friend had told me to be careful: 'Gareth has a terrible temper. He's likely to throw things if he's crossed; anything heavy that's at hand.' I stared at a large, glass ashtray positioned on the coffee table between us. As if he knew what I was thinking, his eyes blazed. What gave him the right to be angry? Did his children starve? Was his wife raped? Lord Byron's poem about the destruction of Sennacherib came to my mind:

> *The Assyrian came down like the wolf on the fold,*
> *And his cohorts were gleaming in purple and gold.*

'Senator Evans,' I said, 'are you going to help Senhora Gusmão or not?' He glanced at the ashtray and then at me. Scared out of my wits in case I was making things worse for Emilia, I copied his every gesture. And if he had thrown that ashtray at me, I would have thrown it back at him with all my might.

Emilia initially gasped at my forwardness, but soon I felt her body straightening. I looked into her eyes and saw a tiny glint of resistance there. As he repeated his words, she spoke quietly and with great dignity: 'Are you going to help me, Senator Evans?'

'Yes,' he barked. His anger could have struck sparks. Perhaps he was ashamed of himself — that could account for his fury. He was used to the rarefied garden party air of diplomacy where reality is routinely evaded. Perhaps he was not accustomed to answering a direct question. His objective seemed to be to avoid any intervention that might interfere with any trade deal with Indonesia. He could claim with perfect honesty that Indonesians are fine, moral people, because he mixed with the rich and judged them by their possessions. And there *are* fine Indonesians, but that did not excuse his carefully cultivated blind spot, which allowed him to ignore the kleptomaniacs, and the killers of children, of old men and defenceless women. Did he have the wit to see that his abuse of Emilia was only once removed from *theirs*? Did he realise that his refined torture was less forgivable then *theirs*? The brutes who had tortured her were hardly human. Either they did not know any better or they had been trained to reduce a human being to blubber. I wondered too about my lack of compassion for the Senator's plight? But, to begin with, he had chosen this way to make a living. As I watched him chipping away at Emilia's natural dignity I wondered how he could justify all her misery.

Emilia's expression telegraphed that she knew she was wasting her time: the minister for foreign affairs did not deserve the respect his position demanded. Even so, there was no call for catastrophic stress at this moment; no one would rape or

The Circle of Silence

beat her, she was in Australia. I marvelled at the dignity in the bearing of each of the Timorese as they rose to take their leave. There was no sign of hatred. They were in control; they were a civilised people.

'They are not civilised,' she had said of her tormentors at our first meeting. 'Civilised people do not behave as they do.' In the atmosphere in the office of the minister for foreign affairs I was reminded once again that Timorese are just not nasty.

I called Senator Evans' office the following morning to arrange to collect a copy of the tape recording and was told I would be informed when the transcription was ready. I called another five times over the following weeks. Each call initiated a descending scale of excuses until the final call when the secretary responded with the words, 'What tape recording?'

The Australian Red Cross arranged for Emilia, Nito and Zenilda to meet Xanana in Cipinang prison. Zenilda was a baby at the time of the invasion, so this was their first meeting. Nito had only a hazy memory of being carried on his father's shoulders to buy an ice-cream. When he entered the room to meet his family Xanana's first words were, 'Don't cry.'

When Nelson Mandela visited Xanana in prison we activists breathed a sigh of relief. They dare not kill him now. In the same year that we gave up all hope of justice from the Sherman report, the 1996 Nobel Peace Prize was awarded to José Ramos-Horta and Bishop Carlos Belo. Since 1975 successive Australian governments had refused to recognise José. He was now in demand to speak about East Timor all over the world, but not in Canberra.

In 1996 when Bishop Belo returned from the Nobel ceremony, thousands of East Timorese flocked to the airport. This was not just a show of public support. Every Timorese crowding the airport was ready to die to save the life of the man who had the courage to write that fateful letter to the UN in

1996 with its startling central message: we are dying as a nation. In Australia I had never had to attend a demonstration of such danger, where the authorities in attendance were liable to turn on me. Just how one goes about making a decision like that is beyond my imagination. Can you imagine making arrangements to leave your children knowing you may not return? Even priests who went to the airport that day were armed.

Murdani was not the only Catholic in the Indonesian army. Someone, maybe several people, had warned of a plan to assassinate the bishop. A Timorese traitor, a corporate in the Javanese army, tried to shoot Bishop Belo – the crowd beat him to death. Eleven of Siga's Indonesian bodyguards were also beaten as they ran away.

John Martinkus, the courageous freelance Australian journalist in East Timor, who had documented the struggles of Falintil guerrillas and the determination of the population since 1994, reported that a few days after the return of Bishop Belo he saw 'a headless body, minus hands or feet floating in the sea'. He thought that was how a dead person would look after a few days in the sea, but this body had been hacked to pieces and it was the first of several. The torturers employed identical modus operandi. The mutilated torsos were part of a retaliation campaign for the death of the would-be assassin. In any other country this would have been a crime; in East Timor at that time it was the authorities themselves who were responsible. John Martinkus said in *A Dirty Little War*, 'Reports of the violence in East Timor were always met with blanket denials from Indonesian authorities. If they did acknowledge any particular incident had occurred, pro-Independence Falintil guerrillas were routinely blamed.'[1]

---

1 John Martinkus, *A Dirty Little War: East Timor 1997–2000*, Random House, 2001.

* * *

The 1997–1998 economic crisis in Indonesia heralded the collapse of the New Order. After months of negotiation the new Indonesian president B.J. Habibie agreed to a democratically supervised referendum for East Timor's independence by the UN, twenty-four years too late. I wanted so much to be there. I *needed* to witness the momentous occasion for Greg, Gary, Tony, Malcolm, Brian and Roger East. The Timorese would vote for independence no matter what the cost. I had seen the chances they took for me in 1989 and so my joy at the possibility of their freedom was frustrated by the thought that if I went I would most likely compromise the safety of anyone who helped me. Accustomed to plundering the country with the impunity of the conquistadors, Javanese vengeance would be terrible.

In the lead-up to the miracle, the Machiavellian behaviour of some of my own government's officials made me wonder whose side they were on. Like the Balibo Five, who had to die because their mere presence had caused a glitch in the plans of the Javanese generals, even more Timorese were going to die. By then I had accepted the unacceptable – Greg and his colleagues had to die. *Had to.* But now what was destined was a new horror-of-horrors. By exposing themselves at the ballot box Timorese would be voting for their own murders.

I recalled the mantra so gloomily reported to me during my 1989 visit by the Javanese helicopter pilot who could not stand the sight of blood – 'If we are forced out of our territory we know we will have to follow orders to kill every male.' When I asked Timorese about this Herod-like threat they confirmed it was common knowledge. Sexual assault would also be used as a weapon. One astonishingly beautiful girl who worked at a local bakery had told me, 'Some will be spared as I was spared – just so I could be forced to produce half-Indonesian children.' This observation was accompanied by a very big spit, and I saw again the terror in her eyes.

'What happens to those children now?'

'Some have love; all have hate.' My eyes had filled with tears as she told me how her two darlings were ostracised. This situation is never fully considered by bureaucrats, who think of themselves as serving their government honourably when they support invading armies. It was painfully clear to me she loved her children dearly. I wondered if she had been punished by Timorese as it was likely she would be blamed for her own condition, in the time-honoured way of blaming the victim. Women in her predicament are readily damned as sluts.

The whole world seemed to shake off its lethargy and take an interest in the tiny half island to the north of Australia. But instead of sharing the joy that I believed was my right, all my fears were being realised. After years of criminal intent and ineptitude towards the plight of our closest neighbour, a confrontation seemed inevitable between Australian and Javanese soldiers. All those years ago, as I had tried to make sense of that telegram – 'the remains are possibly human' – I predicted this tragedy would happen. It was the only possible outcome given the circumstances.

Turning the pages of the notebook I had filled in 1989, I re-read my notes. I wanted an excuse not to go there. I was deeply afraid of the consequences – if I were killed Evan would have to live with propaganda that I had a death wish.

> *capture atmosphere – dread in eyes of inhabitants – repression. People trying to see sideways, heads slightly turned trying to gauge what is happening behind them. Every aspect of life is inverted; metaphor for their art, each half of a design is inverted to form a mirror image. Use to suggest the underworld – stinking drains. Stench*

belies tropical paradise. Underground resistance fighters hidden in cellars, caves, jammed under floorboards. Everyone frightened to make the fateful decision when to go out; when to stay in.

Matebian. Resistance – underground, hide in holes – abrigo. Undergrowth as underground, protection, people seek cover – in clumps of grass, areas of saltbush. Human beings searching at ground level for roots – metaphor: ground rodents searching for food for their young.

How can you take cover when you have to carry your child on your back for fear of repeated aerial attacks? What if you have more than one child?

My last entry for the day: 'spooks everywhere. Dread and determination equally balanced.'

I was envious of my friend and colleague Carmela Baranowska because she was already in East Timor. Her subsequent film, *Scenes from an Occupation – 'The Law Of Violence'*, is a confronting account of the last six months before the UN Registration Process. 'We may all die', observed an East Timorese woman in the film, 'but if one is left, he will tell the story.' The film is a testament to the East Timorese people's courage, strength and determination, and ditto for Carmela.[2]

Carmela told me later that, while she was staying at the Villa Harmonia in Becora, she found the daughter of the owner Pedro Lebre, lying face down on the living room floor weeping hysterically. All the lights were off and her mother was peering

---

[2] Originally screened on SBS TV, the film won Carmela the Rory Peck Award, named after a freelance cameraman killed while filming in Moscow. The award celebrates freelance journalists, and Carmela was the first of only two Australians to receive the prestigious award.

through a tiny gap in the curtains. A military vehicle had stopped. This is what she was whispering: 'They might go on. Shh . . . they're moving. No, they're stopping. Oh no. Shh. Shh.' Everyone feared a visit from the Ninja – these were the death-squads formed by General Prabowo. They were sometimes called militia, but I call them mercenaries, for that is what they were. Clad in black with their faces covered by balaclavas, they were equipped with knives, chains, whips and M-16s. Known to enter houses at will, they raped the women and took the men away – their mutilated bodies were dumped or thrown into the sea.

The estimated two hundred thousand death rate had become an accepted fact, but few had made the mathematical connection – one-third of the population had perished. This is the highest per capita death toll in the twentieth century. I had tried to interest editors all over the world by using the Balibo Five to introduce East Timor's struggle, but my reports plus photographs were rarely acknowledged and when they were the consensus was, 'Our people don't know about this place; they wouldn't be interested.'

You might think that was in the bad old days before the blockade was lifted. When John Martinkus returned to Australia from East Timor in 1994 and then again in 1995, he was told by a string of editors from every major daily in the country that ongoing killings by the Indonesians were not news. In his fine book, John says the response from the foreign editor of one major Australian daily newspaper was: 'Look, we are not going to publish anything on East Timor. Can you stop bothering us.' No wonder Indonesia's government and military got away with genocide.

Over the years I've asked every Indonesian I met what they thought about East Timor. It was usually women I spoke to and most replied that the army was very brutal. Only one man, well dressed and visiting Melbourne on 'government

The Circle of Silence

business', differed greatly in his response. We were in a shop in Prahran, and it was the first time I had been in that shop. When I asked him, he stiffened and walked away. I followed and quietly said, 'I'm not blaming anyone here; I would just like to know your views. I want to know if you realise what is happening in your twenty-seventh province. Australians don't know because we practise self-censorship.' He frowned at the shopkeeper, looking for support, I think. The shopkeeper, looking sorrowful, whispered to him, 'This lady knows what she is talking about, Sir.'

At that the poor man stepped out the door, turned around and pushed the fly-wire door towards me to prevent me following. The latch was defunct and as I continued, without being aggressive, to encourage him to express his views he kept pushing at the door. I wondered why he did not just walk away; perhaps he was afraid I would pursue him. I apologised for upsetting him, saying, 'I really only want to talk with you.' Then he turned and ran. I apologised also to the shopkeeper: 'I hope I haven't lost you a customer.' He was consoling and we speculated that the poor chap, because he looked so guilty, probably knew more than he was letting on.

In 1995, Indonesia's foreign minister, Ali Alatas, was mobbed by German activists. A photograph of him giving them the finger was flashed around the world. The tide was turning and some who were accustomed to getting away with any crap they cared to utter did not like it one little bit. Alatas had coined the phrase: 'Timor is a pebble in the shoe'. By then he had to admit Timor was a bloody great boulder. When Alatas died on 17 December 2008, John Pilger wrote this obituary for the *Guardian* – it was published on 30 December:

> I covered both Cambodia and East Timor as a correspondent; the 'urbanity' and 'peace-brokering'

of the Indonesian foreign minister Ali Alatas was a myth which he deployed to gull western journalists in Jakarta. Quoting Hobbes, Locke, Montesquieu and Rousseau, he lectured the west on the 'cultural differences' that made slaughtering people OK: the British, who were then providing Suharto with machine guns and fighter aircraft, lapped it up. Together, Suharto and his British government backers oversaw the extinction of almost a third of East Timor's population. Not only was Alatas an apologist for a blood-soaked regime, he was a liar par excellence, dismissing evidence of massacres in which he was complicit as 'entirely fictitious' and using American PR firms to smear those who told the truth, such as the courageous Bishop Belo, a leader of the East Timorese resistance. In 1989, Alatas demonstrated his contempt for his victims by flying over their graves and toasting his Australian opposite number, Gareth Evans, with champagne as they illegally carved up the oil and gas wealth that belonged to the captive East Timorese.

EIGHTEEN

When the UN decided to supervise a referendum in East Timor, following Suhato's resignation in May 1998 and the dramatic reaction in East Timor when thousands took to the streets to demonstrate in favour of Independence I thought all my dreams had come true. The usual carping criticisms circulated: the Timorese 'native class' couldn't even write their names, so how could they be trusted to know what was good for them? There was no point in talking about their extraordinary linguistic skills, their art or their common decency, but I could and did state the obvious: 'They know what's good for them because they haven't had it for twenty-four years.' The United Nations represented security, but information emanating from Canberra was alarming for its complacency and ignorance. I was congratulated for 'having been right all the time'. I was not amused. I was now expected to explain how a democratic country had suffered a succession of Australian prime ministers and foreign ministers who had supported Indonesia. I felt like telling them we Australians live in a state of amnesia, but I said nothing. I knew the Timorese would need huge support from all over the world, especially Australia, when the results were announced.

Privately I worried about the success of the referendum because of the scabrous brutes who'd formed mercenary squads and trained them. General Prabowo Subianto is credited with their training in the ways of similar forces common to Indonesia. While their future was being discussed in New York, East and West Timorese were perfecting the art of intimidation, torture and murder with impunity and immunity. The names of their squads are instructive: Thorn, Red and White Iron, Live or Die for Integration, The Brave Ones. Some recruits joined for revenge for a relative killed by resistance fighters, others joined because refusal could result in the burning of their homes or a death sentence, but most were attracted to power and access to money and drugs. They dressed in red and white pirate bandanas (the colours of the Indonesian flag) and they used home-made weapons which were based upon seventeenth-century flint-lock firearms.

Andrew McNaughtan, one of our most dedicated activists, previously reviled by the Jakarta Lobby, was suddenly given his medical title. Meanwhile he was secretly educating Australian military representatives bent on studying East Timor. I supplied all my maps of East Timor and a little book of useful *Tetuñ* phrases, which were compiled by my mate, the World War II commando Cliff Morris (now deceased), and from Dr Geoffrey Hull's splendid dictionary. We did warn the Aussie soldiers that few would now understand their own lingua franca since everyone had been forced to speak the language of the invaders for twenty-four years.

I answered lists of questions put to me by Andrew, who had educated himself brilliantly. Years before, when he first called me with questions about Balibó, he had told me he was completely ignorant about East Timor. On learning he had been working with Timorese torture victims in Darwin, I said, 'The little you know is quite enough, Andrew.' I had set him a course of reading – by then there were a number of books about East Timor – and was pleased by how quickly he picked things up.

The first time I stayed with him in Sydney I arrived with food and that made him angry, 'Don't waste your money on me, Shirley.' Grateful for the accommodation, I preferred to pay my way. He gave me a room of my own, small and compact. I was accustomed to a variety of sleeping arrangements – I had slept on floors, on benches twice as hard as a floor, on the deck of the *Lusitania Expresso*, and one uncomfortable night on a cane lounge, which decorated my body for a couple of weeks with bruises caused by the rungs. Staying with Andrew with a stream of fellow activists offered an intense cultural pleasure. We were alive with vibrancy in our determination to overcome the impossible, and, I have to add, I was blessed to be among people who had nothing to gain except freedom for others.

We worked on the quiet of course, thrilled that someone in high places must understand what was likely to happen when the Javanese were forced to withdraw. It was a comfort to know preparations were being made to protect Timorese civilians. We laughed with unrestrained glee because Aussies (besides the heroes who had operated the secret radio in East Timor) might get to repay the debt owed to Timor since World War II. We spent a lot of time imagining what it would be like for resistance fighters to be reunited with what was left of their families – even one surviving relative would mean the whole world to them. Some were like Alfredo Alves Reinado, who was only a child when he was forced to escape the bombing of his parents' house; he was now a little older than Greg was in 1975.

Volunteers from all over the world poured into Timor to supervise the referendum. It was the *Lusitania Expresso* all over again, but this time instead of one Indonesian journalist, six hundred brave Indonesian civilians volunteered. Kendelle Clark, a Victorian member of the Federal Police, volunteered. The country was thick with journalists, among them Jonathan Head of the BBC. Despite the goodwill, all was not going well.

All over the country undefended people were being murdered by General Wiranto's mercenaries. In Australia, I was confronted by angry people completely ignorant of the previous twenty-four years of untrammelled violence. Once again Timorese were being blamed for their own problems: 'The Timorese mercenaries are worse than the Indonesian army.'

My response to that: 'They have been trained by the Javanese army precisely so you can say that. The mercenaries are part of the vengeance being meted out to the Timorese by drugged and brutalised wretches. Like the general who gives the orders and does not stain his hands with blood, the Javanese rely on you to blame the victims.'

On the last day of campaigning journalist John Aglionby, correspondent for the *Guardian*, and John Martinkus witnessed the fate of the pro-democracy village of Memo. John Martinkus wrote in *A Dirty Little War*:

> Out in the bare, dried-out rice paddies several hundred scared and angry militia [fresh from a demonstration of 4,000 militias headed by pro-Indonesia Bupati Guilherme dos Santos] armed with homemade pistols and knives walked towards the pillars of black smoke that marked Memo. It was like a column moving up to a medieval battle, with the swords, the spears, and rough wooden clubs they were carrying, and the noise of screaming that rose from the village as a line of nearly a thousand mercenaries got out of their vehicles and walked towards the fighting.

Armed with rocks, spears, machetes and swords the people were fighting to save their homes.

As 60 motorcycles roared though, the men of the village ran forward and positioned themselves; then some of the women and children ran away. Five motor buses full of pro-Indonesian supporters stopped and as they all got out, the village men ran up and started smashing their vehicles. As the-pro Indonesian supporters retreated, more than 40 automatic shots were fired at the villagers, still venting their anger on the vehicles. They smashed everything and tipped the buses over.

Women and children emerged from the houses gathering stones; men ran screaming orders to each other, and the makeshift alarms of metal pipes which hung on trees were rung as the whole village prepared to fight back. Men came running out holding clubs and with nails driven through them, plus spears, machetes and knives. One stocky man ran past us with a shovel.

At that point Martinkus and Aglionby left to raise the alarm in Maliana and to shout a report though the telephone exchange. Upon their return:

> 'The pro-independence villagers had beaten back the militia, and we walked down the hill past still burning trucks and houses. The owners wept by the wreckage of their homes or yelled at us that the militia and the Indonesian police were to blame. The police had been firing up the hill at them to cover the retreat of the militia.
>
> There were losses on both sides, houses had been set alight; several men had been hacked to death by a

group of pro-Indonesian militia. One man, Raul dos Santos, was shot dead by an Indonesian police bullet as the police attempted to storm the upper part of the village. No one knew how many had died but fifty villagers went permanently missing. Back in Maliana, the local police commander, Major Budi Susilo, told us his men "hadn't fired any shots – they had orders not to".[1]

On the great day of the referendum, all over the country, thousands of civilians walked for miles, pouring from the hills and valleys, to cast their vote.

For some it was reminiscent of a political demonstration in support of the Fretilin political party in Dili twenty-four years before, when flower-decked ponies made their way down ancient pony tracks. The sun had struck and flashed against tens of thousands of solid gold *belaks*, making the mountains glitter. Timorese wearing colourful traditional garments converged on Dili carrying musical instruments. Teams of dancers performed the complicated movements of the Snake Dance – the art was to dance as close as possible to another person without touching. The dancers slithered erotically with serpentine grace.

The Portuguese police had had a hard time keeping the roads clear as a procession headed by *liurais* and their attendants arrived; their self-important little ponies flared their nostrils and tossed their heads. Silver bells tied to the upper arms of the riders jingled pleasantly; crowns of buffalo horns, silver half-moons and solid silver stars and feathers sprouted from their heads. Red, yellow and black Fretilin pennants fluttered from javelins. Though the red and green ensign of Portugal

---

[1] John Martinkus, *Dirty Little War*, op. cit.

The Circle of Silence

still had pride of place on all official buildings, it was flanked by Fretilin flags.

The procession wound through the streets to deafening applause. From Liquica they came, from Bobonaro, the weavers of Manatuto joining hands with fishermen of Atauro. From rice paddies, coffee plantations and orchards, from mountains and wide rivers they came. From Atsabe came silversmiths and from Baucau, Los Palos and Tutuala and from the forest of Lore came wood carvers and makers of musical instruments.

Xavier do Amaral, president elect, and Nicolau dos Reis Lobato, vice president elect, stood on a dais – the similarities and differences between the two men were striking. Nicolau was tall, purposeful and self-confident, a natural leader, perhaps because he was part of the ruling elite – his father was a *liurai*. He was almost ten years younger than Xavier do Amaral. They had been educated at the Dare seminary and both had intended to enter the priesthood, but each had turned to teaching for a time before accepting careers in government administration.

'Looks like you don't need an election,' shouted Oliver Strewe, Australian photographer to José Ramos-Horta, the minister for external affairs, who was worried by the size of the demonstration.

José Gusmão, now known as Xanana, was jubilant. 'This has never happened before in the entire history of the island,' he cried, 'we didn't anticipate such huge support. It's a vote for an independent East Timor. These people won't let us down.'

All over the city groups of revellers combined in circles to dance the *tebe tebe*, which signifies cooperation. If someone gets out of step and the circle is broken, the dancers start again and by a process of teamwork the dancing is able to continue. The procession had continued all day and well into the night.

How many of that jubilant throng had survived to vote for an independent East Timor? Now the people of East Timor prepared to make another journey. The registration for the UN ballot was almost complete. Approximately four hundred and thirty thousand of the descendants who had travelled to Dili in 1975 had registered. This was ninety per cent of the voting population.

Taur Matan Ruak, head of the Resistance Army since the capture of Xanana, was in contact with his supreme commander, still a prisoner in Cipinang prison, thanks to mobile phones. Taur was under orders not to retaliate to any provocation.

Australians did not understand my anguish – for them it was a victory. I should have been delirious with joy. I could not blame them. What was going to happen was unimaginable. I guess I looked pretty miserable because I was told more than once to cheer up. I would smile and grit my teeth – how could anyone understand? I could only hope the UN were not so easily duped. The problem was this: responsibility for the safety of civilians, no matter what violence was perpetrated, had to be left to the UN, otherwise Indonesia would claim it was a civil war. This was General Wiranto's purpose in recruiting huge numbers of mercenary militias – for them to go on a killing rampage, for that was what they were trained and paid to do.

The tracks and roads were once again travelled, but the travellers were nothing like their countrymen and family members in the past. As described by John Martinkus:

> their emergence was a scene with a spectacularly epic nature about it – the ragged line of long-haired students and a few Falintil fighters with guns all wearing a weird collection of clothes shivering against the cold mountain air, suddenly started streaming out of the mountains to register at a remote post. Argus, a

Balinese journalist who was later murdered by militia, was with the students filming them.[2]

Kendelle Clark was sent alone to supervise the voting process in a bark hut set by a river at the base of a very steep road. Armed Javanese lined the route. Timorese had to walk between them to vote while being told, 'We know where you live. We will come and get you if you do not vote for us.' The entrance to the hut was guarded with armed enemy soldiers and several lounged around inside, their armoury spread out on the table holding the ballot box.

Armed with only a pistol and a mobile phone, Kendelle told the soldiers to stand to attention. She then politely asked the officer in charge to order his troops to leave their positions and line up beside the river where she could see them. 'Put all your weapons away,' she said. Their leader refused. She called her superior and told him to notify Ian Martin, head of the UN Mission in East Timor, she was closing down the voting booth and needed transport to take the locals to the next voting point. Martin returned the call within minutes and ordered the Javanese officer to do as he was told by the Australian police officer.

'That was a very tense moment,' Kendelle told me when she came to my house to be interviewed. 'I stared the officer out. He was in a difficult position; being forced to take orders from a female was not his style. Not his style at all.'

She stayed on duty until the last vote was cast. Having phoned in each soldier's ID, she warned them she would see them prosecuted if any violence occurred. Kendelle was still at her post when the results were announced. Seventy-eight and a half per cent had voted for independence. As soon as the

---

2 John Martinkus, *Dirty Little War*, op. cit.

announcement was broadcast the hut burst into flames. She told the officer to put out the fire. While looking straight at it he replied, 'There is no fire.'

Using her mobile phone she asked for assistance while telling him to look again. He ordered his soldiers to get some water. 'It was hopeless,' she said. They pretended there was no water, but the stream was running fast behind them. Next they pretended there were no buckets. One scooped up water in his coffee mug and sprinkled it on dry ground. The soldiers chatted and smoked as the building burned to the ground.

Later that night a truck sped past with a Timorese man in the front seat. She told me, 'He was covered in blood. He looked terrified. The truck drove so fast there was no hope of intervention and it was too dark to see the registration. He had no chance.'

America engaged in negotiations for a peacekeeping force if sporadic violence increased. Australian officials used the pretence of an impending civil war to pander to Indonesia, agreeing to allow Indonesian soldiers and police to 'protect' the Timorese. I wondered which planet Dr Ashton Calvert, secretary of the Australian Department of Foreign Affairs and Trade, had been living on for the past twenty-four years when I learned he had said, 'The Timorese have to sort themselves out, and to dispel the idea that the UN is going to solve all their problems.' Once again the victims were being blamed for their own problems – shades of the Balibo Five.

William Maley, Australian academic, decried John Howard's refusal to establish a peacekeeping force. He said it was ludicrous given the Indonesian military's reputation for violence. Howard's reluctance gave a clear signal to General Wiranto. His mercenary militias had been trained to provide evidence of an impending civil war in order to prove that his regular army would be necessary to restore peace and order. That was when the killings escalated.

Members of the media continued to pour into East Timor – at last the irresponsible editors had sniffed a big story. Honourable journalists tried to avert the coming disaster.

The violence electrified all activists. I was asked to join a group at the Treasury building in Melbourne where John Howard was holding a meeting. The chanting continued for an hour. I don't know how we did it. By the time I was asked to make a statement by the press I was almost hoarse – though I think we could have continued all day because we could not give up after all the years of the struggle. Several people wanted to speak so I made my statement short and snappy: 'There will not be many chances where John Howard has such a clear line of duty. He is at a crossroads; if he turns one way he will be seen as a hero, if he takes the other road people will say "Howard is a coward".' I finished with a plea for decency. I was told the next day that my statement was cut; all that was left was me saying, 'Howard is a Coward'. I'd like to get my hands on that editor. I wouldn't blame John Howard for despising me. I would have reported that criminal editor to the Press Council, but there was too much to do. He remains lost to history.

Asked to speak by the Timorese at a rally outside the Melbourne Post Office I was very surprised to find the tram packed with protestors, most of whom I had never seen before. I had spoken many times at that meeting place, quite often in terrible weather to small crowds, so I was unprepared for the numbers – estimated to be between fifty and sixty thousand. They were very, very angry. In Sydney the number of protestors was said to be over a hundred thousand.

I made my way towards a tray truck set up with a microphone. A couple of men offered to help me up. Unionist Leigh Hubbard, who had been one of Timor's staunchest allies, waved me away. 'No, Shirley, we've got enough speakers.'

I looked at a woman addressing the crowd. I had never seen her at any previous protests or meetings. Timorese standing on the opposite side of the tray truck smiled and acknowledged my presence. I thought of all the thankless meetings, protests, processions, letters to editors, articles and overseas visits – one meeting in Arnhem stood out, where I was persistently heckled and threatened by a group of furious Dutch men and women and by Indonesians who hurled personal insults.

I turned to the men standing behind me and asked, 'Will you give me a leg-up, please?'

'Good on you,' they said. 'Don't let them do that to you. How dare they?' Actually, the words they used were extremely impolite. Emboldened by their support and good humour I reached up and grasping the edge of the truck said with all the emphasis I could muster, 'I am going to speak.' A little cheer went up and I was shoved unceremoniously aboard.

I did not say much, there were *far* too many speakers. I told the crowd about the schoolchildren I had heard in Dili singing the Indonesian national anthem. After explaining how even the children wanted freedom, I chanted their version of the Indonesian national anthem: 'Indonesia is an arse-hole country.' A great cheer went up.

On the train home I reflected that there are times when you have to fight small battles in order to object to big ones. That was the day I heard from someone I had met at one of my many talks to schoolchildren. 'You are going to win,' he said. 'Timor is a war zone. Ninety-eight per cent of the population is showing incredible courage. They wore their best clothes knowing they were going to be murdered on the way back from the polling booths.' He was very emotional and claimed he worked in DFAT. He told me the town of Maliana was in flames. 'Keep going, Mrs Shackleton. The fax machines are burning up; the phones keep ringing; people are hysterical; they

The Circle of Silence

are demanding armed intervention: we've never had anything like this before, ever.'

While democracy died in East Timor all was calm in Canberra. A detailed account of the machinations of government officials discussing what to do about our troublesome neighbours reads like a script for a thriller – spies, lies, damage control and stonewalling. And their reason for the delays? Support for East Timor would require a historic policy shift.

In Maliana, UN officials assured terrified residents that they would be safe at the police station. After the UN pulled out police, militia death squads and TNI Kodim 1636 staged a massacre. Hundreds were similarly murdered at the cathedral in Suai on the south coast. A few days later Balibó was the scene of another massacre – this time of students trying to return to Dili after completing their work at the voting polls.

Damien Kingsbury, the second and last recipient of the defunct Greg Shackleton Scholarship, told me:

> The day after the ballot, my house in Maliana was in flames. At one of thirteen militia roadblocks between Maliana and Dili, a screaming militia member affected by drugs and alcohol put an M-16 rifle to my head. The TNI gave the militias amphetamines the locals called *anjing gila* ('mad dog'), describing its effect. East Timor began to burn more furiously with the police, sent under a deal with the UN to protect it, standing by and watching, or helping to burn it.

Two days later the giddy joy at the prospect of freedom turned to yet more horror as mercenaries attacked public buildings and ramped up killings and intimidation. Film of unarmed BBC reporter Jonathan Head being attacked by a killer wielding a machete was broadcast all around the world.

At the last minute his assailant twisted the machete and smashed the flat of the blade on Head's arm.

I heard Matt Frei from the BBC describing how he had run towards the UN compound as a man nearby was hunted down like an animal. A colleague filmed the attack (which I saw on the ABC news) while hiding in a shack opposite the compound gates. Frei reported, 'It took only 30 seconds to hack the man to pieces. The attack was so ferocious bits of him were literally flying off. The sound reminded me of a butcher shop – the thud of cleaved meat, I will never forget it.'

Visibly shaken by the escalating violence, journalists and UN staff crowded into the UN compound. Max Stahl filmed desperate parents trying to throw their children – unsuccessfully in some cases – over razor wire at the top of the perimeter wall.

At Liquiça, thirty-five kilometres from Dili, four hundred people and their parish priest were massacred in the local church.

After the massacre at Suai, Lieutenant Colonel Siagian was ostensibly removed from duty. Disguised as a civilian he continued to work with chief of police and militia boss João Tavares. Tavares died recently and his obituary published on the ETAN (the East Timor and Indonesia Network) Network website described him as a Timorese hero.

Some memories stay with us forever: nuns attacked and burned to death; General Wiranto singing 'Feelings' at a karaoke club; Sister Susan Connolly of the Mary MacKillop Institute of East Timorese Studies on the hustings in Sydney chanting, 'Send the troops in'; Bill Clinton accusing the Javanese of direct involvement in the violence sweeping East Timor. The police force worked under the control of the military. Andrew McNaughtan's comment on this was, 'Two lots of shits in different uniforms.'

Before the referendum a huge oil tanker had moored out to sea. This added to the dread. Many applied to the UN for information about it but none was forthcoming. If you had called for firemen in Timor before the referendum water carts on wheels were available *if* you could pay cash on the spot. Otherwise the firemen watched your house burn down. The reason given for this practice was that 'Indonesia is a poor country'. This, though, did not prevent the making of many thousands of water carts in preparation for retaliation if the Timorese dared to vote for freedom. Javanese forces strolled at their leisure down every street and road in the land. As soon as the result of the referendum was announced, they trundled their carts and drenched buildings with hoses now filled with high-octane oil. All that needed was a match or a cigarette lighter. In the event, seventy per cent of buildings were burned beyond repair and the telephone system, electricity and water supply were destroyed.

While East Timor was burning, the minister for foreign affairs, Alexander Downer, said, 'I get the impression that President Habibie, Mr Alatas and General Wiranto are all trying to do the right thing and some of the commanders are clearly trying to do the right thing.' Captain Clinton Fernandes, principal analyst for East Timor in the ADF INTEL Corps 1998–1999 reported that the Australian government was not ambivalent about a peacekeeping force: rather, it worked assiduously to prevent such a force.

The rape of Dili in 1975 was now repeated with a slight difference – houses though ransacked then had been left intact because the Javanese had intended to 'acquire' them. Now everything was removed while the owners were held at bay by mercenaries and Javanese, threatening to drench their children and set them alight with the petrol. Electrical wiring was pulled from timber and plaster walls along with anything that could be sold. As before, doors, windows, carpets were stolen, but now plumbing pipes, roofing tiles, floorboards, bricks, and of course, all children's toys, crockery, furniture, electrical goods, bedding and food was loaded onto waiting trucks. All animals, including pets, were killed one way or another.

Then, at least two hundred thousand Timorese were forced onto trucks and taken across the border into Indonesian-occupied West Timor. The ploy was to convince the world that all those poor terrified people had disagreed with the referendum, but it was enforced deportation on a massive scale.

After all its promises, the UN decided to pull out and they ordered all foreign nationals to evacuate with them. This would leave Timorese unprotected even if they remained in the UN compound; they were lambs to the slaughter. They had no option but to face the terror and at least try to escape certain death. They could not leave by the gates as the mercenaries and Javanese waited outside. Kendelle Clark asked for permission to break down part of the perimeter wall. She told me the official in charge of safety was a hopeless drunk. 'He sat on his bunk scoffing Mars Bars and Whisky,' she said. 'He was a disgrace.' Kendelle took matters into her own hands and broke down part of the wall. After scouting the immediate area she escorted Timorese to safety in the early hours of the morning. She has died since of cancer, a heroine. Vale Kendelle – you were a credit to us all.

Liam Phelan reporting for the *Australian* and the *Irish Times* decided to stay, despite being targeted by snipers. 'The UN were just walking away from them [the Timorese] leaving them to be deported, beaten and killed. I just couldn't walk away,' he said.

As Liam Phelan observed in the *Pacific Journalism Review*, 'When we arrived back in Darwin, we were met by a huge groups of Australian and overseas media desperately trying to follow the story from the Northern Territory. It was strange to face the media scrum desperate for footage. There were too many journalists here and not enough news, and yet just one hour's flight away was the biggest scene of destruction happening virtually unrecorded.'

* * *

In Australia the fight was on to save what was left of the East Timorese nation. We activists were in for a big surprise. We were about to discover that all our years of hard slog had not been wasted. No longer were we ratbags, scum of the earth, professional whingers and haters of all Indonesians. We had been exonerated . . . we were in demand. It was a very odd person who was not touched by the bravery of the Timorese. People stopped me in the street to voice their admiration and anger. 'Thanks but don't tell me,' I would say. 'Get on the phone to Canberra, make your feelings known. Our troops are ready and willing. Please call Canberra as soon as you get home. Next week will be too late. Tomorrow will be too late. Innocent people are dying right now.'

Australian public response to the destruction swelled as reports of atrocities increased. Hundreds of thousands rallied publicly. The government came under pressure from major unions, who put bans on everything from loading Indonesian flights, rubbish collection from Indonesian institutions, mail deliveries and repairs on Indonesian consulates. They impounded containers, banned all incoming and outgoing sea and air traffic, including Garuda Airways. The Construction, Forestry, Mining and Energy Union, aided by the Labor Council of New South Wales, implemented union bans worth seven million dollars. Thousands walked off construction sites to protest. Footwear and textile clothing workers joined the protests. The Maritime Union of Australia declared that all Indonesian shipping and freight was banned, which caused major holdups with wheat exports worth millions. Workers warned oil companies Shell, BHP and Caltex against ordering Indonesian oil as their workers would refuse to process it. Printing works refused to handle Indonesian paper products. Schools, community organisations, churches and individuals lobbied Canberra to intervene. The World Bank froze an aid program to Indonesia worth one billion dollars. Even the Sydney Organising Committee for the Olympic Games was pressed to suspend contact with Indonesia.

We were astonished by the rapidity with which the protest grew. I had said at a meeting way back that when push came to shove we activists would be swept aside in the rush. Though I was fully occupied answering the phone, giving interviews and attending protests, I was sustained by the extraordinary evidence that my words were being realised. Frankly, I could now have taken a long hot soak in the bath, had an early night and stayed in bed all day and it wouldn't have made a scrap of difference to the outcome of one of the greatest tragedies of the twentieth century.

The impetus was dynamic; nothing could stop it in Australia. Public demonstrations proved that we had not wasted our lives after all. They believed us. Some told me they had always believed me. When I had time to think I remembered John Pilger telling me in London in 1990 that he could not understand the silence surrounding Balibó. I assured him, 'Everyone knows about Balibó, they are disgusted but they can't think of a way to influence the government. Australians don't like to object; they're afraid of drawing attention to themselves.'

The fierceness of the reaction was proof-positive that the conscience of the people had always been ashamed of our moral cowardice and abandonment of the Balibo Five and of the East Timorese. In 1991 John Birmingham in the *Quarterly Essay* wrote:

> While Whitlam, Fraser, Keating and Evans all have reason to examine their conscience, the agency which advised, guided and ultimately misled them all was the Department of Foreign Affairs (now Foreign

Affairs and Trade). It is arguable that in pursuing what it thought to be a hard-headed assessment of Australia's best strategic interests, the Department in fact undermined those interests by creating a totally unsustainable paradigm for a relationship between a liberal democracy and a para-corporate military dictatorship.[3]

My only argument with Birmingham's point of view is that he used the past tense; there is nothing I can see that has changed, particularly in the matter of repatriation of the remains of the Balibo Five and war crimes charges for their murderers, or indeed, war crimes trials for Indonesian generals who gave the orders for the genocide.

---

3 John Birmingham, *Appeasing Jakarta*, op. cit.

NINETEEN

The name of the leviathan unleashed upon unarmed Timorese for twenty-four years was Carnal Brutality; the monstrosity facing activists was Official Indifference.

Why did successive Australian governments bother to cover up for the Indonesian president and his rapacious army? Could trade deals that disregard human rights be the catalyst for something as repulsive as the lust for power? Could it be an erotic charge or could the motive to betray one's own constituents be as primeval as the survival of the fittest — I'm the monkey with the largest brain so I get to ignore the ethics? Is pitiless indifference the result of inward-turning guilt for consigning humans into years of unremitting fear and suffering?

Governments have every right to make money through trade, but where exploitation over human values take precedence, politicians, ambassadors and bureaucrats must be called to account, for they are in Long John Silver territory. I believe they do start out with good intentions, but years of compromise lead some of them to having less social conscience than a gnat.

I am often asked why I spent a third of my life working for what appeared to be a hopeless cause. Well, I want a better world. I want moral responsibility to be part of the charter for elected governments. I want recognition of the damage done to the families of the victims, including the families of the Javanese who died in their government's bid to seize East Timor for private gain.

The Timorese youths I had met in Perth in 1990 were not unique in lacking knowledge of their recent history; Australians are shocked when they learn how a democratically supervised referendum could have led to catastrophe.

When I began to record the events for this book, I could not believe the dates on which Australian prime ministerial decisions and statements had been made in 1999 when everyone knew that the safety of the Timorese depended upon them. I checked and rechecked the facts. I could not believe them for a very simple reason: they are unbelievable.

Consider the sequence of events. In 1997 Hugh White, deputy secretary at the Department of Defence, writes that 'Indonesia's economy will likely become the biggest in our region'. After this confident prediction is tabled, Indonesia's economy begins a downward slide towards the point of collapse, leading to the fall of the house of Suharto.

Even after all the death and destruction during General Suharto's occupation of East Timor, John Howard's foreign minister, Tim Fischer, expresses the startling belief that Suharto is 'perhaps the world's greatest figure in the latter half of the 20th century'.

In August 1997 the Australian Labor Party spokesperson for foreign relations, Laurie Brereton, calls for a referendum on the grounds that it is 'the only real solution to the problem of East Timor'.

While the Department of Foreign Affairs and Trade

prepares a brief to dissuade Labor from supporting Brereton, activists worldwide are inspired to exert renewed pressure on their governments in support of Mr Brereton's inspired foresight. As a result, criticism of military excesses in East Timor increases in direct proportion to the decline in Indonesia's economy.

In 1999 the new Indonesian president, B.J. Habibie, announces that he is prepared to pull some combat troops out of East Timor. That night television news shows departing troops entering barges leaving Dili. The pubs are full as we celebrate this evidence of Habibie's goodwill.

The next day the same troops are secretly filmed going ashore in another part of the island, and Andrew McNaughtan smuggles out the entire Indonesian army personnel records for East Timor, which confirm that the combat troops in question are being rotated, not withdrawn.

In April 1999 attacks by General Wiranto's mercenaries (also called militias) are launched on people living in and around Liquiça, and the attacks increase in violence until 6 April, when a massacre takes place in the church at Liquiça. Four hundred people and their parish priest are slaughtered.

Foreign Minister Alexander Downer's comment: 'It's very hard given that we ourselves had no eyewitnesses there.'

Leaked classified Australian intelligence material later confirms that 'ABRI [the Indonesian military] is culpable [for the massacre] whether it actively took part in the violence or simply let it happen'.

Some very serious problems regarding Australia's national security upset Mr Howard's equilibrium; among them are attempts to sell fifty-six unauthorised disclosures plus seven hundred classified defence documents to foreign governments and the passing of state secrets to a prostitute leads to the disclosure of other scandalous goings-on involving government departments, senior personnel, federal agents and citizens innocent of any crime. Though the Defence Intelligence Organisation's senior Washington official's job is to pass on intelligence to, or share intelligence with, his American counterparts, Merv Jenkins commits suicide in 1999 after being threatened with prosecution for doing precisely that. He leaves behind a young family. Attorney-General Daryl Williams rules that there is no need for an enquiry into the suicide of Mr Jenkins.

I would like to know what threats were made to cause Mr Jenkins to take his own life.

In 1999, on 16 September 2000 Australian Federal Police accompanied by members of the Defence Security Authority served search warrants on the political advisor to Mr Brereton and a number of like-minded citizens. The timing is significant, as media coverage of the 2000 Olympics coupled with the scarcity of Sydney lawyers (apparently they are all at the Olympics) makes legal advice scarce. Those under suspicion include Laurie Brereton and his political adviser, Dr Philip Dorling, who has just returned from his honeymoon. Government agents open Dr Dorling's wedding presents and discard wrapping paper and cards which means that the unhappy couple have no hope of knowing who sent which wedding present.

On 27 April 1999, immediately after the conclusion of the Bali summit, Alexander Downer tells ABC Radio: 'We've been given firm commitments by the Indonesians – that is President Habibie, General Wiranto and the Foreign Minister, Ali Alatas. And their success in fulfilling those commitments, well, all I can say is it remains to be seen, but we have no reason at all to doubt their goodwill ... I think people will feel more confident with the police playing a much more substantial role on the ground rather than the armed forces.'

What? The reputation of the Indonesian police in Indonesia, their provinces and in East Timor is equal to their Javanese forces for brutality, rape and the running of protection rackets.

On 5 May 1999 the Australian government signs an agreement giving full responsibility to Indonesia for security in East Timor, despite its role in the ongoing violence.

Even though he had received a letter from John Howard proclaiming his government's unflinching support for Indonesian rule over East Timor, Habibie tells Australian ambassador to Indonesia John McCarthy that he will move very quickly rather than support Howard's proposal for a postponement of a democratically supervised referendum. Alexander Downer voices his prime minister's rejection of all moves for a peacekeeping force. This statement made by Downer on the ABC *AM* program on 15 March 1999 is typical: 'We hope that there won't be a need for a peacekeeping force because if you need a peacekeeping force, you need a peace to keep and peace first has to be negotiated and we hope that when the peace is negotiated it will be a peaceful peace that won't require a peacekeeping force.'

The Australian National Audit Office later reveals that the Department of Defence could not provide evidence that formal planning for a multilateral operation had even begun before late 1999 – the referendum was not due for another four months (30 August).

In September 2009, the *Australian* publishes an article claiming that Ashton Calvert, DFAT departmental secretary, believes that Australia had finished with an untenable stance on East Timor: 'In public we had to criticise Indonesia's conduct, yet in private we were largely supportive of Indonesia's policy.'

Well, you could have fooled me! I have read every published pronouncement of Prime Minister Howard's and those of Alexander Downer, and I have never seen a single criticism coming from either of them regarding Indonesia's policies. Immediately after the result of the referendum is announced an upsurge in Javanese-led violence occurs all over the island. The civilian population is unprotected for two more terrible weeks. Nevertheless, all the years of lobbying by American activists is about to pay off. US envoy Richard Holbrooke warns the Indonesian president that he faces 'the point of no return in international relations if he does not accept an International Peace Keeping force' and Admiral Dennis Blair, commander-in-chief of US forces in the Pacific, personally tells General Wiranto on 8 September 1999 that 'military ties [with Indonesia] are being suspended'.

Six days after the result of the referendum, UN Secretary General Kofi Annan asks Howard to lead a multinational intervention force. The Australian prime minister agrees.

Eight more days pass while unchecked violence sweeps Timorese families off the face of the earth. In a macabre repeat of the scene of the invasion, the sun emerging through pillars of black smoke turns the corrosive pall into murky ochre. David Usborne of the *Independent* reports that any Timorese suspected of supporting independence are made to disappear by the grisly process of being hunted down. Any suggestion that citizens want to leave is scotched by the number of planes, buses and trucks laid on to forcibly take them to West Timor. Some suspected of being in favour of the vote are forced onto boats, stabbed and their bodies thrown overboard.

At the height of the great burning when seventy-eight per cent of buildings throughout East Timor are being razed, I am told that President Bill Clinton has demanded transit rights through Darwin for fifteen thousand US marines bound for East Timor. In fact, a large contingent of marines is conducting manoeuvres *somewhere in the Pacific* at that time. We will probably never know if this swayed the reluctant Mr Howard to finally act, but when I study reports detailing the sexual violations endured by males and females, and the ferocity and sadism of the murders while he prevaricated, I wish that the US Marines had been able to stop the carnage.

On 21 September 1999, Sander Thoenes, a *Financial Times* journalist, is shot as he rides pillion in Dili. His body is mutilated. In November 2002 the Dili district court issues indictments against two military men, Major Jacob Sarosa and Lieutenant Camilo dos Santos, for 'crimes against humanity', which includes charges against them for the death of Thoenes. Indonesia has never fully investigated the reporter's murder. In Melbourne I waver between being glad I am safe and trembling with fear that John Martinkus, Andrew McNaughtan, Carmela Baranowska, Max Stahl and Alan Nairn are all likely to perish.

Along with four hundred thousand Timorese trying to avoid the slaughter, Max Stahl and Alan Nairn save their own lives by retreating to the hills towards Dare. Carmela is ordered to leave. An English journalist I have never met and whose name I cannot remember calls me from Darwin. His voice quivers as he describes Dili. 'That beautiful, languid, anachronistic, Latin city looks like "an uncontrolled demolition site".' Sir Jeremy Greenstock, the British ambassador to the UN, describes the scene as an 'empty shell gutted by an orgy of extraordinary evil'.

Andrew McNaughtan and Sister Joan Westblade drive a truckload of supplies into the hinterland, a feat of extraordinary courage, since Wiranto's mercenaries are on the rampage. One morning, as they prepare to leave the bridge under which they have been trying to sleep, Andrew pauses to watch the sun rise. He says he has never been happier. They save lives with their food, water and medical supplies. In 1999, with the help of grateful local people, Joan erected a monument to Andrew at that very place. He later died of a coronary occlusion, at the age of fifty, in December 2003.

In Melbourne it is hard to believe in the possibility of peace when reports come in every day detailing wave after wave of sexual violations and particularly gruesome killings after General Wiranto unleashes his drug-crazed mercenaries and his soldiers disguised as Timorese. I can only imagine the suffering and frustration of Taur Matan Ruak and the Resistance Army. Taur, who replaced Xanana on the ground, has to restrain his fighters. Driven to tears he pleads with Xanana, who insists that retaliation will give the enemy every excuse to increase their butchery. By following orders from his commander-in-chief, who issues them from Cipinang gaol in Jakarta, the Resistance Army achieves two goals: they do save some lives and they scotch twenty-two years of lies claiming they are a rabble. The pot can no longer call the kettle black.

On a surreal note, while attending a military function for army wives and widows in Jakarta, General Wiranto smiles impishly at the rolling cameras and says, 'I see you have the same feelings like me about East Timor,' and he proceeds to serenade the audience with a syrupy version of 'Feelings'.

British ambassador to the UN Sir Jeremy Greenstock is 'trying to reconcile the awfulness of the tragedy': he and other ambassadors have been attempting to reverse with the 'frequently jaw-dropping tactlessness of their Indonesian hosts'. He accepts a Fokker aeroplane from General Wiranto in order to get to Dili to support eighty UN personnel who have refused to leave the besieged city. When the plane makes an unscheduled landing at Denpasar airport, the ambassador and his colleagues are alarmed to see two army buses and a 'gaggle of generals' waiting for them on the tarmac. They are told that they are required to alight. 'No thank you,' declares the startled ambassador, 'we are all staying on board.'

The arrival of InterFET on 19 September is presented as an achievement of the Howard government, but it is too late.

The principal analyst on East Timor for the Australian Intelligence Corps reports that the Australian government is not ambivalent about a peacekeeping force: rather, it worked assiduously to prevent such a force.

The first troops to land expect a serious firefight. The outcome will depend on the intelligence of the officer-in-command of Comoro airport in Dili. After a bumpy five-hour flight many are still retching as they vacate their C-130 Hercules transport aircraft. To their surprise and relief they are able to secure the control tower without a fight. They have the luck to encounter a rare creature in the Javanese commander, a realist evidently, who sees the futility of mounting a defence against a numerically superior force that includes light infantry troops and air assault operatives being followed by heavy forces. They replace the Javanese, having informed them that a transfer of control by InterFET forces has been successful.

InterFET consists of ten thousand troops from twenty-two countries whose first impression of Dili's Portuguese villas and wide, tree-lined streets is the stench of dead flesh, excrement and ashes.

Australian army officer David Kilcullen, a leading expert on guerrilla warfare, reports his thoughts upon entering the city of Dili. 'Where are the people?'

A RAND Corporation report estimates that the violence 'displaced close to 80 percent of the population in the territory [of East Timor]'.

Firefights and serious stand-offs occur between Javanese, mercenaries and InterFET forces. Sérgio Vieira de Mello, the Brazilian diplomat who supervises the transition to independence, finally admits that the UN lacks the funds to prosecute criminals even when victims are prepared to confront the perpetrators. The word he uses to describe this shocking state of affairs is 'failure'. He is killed four years later when al Qa'ida bombs the UN compound in Baghdad, on 19 August 2003.

And so, instead of justice, women like Nancy Sanchez Nacimiento have to endure the fact that Colonel Tono Suratman, whom she accuses of raping her, is cleared of all charges in an Indonesian court, after which he is promoted to brigadier general in the words of the judge 'in order to restore his dignity'.

Many of our InterFET soldiers still suffer nightmares and some are deemed to be mentally ill for what they saw but were unable to prevent because of the terms of engagement. When they reported rapes (against young children), murders and kidnappings, they were ordered not to intervene.

Accounts of miscarriages of justice abound and I do not think I am deluded in my belief that the conspiracy that started with the murder of the journalists at Balibó continued after InterFET arrived. Max Stahl was taken to a very deep well filled with human remains. He reported this to the UN and later told me that the area was promptly bulldozed.

> But there were many acts of kindness that suggested the hope of redemption. On a boat moored at Dili wharf, an old woman – who was taking the desperate chance to return home after being forced into West Timor – was carrying her dead grandchild. An official refused to allow the old lady ashore. She pleaded to be allowed to bury the baby in the backyard of their house.
>
> An Australian private, seeing the woman's plight, walked forward, reached down and ever so gently lifted the baby from her arms. Cradling the baby he assisted the grandmother to alight and then escorted her to the waiting truck. When she was safely on board he handed the baby back with great tenderness, then whacked the side of the truck with

the flat of his hand and as it drove off turned to face down the official.

There is nothing new in rape being used as a weapon of war, but men, women and children suffered sexual violation for twenty-four years without a shred of hope that their predatory invaders would be brought to trial. Javanese who gave the orders for these crimes and the men who committed them live today in comfortable retirement in Indonesia, feted in public as heroes; but we don't get to hear what it is like for their families to live with someone capable of such inhuman behaviour.

The Javanese officer who arrested a young woman after she had urged a group of villagers to cast their vote submitted her to gang rape by his soldiers that was so brutal she was unable to walk. Then, he dragged her by her long hair to her home and raped her in front of her widowed mother and her children who wept hysterically while entreating him to cease. The poor young woman's body was found a few days later under a bush at a rubbish dump not far from her home. She had sustained internal and external injuries, including fractured bones.

While many Timorese women are held to blame by unsympathetic husbands, neighbours and (some say) even the church for being raped, male victims are particularly prone to shame and guilt. Both sexes of all ages suffer physical, reproductive and psychological ill-health. The report from the Timor-Leste Commission for Reception, Truth and Reconciliation (CAVR report – also known as Chega! which roughly translates as 'no more, stop, enough') is available on the internet. It contains sworn testimony of the scale and magnitude of the crimes committed against unarmed Timorese. You can read the two and a half thousand–page report, which contains eight thousand compelling and abhorrent sworn statements.

The problem with the CAVR report is rather like the 24-year-old United Nations Security Council Resolution (384) that called on Indonesia to withdraw all its troops from East Timor 'without delay'. The precious paper in young José Ramos-Horta's hands was meaningless and so is Chega! as long as the means to implement the rule of law are withheld.

Timorese were stripped of all dignity by being persuaded to give humiliating accounts of their sexual abuse in the belief that their tormentors would stand trial. They suffer still in silence, while those who carried out the crimes or on whose watch they occurred have not been brought to justice. For example, on 14 March 2002, at a special tribunal in Indonesia, the former chief of police in East Timor, Timbul Silaen, the regional commander Major General Adam Dimiri, militia leader Eurico Guterres and five officers were acquitted of all charges, including rape and murder. The last governor of East Timor to serve under Indonesian Rule, Abilio Soares, was sentenced to a mere three years in prison.

We cannot expect the Timorese to bring Javanese criminals to justice. The whole world has to do it for the sake of all our children, and this includes Indonesians, who should be able to trust their own justice system. Chega! will remain worthless as long as we continue to behave as if it does not exist. Silence is the same as giving tacit approval. Yet another circle of silence.

While women struggling alone to support their children were easy pickings for predatory Javanese, some women did fight. As Xanana Gusmão said in 1999: 'Our women fought shoulder to shoulder with the men, when the men were cowards and ran away, the women held the line.'

I have only had an opportunity to speak with one woman who fought shoulder to shoulder with the men, but I have first-hand knowledge of several who bore messages and provided food and water at great danger to themselves. They are unsung heroines. For example, Dona Enduré regularly carried cases filled with bottles of water up the steep, craggy lopes of Matebian – if she had been discovered carrying water anywhere near the mountain, she would have been abused and killed on the spot. I hope there is some wonderful scribe busily taking down stories of women like Dona so they can be remembered for all eternity.

I had met Xanana several times in Melbourne after liberation. The first time, in September 1999, was particularly fortuitous. This was at the Trades Hall. From the top of the wide steps to the second floor I watched him and Kirsty Sword arrive with an entourage of adoring women. As I stepped into the room where he was to speak I was surprised to see it was crammed with people I did not know. They were packed tightly together near the stage and the side door by which he was to enter, so I moved to the back of the room, where I knew I would not be able to see him, but just to know he was alive and there would be enough. Everyone was tense with expectation when the door at the back of the room opened and Xanana strode in. He saw me straight away. I expected him to make his way to the dais, because he was obviously running late. Not a bit of it. He moved forward and embraced me with the tightest hug. He certainly knows how to communicate his feelings. I, on the other hand, was too shy to say anything. We looked into each other's eyes and smiled: we didn't need words.

Nine years later, on a visit to Timor Leste, Xanana invited me to attend an assembly of the Resistance Army. What an amazing thrill that was. I met the fighters and was struck by a line of youngish men sitting on a stage behind a long trestle table who wrested the microphone from each other in order to speak. Just as some of us hog the microphone, so did they, until a woman sitting with the ranks of weather-beaten fighters stood

The Circle of Silence

and indicated with great authority that she wanted to speak. I did not understand a word, but I thought she was making fun of the young men (future politicians no doubt) for their presumption.

A week or so later I visited a friend at his uncle's restaurant. Fernando had managed a stall at the South Melbourne market ever since his escape. He had recently returned to Timor Leste to help save another uncle's business and I had invited a group of people there for dinner. Francisco Guterres, otherwise known as Lu Olo (his resistance name) had joined Nicolau dos Reis Lobato's Resistance Army at the age of seventeen. He paid a terrible price for freedom. His relatives were tortured simply because he had chosen to fight, and he had survived deprivation, fear and hunger for twenty-four years. Like many fighters who returned after liberation, his family refused to take him in. 'We already buried you,' they said. 'You are a ghost.'

'I know who you are,' said a woman sitting with Lu Olo. She was Bemesak, the woman I had witnessed speaking at the meeting of the resistance fighters. She was a farmer's daughter who was working in the fields in 1975 when her father raced towards her and handed her a rifle. 'He told me to run to the mountains. "Don't look back", he said.' She spoke with a sad little smile. 'I was obedient in those days. I did not hesitate to do as I was told. As I began to run shots rang out. I did not look back. I was terrified and finally threw the rifle away because it slowed me down. I didn't know how to use it.'

Members of her extended family arrived on Matebian, the Mountains of the Dead. Something in her expression warned me not to ask about her father. Over the following two years every family member who sought the safety of the mountain died from starvation, disease, attacks by Javanese or from bombing raids. Her resistance name means Woman Alone.

At our next meeting I asked her to tell me what training she had received in order to fight. She gave interesting details:

for example, no one had a personal weapon; they were stacked in the centre of a circle of fighters who positioned themselves in order to grab a gun if they had to repulse an attack or launch one. 'But how did you learn to shoot since there were so few bullets?' I asked innocently. I will never forget the smile on her face as she gently replied. 'Ah, there's something about being shot at; you know instinctively what to do. If you have a gun you fire back and then go to ground. If you have no means to counter-attack you go to ground.' We laughed and laughed, but I felt so sad. Underneath my laughter I was shocked at my ignorance and I contemplated what a terrible life she had been forced to live.

Soon after InterFET chased the Javanese out of Dili I received a phone call from John Skeffington, a retired West Australian policeman who was seconded to CIVPOL (civilian police). He apologised to me for his ignorance – until he landed in Dili he had not heard about Balibó – and he asked my permission to go ahead with an investigation. After an initial visit to Balibó he decided there was enough evidence to warrant a full investigation and he set about it in the same way a murder would be dealt with in Australia. He arranged for aerial photographs to be taken and made a detailed map of Balibó and its environs. He then interviewed every adult resident of the destroyed township and found several previously unknown eyewitnesses to the murders.

When UN CIVPOL investigators in East Timor recommended prosecution of Balibó murderers, John Howard immediately recalled Mr Skeffington and the Australian police officers conducting the investigation, and his decision was enforced, despite the fact that the officers and Sérgio Vieira de Mello – then the UN special representative for the secretary general to East Timor – made an appeal to Howard to allow them to complete their inquiries.

TWENTY

In March 2000 SBS offered me the opportunity to return to East Timor with documentary-maker Mark Davis. This was my second visit. On arrival at the derelict, burnt shell that used to be Comoro Airport, I experienced pure joy. This did not come from anything I saw, but by an absence. I wanted to kiss the ground but felt it was too dramatic. I remembered the airport under Indonesian occupation swarming with hard-eyed men in combat uniform and officials clicking their fingers impatiently at Timorese who looked tired and harassed. I felt I was looking at a double exposure. The atmosphere was calm and all the Timorese were smiling.

On the drive from the airport on my first visit I had seen underfed Timorese walking barefoot in the dust and overfed Indonesians driving recklessly. This time laughing children waved and called out greetings. Even the plants seemed greener than I remembered, and when I mentioned this to Timorese friends they agreed that they too thought the vegetation looked more lush.

The extent of the destruction in Dili had to be seen to be believed; I was reminded of Londoners in the Blitz sitting on all that was left of their houses – their front doorsteps. Inscriptions were painted on burnt-out houses: 'If your children are hungry, feed them stones.'

The biggest surprise was twilight. Where citizens had once gone inside, drawn the curtains and sat in the dark for fear of being targeted through their windows, they now promenaded in the streets and sat in their ruined gardens, taking great pleasure in talk.

There are as many gripping anecdotes as there are people in the wonderland of freedom. I was told many times how lucky my friends were, but when I heard how they had suffered, I could not help wondering about the tenuous difference between good and bad luck.

I talked with an elderly married couple whose house was destroyed along with all their possessions. They were now living in what used to be their garage under a blue plastic roof. They had two chairs, bedding on the floor and a burnt garden; they were planning to plant some vegetables. I asked if they would have Indonesia back if it meant they could regain their house and possessions.

'No,' they said, 'we haven't heard any shooting since our return and it makes us feel lighter and younger. There was always shooting before.' They added that they would choose to stay in their garage 'rather than suffer *their* presence'.

This gentle couple had survived terrible experiences, including being threatened with being burned alive with their house and forcibly taken to West Timor – they had escaped and walked all the way back to Dili.

Mark went to see the Australian army in Dili to arrange for us to go to Balibó. The officer there was absolutely delighted. 'The boys will be rapt,' he said. He offered to put me up in secure accommodation and was quite insistent that he would fly us there in a chopper. It was all going to be laid on. But when

The Circle of Silence

Mark walked into his office to make final arrangements, it was as if a different man had taken his place. The officer was clearly embarrassed and could barely look at Mark. He had obviously sent his request up the chain of command back to Australia. His instructions were that no helicopter or other transport would be provided. Furthermore, no accommodation was to be made available; no assistance of any kind provided; and no contact allowed with any Australian Defence Force (ADF) personnel. He further advised that Javanese troops were still active in the area, and the road was too dangerous for travel. If I had been present I would have told him I had travelled that road on a number of occasions in 1989 on the back of a motorbike, when large parts of the road had fallen down the cliff edging the sea.

I did not know any of this, of course, until later. Mark had told me we were not supposed to go to Balibó. Then his face broke into smiles when I replied, 'Okay, when do we leave?'

Years later when Mark filled me in, he said, 'We'd come that far and you had waited that long – there wasn't much chance of me turning back if you were up to it. I didn't tell you because I didn't want the nastiness of it to overshadow your trip.'

He had been expecting a much tougher time from the Australian troops when we arrived. Under the circumstances, they were incredibly generous. The local commander had received similar instructions to the Dili officer. He followed his orders, but also did his best to mitigate them. He said mercenaries and common criminals were still moving through Balibó and he shared Mark's anxiety about where I was going to stay. He pointed out a rotunda on the other side of the wire fence from the ADF camp.

We were greeted wherever we went. I was even given a tour by a lovely soldier in full battledress armed with a machine-gun. Unfortunately Mark could not film this as it would have caused ructions in Canberra. Why was that? What possible affront would that have been to the Indonesian government? We were invited for a cuppa in the old Portuguese fort that Greg had described. We were invited to dine in the Mess and I think we even watched a movie for a while. I had a very lively debate with an officer over women being admitted into the army. I won the argument hands down, which he graciously conceded. I had previously researched the subject: women have always fought – they died in their hundreds defending Paris after the Battle of Waterloo was lost, and they fought side-by-side at Bull Run, the bloodiest battle of the American Civil War, and I cited spies Nancy Wake and Violette Szabo. Enough! I could write a book.

While we prepared to sleep in the building that seemed to be a rotunda, I decided I was not going to venture up the steep trail to the hole in the ground that served as our dunny. The path was slippery with what I did not care to discover and it was pitch dark. While Mark erected our mozzie domes (he is one of nature's gentlemen) I pulled down my pyjama pants and hanging onto a piece of wreckage in a wobbly fashion, stuck my bottom over the edge of the raised floor and had an enjoyable pee when he was not looking my way. When I talked to him recently about this, I wish I had taken a photograph of his face as he told me, 'You were heavily if discreetly guarded all night. You were well protected and observed in those ruins and all the soldiers had night-vision, Shirley.'

During his visit Mark discovered more about the killing of Roger East and the Balibó Five in nine days than any Western government had in a quarter of a century. He had also discovered evidence that the money to pay Wiranto's mercenaries was channeled from the World Bank come from Ali Alatas' office.[1]

In an interview with us, Thomas Gonçalves, a UDT

---

1 'Blood money' SBS documenary, Mark Davis. Dateline 16 February 2000.

supporter, admitted he had led Yunus Yosfiah and his troops across the border into Balibó. He said one journalist came out of the house with his hands up; he was followed by three obviously unarmed journalists. Yunus Yosfiah, who was later appointed information minister in the Habibie government, shot them down with his machine-gun and all his men followed suit. Gonçalves was told to go away and claimed he did not see what happened to the fifth man, but when he returned five bodies were being burned.

One interview in the documentary was roundly criticised by those who were critical of Roger East and his bravery. João, who had given me coffee when I waited to confront General Murdani – 'Double strength for courage' – told us that he had served Roger East the night before the invasion. He said that Roger had been wearing Falintil fatigues and was armed. This was such a departure from his normal mode of dress and it showed his serious intent not to give up. Mark hit him with a barrage of questions designed to trip him up if he was embroidering the facts.

Some have said that Roger would not have jeopardised his 'safe' status as a journalist by wearing a uniform and being armed, but I never doubted João's account. I can imagine Roger meeting with Falintil for an inspection of his gear. No one knew when the invasion was coming; it would have been impractical not to make sure Roger was capable of carrying his own equipment and stupid for him to remain unarmed.

As to the reason why he was dressed in yellow shorts at the wharf on the day he was killed and didn't wear shoes – some say he had a bad case of dysentery. Yellow shorts sound like shorty pyjamas to me. I wonder if Bali Belly was deliberately inflicted upon him – Dili was full of spies posing as itinerant hawkers. To give Roger a case of the squirts (as the 2/2nd boys used to say) would have been an easy and an effective way to make him too ill to carry out his plan to withdraw. I wonder if they arrested him before the pre-invasion bombardment began. A Falintil jeep was sent to rescue him but the occupants were killed by paratroopers.

Mark's documentary was shown on SBS in April 2000. It was nominated for a Logie and the moment we heard the name of the other nominated entry, *Crooked Cricket* by *Four Corners*, we relaxed, as it was the obvious winner. As I walked up the red carpet with SBS executives a bystander called out, 'Have a good time, Shirley.' I wore my 1920s Chinoiserie out-coat decorated with peonies over a long black velvet skirt and a black silk blouse. As we approached the big glass doors I caught sight of dozens of young women dressed in black that exposed about as much of their bodies as a skin-tight bathing suit. I was still surprised, however, when a young man, also dressed entirely in black, bowed and asked, 'Are you the wife of the ambassador, Madame?'

'No,' I replied. 'I'm just dressed like her.'

It turned out to be a very fortuitous night. As I sipped my champagne, still goggling at the multitude of bum-cracks and scarcely covered nipples, Victorian premier Steve Bracks smiled at someone sitting behind me. I turned to see who it was. There was no one there. I returned the smile and stared into the champagne glass – *you've got ten seconds to think of something to ask him to do*, said that voice in my head. I had seen Mr Bracks being interviewed in Dili after InterFET had cleared the Javanese out. He was genuinely upset. I thought then that I must find a way to persuade him to do something to help the people of Timor Leste.

Feeling rather light-headed I rose and walked to his table. He stood and shook my hand; a memory of Greg's last iconic report repeated in my brain, in what must have been an electrifyingly charged moment when the men in the hut heard Greg's words and rose to their feet to say, 'That's all we want, camarade journaliste!' Looking up to stem my tears, I asked if he would consider buying one of the houses that had sheltered Greg, Tony, Gary, Brian and Malcolm. 'They have nothing in Balibó, I would love the building most suited to the purpose to be used as a clinic.' He explained that a clinic would be too costly to run. I asked if he would approach the local people to see what they wanted, and he agreed immediately.

I was told much later that he had already thought of doing something worthwhile but would never have gone ahead without being approached by a family member. In 2003, the Victorian government, with assistance from the Balibó House Trust, World Vision, Multiplex, Channels Seven and Nine and the Australian peacekeeping forces in East Timor, reconstructed and refurbished the Balibó Flag House to provide a Community Learning Centre with a wide range of programs, including a crèche, sewing and cooking classes, computer training, mechanics, carpentry, literacy, sport and music activities. It is a matter of great pride to me that everything unavailable in Timor at that time – every nail, every grain of sand, doors, windows, cans of paint – was donated by forty Victorian businesses.

Australian troops stationed at Balibó volunteered to work on the house – after doing the hard yards protecting the border they broke their backs working miracles. The owner of the house had painted over Greg's original painting for fear of Javanese reprisals, and one Aussie peacekeeper dedicated to finding the flag that Greg had painted spent hours painfully scrubbing the walls with steel wool in order to reveal the painting without destroying it. My first reaction when I saw the photograph was horror – it was a ghost image, a nasty reminder of the past – but I agreed to leave it exposed to allow the next-of-kin to decide its fate.

Twelve Australian family members, including Evan, his

wife Julie and me, along with three family members from Britain, attended the opening by Steve Bracks, the president of Timor Leste, Xanana Gusmão, and the senior minister for foreign affairs and co-operation, José Ramos-Horta. Most moving was the presence of hundreds of Timorese who had walked all night from outlying districts in order to pay their respects. The ceremony was dedicated to all those who died, including Roger East, Timorese civilians and members of the Resistance Army.

Anna, the wife of Gary Cunningham's son, John Milkins, sang 'Ave Maria'. I decided not to speak about Greg since everyone could guess what I was likely to say; instead I spoke for Glenise Bowie, Roger East's sister. A few days before his murder, Glenise and her husband, while flying over Timor at the start of a holiday, heard the pilot's message, 'Below us is Dili.' Glenise looked down and saw one tiny light flickering. Her husband said, 'Roger's down there.' She told me, 'We were both profoundly moved just to think of him.'

Roger had been Glenise's hero from when she was a tiny child. She chuckled as she spoke to me:

> I was a fat little thing, the youngest of four. My older brothers used to climb the fence and leave me crying my eyes out in the back yard. Roger always came back for me. He would carry me on his back, his skinny little legs wobbling like mad, but he never let me down either then or later in life. He was loyal and the most generous man I have ever known except for my husband.

My son was eight years old when Greg was murdered. Balibó was the last place on earth he wanted to be. But he faced the ordeal. There were great outpourings of joy from Timorese as well as us. 'That's the first time I've ever heard an official say something good about my dad,' Evan observed. There were a lot of tears, except for one ghastly moment when the translator who was doing a great job of speaking in *Tetuñ*, Portuguese, Indonesian and English mentioned Greg Shackleton. As we tried to stem our tears we heard him say Gregory Skeleton. Evan, Julie and I almost suffocated trying not to laugh. It was dreadful, but we felt so sorry for the young translator and this unfortunate trip of the tongue. Though it was horribly gruesome, it actually saved us from dissolving into sobs. Some things that seem dreadful at the time turn out to be heaven sent.

When the flag Greg had painted on the wall with a piece of cloth was revealed it appeared to me as a kind of resurrection.

The Community Learning Centre is thriving. For me the flag no longer holds horror; like the restored house it is a symbol of renewal and of hope for a better future for the Timorese nation. Like an archaeological mural – it is a precious remnant from the past, a sad and ghostly artefact of a vile and unfinished business.

In 2010 all the computers have been replaced and a modern playground is to be installed. Next we plan to put up a satellite dish to augment the computers.

Mark Davis flew back to Australia in order to facilitate my attendance at the independence celebrations of the new nation of Timor Leste, which were to be held at Taci-Tolu, on 20 May 2002. Taci-Tolu is the place where the papal mass had been held nineteen years before and was called Cactus Flats by Australian commandos in World War II. This was my third visit and I thank Mark with all my heart, because I would have missed out on one of the most memorable experiences of my life.

On the day we arrived a demonstration was held against the presence of six Indonesian warships that had sailed into Dili Harbour several days earlier. One of the warships had 2000 troops on board. This arrogant and insensitive behaviour was not appreciated by the Timorese, who expressed their disgust and determination not to be intimidated by demonstrating in a dignified manner. I could not but help remember the interview I had conducted with an eyewitness to Roger East's murder on the same wharf where the demonstration was taking place. While showing his contempt and rage, when the end came Roger had also behaved with dignity. Needless to say my thoughts were with Greg and his colleagues, Shonny, Dr Andrew McNaughtan and Michele Turner, for Michele had committed suicide. In my small way I felt closer to the Timorese than I had ever felt before; I had lost people I loved and though they had whole families to mourn, grief does not require large numbers to cause acute pain.

The independence celebration was more like a commemoration; the Timorese deserved to feel joy, but for those of us who recalled the price that had been paid by so many innocent of any crime, our thoughts were drowned in tears.

I sat in the dust in darkness next to Cathy and Andy Alcock, two most loyal activists from Adelaide. With us were two hundred and fifty thousand Timorese. We could see the illustrious guests sitting under cover in a huge, brightly lit stadium. They included Kofi Annan and Bill Clinton.

The proceedings were stage-managed by the same organisation that had conducted the opening ceremony of the 2000 Sydney Olympic Games. The vast arena was encircled with gigantic screens, which showed every moment of the celebrations accompanied by stereoscopic sound. Xanana was the star of the night. When even a small part of his ear appeared on the screens, the Timorese cheered ecstatically. In fact, the more they saw of his image, the louder they cheered.

Needless to say some guests should have been publicly hanged for the atrocious part they had played in the tragedy, but politics heralded a whole new set of polite procedures that would have to be observed in the future.

A mass was held to start the proceedings. It was the first of several moving ceremonies. Soon after the mass concluded, we were told that Xanana was leaving to welcome President Megawati's arrival at the newly named Nicolau Lobato International Airport. He had agreed to escort her to the Indonesian Heroes Cemetery in Dili before bringing her to the stadium.

This announcement was received with studied politeness down on the flats.

The timing was dreadful. Xanana would miss the most important parts of the program.

The lights were dimmed as 200 young people wearing long white gowns carried candles into the arena. *Kadalak* (Small Streams) and traditional Timorese music was played. A group of elders (the *Li'a Na'in*) wearing traditional *leipas* (sarongs) entered the arena and they proceeded to bring in the souls of the departed. I wondered how many who had attended the Declaration of Independence on 28 November in 1975 had survived to meet the spirits of the deceased. My eyes stung with tears – it might have been an illusion in that place of the dead, but I felt a presence I cannot explain.

The next part of the ceremony was also missed by Xanana. He had led the Resistance Army for twenty-one years of the bloody occupation against near-impossible odds. As supreme commander he should have been there to honour his troops.

Wearing black trousers and long-sleeved shirts the line of resistance fighters was suddenly spotlighted in the general gloom. Murmurs began to reverberate amongst the Timorese. I expected wild cheering, but the demeanour of their heroes standing silently had the desired effect – the murmuring ceased. We were in a circle of silence never to be forgotten. As a deep hush fell over everyone present, men and women, heroes of the resistance, commenced a controlled military walk with such discipline and in such a solemn manner that everybody got it – these fighters were not there to celebrate a victory, they were honouring their dead.

What other country in the world would parade their military heroes in that sensitive manner? They would be in full military uniform covered with medals, carrying state of the art weapons and marching to a military band.

The announcement that Megawati had arrived was met with a sullen silence on the flats and a smattering of clapping in the stadium. She appeared at the top of the steps dressed in black. The silence was profound as Xanana ushered her into a front row seat and, standing next to her, raised her hand high with his own; that's all that was needed, everyone applauded. But it would be a mistake to assume that the ovation was for the Indonesian president.

Lu 'Olo made the only unscheduled speech of the night. He paid tribute to the fighters and especially the leaders who had lost their lives in the struggle, and he spoke about the crimes committed by the Javanese.

Speeches followed and the night ended with a sensational fireworks display. The Timorese were entranced and they made a very appreciative audience for an exciting and beautiful finish to a sad and reflective night.

I met Peter Gordon in Dili the next day and he told me the rest of the miracle that led from my original interview on the BBC *Woman's Hour* to the making of his documentary *In Cold Blood*, which exposed the Santa Cruz massacre. On the morning of my interview his wife had parked her car behind his. He was running late and in too much of a hurry to wait for her to move her car, so he drove hers without changing to his usual radio station and so heard my interview. My goodness, people like me who operate without power get a terrible shock when they realise how tenuous are the steps that lead to any tiny achievement.

TWENTY-ONE

The film *Balibo* opened the Melbourne Film Festival on 24 July 2009. Before that momentous occasion, which had people in the audience sobbing uncontrollably, at least twelve film-makers had assured me that they were going to make the definitive film about the Balibó atrocity. I had always been afraid that any film would depart from the truth on the grounds of poetic licence. Lies were and are still being told about East Timor and a film makes an indelible impression, which is well-nigh impossible to erase.

Films that ignore vital information in favour of dramatic fiction are legion. In a film made of his life, Tom Lawrence's considerable achievements were largely ignored. He had translated *The Odyssey*, had extensive knowledge of the Hittites, was able to write knowledgeably and accurately about the development of high-speed motorbikes and had successfully set up a printing press. He had written a thesis about castle architecture in England, Europe and the Middle East, and was a respected archaeologist – many of his 'finds' are in the British Museum. He was a polyglot who spoke perfect

English, French, German, Latin, Greek, Arabic, Turkish and Syriac. All pretty amazing stuff when you consider that all of the above was accomplished by the age of 29 when he became famous as Lawrence of Arabia. David Lean's film is a classic admired all around the world. Perhaps the power of film compels the viewer to discover the guts of what is called the back story.

When I first read Robert Connolly's screenplay I was horrified. Even though I was conceited enough to think I could put my personal feelings aside if the film made a contribution to sorting fact from propaganda, as a dedicated activist I wanted the dirty deeds by Australian officials, prime ministers and their foreign ministers exposed.

There certainly were enough books to make the task easy, among them Jill Jolliffe's *Balibo* and *Death in Balibo, Lies in Canberra* by Desmond Ball and Hamish McDonald, exposed Australian governments' multitude of crimes against humanity. For example, *Death in Balibo, Lies in Canberra* details how senior officials in the Australian embassy in Jakarta, Malcolm Dan and Allan Taylor, received detailed briefings on Indonesia's plan to destabilise and invade East Timor. The authors conclude: 'This is a rare case where officials decided, in peacetime, to sacrifice some of their fellow citizens to protect security and intelligence interests. At the very least, it is a case of official negligence, failing to connect the intelligence with the known movement of the journalists.'[1]

There are many nasty, jealous fools who depicted Roger East in their writings as an old hack when he decided to report East Timor's unequal struggle. But over the years following the Indonesian invasion, the more I discovered about Roger, the

---

1 Desmond Ball and Hamish McDonald, *Death in Balibo, Lies in Canberra*, Allen & Unwin, Sydney, 2000.

more I liked him. Little insights were endearing. His manner of walking (he did not walk, he bustled), his adventurous background (he had started a newspaper under the noses of the secret police in the Spanish Civil War, and had put up his age to join the navy in World War II). He did not swear or drink beer; he was courteous and a connoisseur of fine wine. He could not stand snobs and had a keen sense of fun.

The Roger in Robert's screenplay is a beer-drinking slob.

There were minor mistakes, easily fixed, so I offered to write a report pointing them out, and Robert Connolly accepted this offer – for example, the child who welcomed Roger to the Turismo would not have called him Mr East; she would have addressed him as Senhor.

I would have loved to be present during the filming, if only for the learning experience, but I stayed away in case I would need to criticise the finished film. As merely one of the family members, the others of whom were thrilled at the prospect of a film, I was powerless.

However, I was able to give a tutorial for Anthony LaPaglia and the actors playing the Balibo Five, and I told them all I knew about the men they were to play. I encouraged them not to think of them as heroic or as fools as they are so often depicted. They were just doing their job, though, the night before their murders, they did make a courageous decision to stay. Even the feared North Vietnamese did not target the media during their invasion of South Vietnam and when they burst through the gates of the presidential palace in Hanoi they did not harm Australian photo-journalist Neil Davis who was waiting to film them. Roger East, however, was heroic because he decided to stay after the killings in Balibó. There should have been no danger for any Australia-based journalist because of the greatly lauded relationship between General Suharto and Prime Minister Whitlam.

Greg was a courageous person and he had an open mind on the delicate matter of who had been attacking the border over the previous year. The Timorese accused the Javanese and the ever-so-truthful Indonesian president was adamant that not only were his soldiers innocent of the charges, he had no plans to start a war.

Greg faced death every day. He was an asthmatic who fought his disease with determination, self-control and, yes, courage.

A lot of money was spent on spreading propaganda to denigrate Greg, and some really creepy people did it for their own sick reasons – this practice continues today. They are to be pitied, for they are envious cowards. They might persuade some to believe that the Balibo Five were stupid and they were clever, but the five who were murdered were braver and better journalists. They chose to cover one of the biggest stories that was unfolding in the world at that time. It was important to discover if any Javanese troops were attacking the border and that they were not merely disaffected Timorese mercenaries. If they had wandered into crossfire on an active battlefront as the Indonesians maintained, it may have been a foolhardy risk. But they didn't. They were murdered. Not in the heat of battle, but in cold blood.

Greg bears the brunt of carping criticism and I think I am responsible for that – I believe if any of the other families had demanded a full judicial enquiry from the first day, as I did, their relative would have been denigrated. I do not blame them for this: they were not given the opportunities I was given, they did not have a media background.

Neil Davis is eulogised for waiting at the gates of the presidential palace to greet the North Vietnamese invasion of South Vietnam and for having crossed the line to report the other side in other conflicts. Greg would have relished the opportunity to report a Javanese invasion, not because he idolised Davis – he was far too sophisticated for that – but because he believed in balanced reporting.

I was invited to see the completed film of *Balibo* just before it was officially released, but I told Robert I would wait for the DVD as I could not possibly see the film with an audience. The manager of Cinema Nova, Kristian Connelly, gave me a cinema to myself.

I cried a lot, starting at the first scene showing Roger on his knees at the wharf. The image was so powerful that I was with him at the sea-wall; here was a healthy human being who loved life; a strong, athletic man who had every reason to live and he was going to be butchered in another fifteen minutes. I had to leave the cinema to throw up during the murders in Balibó.

The blueprint for *Balibo* is Joseph Campbell's concept of a hero's journey in which a protagonist refuses the call to adventure, until an initiating event causes him to accept the challenge and, hey presto!, Indiana Jones is born – everyone loves the film, and Steven Spielberg earns enough to make another movie. Though Roger was certainly determined to discover what had happened to the Balibo Five, and he came to the decision to continue to do his job by staying to report the Indonesian invasion, the film does bend facts, but the gravitas is maintained by the power of the acting, the director's skills and the overall tragedy.

Roger was absolutely nothing like the character Robert created, but it did not matter, because Anthony LaPaglia made him believable and, more importantly, memorable. I was not offended by the use of fiction as I had expected to be, partly because Anthony portrayed Roger in a way that mirrored Greg's determination in getting to the truth, which I found poetic.

Robert was going to show the actual footage of Greg's last iconic report, but Damon Gameau, who played Greg, wanted to have a go at it. He did a remarkable job. Damon pauses where Greg paused, pronounces Balibó correctly, as Greg did, and captures all the correct inflections. In fact, he emulates Greg in a way that sends shivers up and down my spine.

Robert arranged to use the same equipment for the filmed sequences in Balibó village that the journalists had used to film their reports, which gives the film a grainy texture that works on several levels, from capturing the fidelity of film-stock in 1975, to demonstrating the professional capabilities required in those days, so different from today's flexible and lightweight equipment. In manoeuvring the heavy cameras and fiddly sound recorders the actors learned to respect the achievements of the men they were playing. I like to recount how Damon's re-creation of Greg's last iconic report took nine takes; Greg did it in one. He would have written the report, memorised and performed it straight to camera; no sweat, as they said back then.

Arena Film dubbed the *Balibo* soundtrack in Indonesian and *Tetuñ*, and John Maynard, the producer of *Balibo*, showed the film in Dili on the tenth anniversary of liberation, 30 August 2009, at the presidential palace on a large portable screen. He and his son subsequently followed the Tour de Timor – a hair-raising bicycle race described by participants as thrilling beyond belief, as they would turn a corner to see incomparably beautiful scenery of enormous depths and rises in the mountainous territory so useful to resistance fighters. John showed the film at night to audiences many of whom learned about the hidden history of the start of their long journey.

In the meantime, at a question and answer session I attended in Melbourne regarding *Balibo*, film critic Julie Rigg read part of a statement by the Indonesian foreign ministry spokesman, Teuku Faizasyah, who said that the film wouldn't change anything as far as Indonesia was concerned. 'The film may stir some controversy in Australia, but for us, it's a finished problem, case closed,' he said.

As far as Indonesia is concerned the case was never opened.

The Indonesian press reported further government statements that the film was 'fictional' and that the journalists in Balibó had been 'killed in crossfire' in what 'the Australian Government called an accident'.

Balibo won acclaim all over the world, including in Indonesia, where it was banned. The Alliance of Independent Journalists screened the movie in venues around the country, and sales of pirated DVDs flourished.

Andreas Harsono, founder of the alliance, said Indonesian journalists would lodge a constitutional court challenge if the government took the next step of enforcing the ban, which was instituted on 1 December 2009. 'This is all the legacy of the Suharto regime that we are trying to scrap piece by piece,' said Harsono, whose group began as an underground free speech movement under the Suharto dictatorship.

Then, ex-Kopassus officer Gatot Purwanto revealed in the respected *Tempo* magazine that he had participated in the deliberate killing of the Balibo Five in October 1975.

I suspect this was designed to provide a justification for the killings, to provide a smokescreen for his superiors, Yunus Yosfiah and Christoforus da Silva, so that they are able to say, 'We've got eyewitnesses.'

The article in *Tempo* magazine made the point that 'if taken at face value, it could absolve his [Purwanto's] superiors and leave largely intact the Indonesian version of events that crossfire was ultimately responsible for the killings. The censorship

The Circle of Silence

shows that in post-Suharto Indonesia the establishment is still more interested in covering up past crimes, and protecting the military officers who committed them, than in expanding democratic freedoms.'

Purwanto was quoted in *Tempo* as saying: 'If we let them live, they would tell everyone it was an Indonesian invasion. If they died and we abandoned them, there would be evidence that they were shot in territory controlled by Indonesian guerrillas. So, the simple way was to eliminate everything. We just claimed not to know anything. It was the instant reaction at the time.'

My response to this in the *Sydney Morning Herald* on 8 December 2009 was: 'He's saying it wasn't crossfire, he also says that the troops fired after a shot came from behind the journalists. [But] there was no one in that village, it was completely deserted. That's bullshit. Team Susi was an assassination squad sent to shut them up. This was bloody murder.'

An article like the one in *Tempo* achieves unprecedented publicity for the goal of justice in Indonesia. At every interview I did at that time on TV, radio or in the press I made my plea for justice. 'Justice is not about vengeance, it is about accountability.'

When Gary Cunningham was murdered at Balibó he did not know he had a five-year-old son. Heather Norman had made a decision to have her baby adopted and she had never told Gary about the boy. Her wonderful brother Peter Norman, the Australian track athlete who won a silver medal for the 200 metres sprint at the 1968 summer Olympics in Mexico City, looked after her during the pregnancy. Though Peter's time of 20.06 seconds still stands as the Australian 200-metre record, he is admired and remembered for his support of Tommie Smith and John Carlos when they gave the Black Power salute as the three Olympic champions stood together on the Olympic dais.

When John Milkins turned nineteen he found his natural mother. Heather told him about his father's death and she put him in touch with Gary's relatives. They were amazed and delighted to meet John as they had never known of his existence. He has become an outspoken supporter for justice for this father and his colleagues, and he wants their remains brought back and laid to rest in Melbourne.

Soon after a son, Benjamin, was born to John and his wife Elizabeth, Heather Norman returned home from the Falklands – where she had been teaching since 1997 – to meet her grandson. I was delighted to join them for dinner at a Melbourne restaurant. MP Rob Hudson and his wonderful wife Marie attended and we were all charmed to be able to watch Heather cuddling her grandson. When Rob saw how excited I was to be sharing in the joy he suddenly turned to me and asked if I knew how John had made contact with Heather.

His wife Marie had also relinquished her baby when she was seventeen for the same reasons that Heather had given up John: both had acted out of a determination to give their babies the best life possible, which they knew they could not do alone. Later in life Marie and a group of her friends created Vanish, now known as the Association of Relinquishing Mothers, and it was through that organisation that mother and son were reunited.

As we sat around the circular table I was reminded that not all circles are unremittingly sad or evil and this one filled me with inconceivable joy.

TWENTY-TWO

*They were free to roam
the world their oyster
their hearts at home,
long before Balibó.*

*Seeds in the wind?
too romantic by far;
they're stuck together
like pitch and tar.*

*Their bodies were burned
three times in all.
Imagine the stench?
Consider the pall?*

*Ashes to ashes; dust to dust
described as 'bone fragments'
'the remains' were stuffed
in four small boxes*

Shirley Shackleton

*and hidden away
in the murderer's land
by the Australian Ambassador's
Blood-soaked hand*

*Together in bondage
no longer afar;
still stuck together
like pitch and tar.*

Seven investigations have been held over the years into the murders of the Balibo Five – but since they agreed with the propaganda that the men were killed in crossfire by warring Timorese, I don't propose to describe them. Conducted by the government the investigations were a complete waste of time and money.

Between 1975 and 1980 I sought advice about taking legal action that might lead to an inquest. I was told by three Melbourne lawyers that there was no way in Australian law that I could do this. However, late in 2005, the chairman of the Balibó Committee, Rodney Lewis, told me that George Masterman, QC for the New South Wales Ombudsman and a serving member of the International Commission of Jurists, had found a loophole that could lead to an inquest. He then told me only Brian Peters, who had been a resident of New South Wales, was eligible to take action. I happened to know that Brian's sister, Maureen Tolfree, was thinking of coming to Australia, and that she had suffered greatly, since the British government appeared to care even less than the Australian and New Zealand governments about the murders of their citizens in this particular case. Soon the wonderful day dawned when Maureen and Rodney Lewis, representing the International

Commission of Jurists, reported Brian's murder thirty years after the fact. I trembled with anticipation, for if an inquest came to pass the circle of silence might finally be broken.

I felt very strange and lonely when I attended the preliminary hearings in Sydney. I had not expected to be the only non-legal person in the courtroom. Submissions made to the coroner, Judge John Abernethy, were absolutely fascinating and compelling.

We would have to wait two years before His Honour Judge Abernethy announced that a formal inquest into the death of Brian Peters would be held in an independent, open courtroom.

I had decided to stay away for the first week of the inquest in February 2007 to give Maureen full benefit of speaking to the press, so I was at home when the *Australian* published an extraordinary article, 'Conspiracy of Silence', by Dan Box.

> Australia's former chief intelligence official confirmed that members of the Whitlam government deliberately withheld news of the deaths of the Balibo Five from their families for fear of revealing the information came from intercepted Indonesian military communications.
>
> Gordon Jockel, director of the Joint Intelligence Organisation at the time of the 1975 Indonesian invasion of East Timor, yesterday said he broke the news of the deaths to the then defence minister, Bill Morrison, and the two men agreed not to release it.
>
> The *Australian* revealed yesterday that the then foreign minister, Don Willesee, attempted to break this embargo and privately pass on word of the deaths, most likely through an unidentified military officer who spoke to two of the men's employers at the Nine Network.

This account of a conspiracy of silence at the highest levels of government is in contrast to that given on oath by Gough Whitlam at the coronial inquest, due to report next week, in which the former prime minister stated that he had not been told about the deaths for five days. Mr Jockel said: 'I learned about the deaths about 11.30 in the morning [of 17 October, one day after the invasion]. I went over to Parliament House and told Morrison straight away. I didn't have to argue with him, we agreed we simply couldn't release it,' he said.

'That was the general view at the time, that officially it would not be in our security interests. Simple as that.'

Peter Cronau told me that the court was packed every day, and that I should come up to Sydney immediately: 'Indonesia is on trial in that courtroom, Shirley, for murder.' I had wondered how most of the reporters would view the proceedings – after all, some were not even born in 1975.

On the same day I heard from Peter, I was asked by journalists if I was staging a boycott by staying in Melbourne, so for the first time since 1975 I reversed my practice of waiting to be asked to give an interview. As soon as I booked my air ticket I called AAP Reuters. This worked so well that I wondered if I should have taken the initiative on other occasions, but I still believe that, though I had earned my living in the past by promoting others, it is unwise to promote oneself.

On 15 September 2006 Rodney Lewis informed me that:

the Coroner, in rejecting our arguments on broadening the scope of the inquest, had announced a call to the communications intelligence operators today to come forward if they have evidence. This is, at least in my experience and recollection, an unprecedented excursion by a State Court into the realms of the Federal government's operations and will certainly not go unnoticed in the intelligence circles from which we hope to draw more information.

However, all my fears were to be realised, because inferential evidence from Australian intelligence intercepts, showing that prior knowledge of the imminent invasion of East Timor by Indonesian armed forces and of the Five's location near the border, was to be heard 'in camera'. The Javanese military incursion on 16 October 1975 was designed to be a deniable action and the Department of Foreign Affairs had obliged by deeming the information 'black'. As far as the public was concerned the information would still be 'black'.

After thirty-two years the excuse of 'security reasons' was designed to restrict the scope of the inquest. But was this excuse valid, or merely a ruse to prevent embarrassment, or cause offence to the Indonesians? The Department of Foreign Affairs and Trade and Australian government discrimination against the Balibo Five was apparently still gutless and unforgivable.

Hamish McDonald wrote a piece in the *Sydney Morning Herald* ridiculing the arrangement. The coroner heard evidence to this effect in closed sessions and subsequently changed the rules, but the public had to leave the courtroom and wait outside while vital evidence was given. It was very disappointing. Nevertheless – though the inquest was originally restricted to the fate of Brian Peters – Tony Stewart, Malcolm Rennie, Gary Cunningham and Greg Shackleton came strolling in through the back door.

Another deep disappointment occurred when the barrister assisting the coroner pleaded for Whitlam to be excused. However, Coronor Dorelle Pinch insisted, and then we saw the difficulty — apparently an inquest does not have the power to cross-examine.

General Sutiyso, former member of the force that attacked Balibó, was on an official visit to Sydney in his role as Governor of Jakarta. Although Coroner Pinch wished to subpoena him to appear as a witness, solicitors from the Department of Foreign Affairs and Trade drew her attention to the Foreign States Immunities Act 1988, implying that Sutiyoso might enjoy diplomatic immunity — as though interviewing a local mayor would really impair the conduct of Australia's international relations! Pinch instead 'invited' him to appear, but he fled to Sydney airport and got on the first plane to Jakarta. Sutiyoso's background is informative: in the late 1980s and early 1990s, he was trained in Australia, the United States and Britain, and from 1992 to 1993 he was deputy commander of the Javanese army special forces group, Kopassus. In 1996 he commanded the attack against Indonesian pro-democracy activists in Indonesia during which time he issued shoot-on-sight orders.

Sutiyoso declined the court's invitation, and complained that his dignity had been outraged and he was far too busy to attend the inquest. The very next day he took the first available flight to Jakarta.

The premier of New South Wales, Morris Iemma, failed to apologise for the coroner's invitation to General Sutiyoso. He was ordered to do so by the minister for foreign affairs, Alexander Downer, who flew into a tizzy and told General Sutiyoso to take no notice of the inquest. This was an unprecedented attack on the Australian judiciary, which was bad enough, but there was far worse to come.

A second apology was made by the Australian ambassador to Indonesia, Bill Farmer. John Milkins, son of Gary Cunningham, publicly complained in the *Canberra Times* on 14 July that 'spineless federal state government employees were apologising to someone who was, in fact, close to the Balibó murders'.

A third apology came from the chief of the defence forces, Air Marshal Angus Houston, who flew specially to Jakarta to placate Sutiyoso.

Believe it or not these abject apologists were soon to be joined by the governor of New South Wales, one Marie Bashir, who not only flew to Jakarta to voice her regret over 'the incident' but also added that she was 'outraged'. General Sutiyoso graciously accepted all apologies from these morally outraged Australian office-holders.

Jill Jolliffe subsequently published an account of General Sutiyoso's activities in East Timor (Joyo Indonesian News Service, 14 July 2007), in which ten Timorese gave detailed personal testimonies alleging that General Sutiyoso was a sadistic torturer.

The truth is that anyone making excuses for Indonesian crimes, in Timor Leste, any of the Indonesian provinces and, especially, against Indonesian citizens, are in fact aiding and abetting Indonesia's moral and political decline.

The inquest held in the Glebe Coroner's Court was thorough and it was found that the Balibo Five were unarmed and attempting to give themselves up when they were slain.

The killing of the Balibo Five was now officially a war crime. War crimes can be prosecuted wherever they occur and regardless of the nationality of the victims or perpetrators. There is no statute of limitations. This means that the alleged killers of the Balibo Five could be prosecuted in Australia following extradition from Indonesia. The attorney-general could make an extradition request under Australia's 1995 extradition treaty with Indonesia. Indonesia may refuse to extradite, but must then submit the case to its prosecutors. Since the killings were associated with, and occurred in the context of, an international armed conflict, the case was referred to federal authorities for possible war crime prosecutions in 2007.

A week before the 2007 election, Mr Kevin Rudd responded to the Balibo inquest by saying, 'This is a very disturbing conclusion by the coroner concerning the fate of the Balibo Five back in 1975. I believe this has to be taken through to its logical conclusion. I also believe those responsible should be held to account.' He also said, 'My attitude to this is dead set hardline. I've read a bit about what happened in Balibó, I've been to Balibó, walked up there, I've seen the fort, I've seen where these blokes lost their lives. You can't just sweep this to one side.'

On 27 May 2008 the assistant secretary of the criminal law branch of the Attorney-General's Department, Karl Alderson, confirmed to the Senate Standing Committee on Legal and Constitutional Affairs that the Attorney-General's Department had liaised with the Australian Federal Police to ensure that they had all the documents necessary to investigate the war crimes committed in Balibó in 1975.

Some say that repatriation of the men's remains and the Australian Federal Police investigation into the deaths at Balibó will damage Australia's relationship with Indonesia. This is piffle. Australia gives half a billion dollars of aid to Indonesia every year and fifteen billion dollars a year changes hands in bilateral investment and trade. In June 2008 Prime Minister Rudd announced a strengthened two and a half billion dollar five-year development partnership with Indonesia – the Australia–Indonesia Partnership.

On 13 June 2008 the Australian media buzzed with the astonishing news that Prime Minister Rudd on a visit to Jakarta had gone to the Indonesian Military Heroes cemetery and placed flowers on some of the graves. In an interview on ABC Radio at the time I said, 'I think he could pay respect to his own people. If he can pay his respects to Indonesian soldiers with a fairly murky past, I think he could visit the grave of the Balibo Five. I am just amazed that no-one suggested it and I am trying to get a message through to him to ask very respectfully, would he consider doing that.'

Mr Rudd failed to pay his respects to the Balibo Five while in Jakarta.

A lot of questions need answering. The remains of the Balibo Five were moved in 1979 and re-interred down by the railway line to make way for a big residential complex. I want to know if this was done with Australian government approval. If so, who gave permission? Was the new site consecrated? The original plot was purchased. Did any money change hands over the acquisition of the second plot? If so who paid them? The new site is a crime scene. I have asked Mr Rudd and Foreign Minister Stephen Smith to treat it as a crime scene. I want to know what is in that coffin.

I want the Australian government to pay respect to the next-of-kin by working with us to achieve repatriation. Everyone can have what each of us wants for our relative. The majority are in agreement: we want them back in Melbourne. The British next-of-kin want their relatives repatriated to Melbourne too.

On 23 November 2009, the *Canberra Times* reported that the Defence Department, after a request made by Australian Defence Force Academy senior lecturer Clinton Fernandes more than two years before, had finally released to the National Archives hundreds of pages of material, including Office of Current Intelligence situation reports formerly classified Top Secret Australian Eyes Only. However, almost all of the contents have been blacked out on the publicly released copies.

In justifying the decision to withhold almost all of the content, the National Archives cited advice from Defence that the information 'continues to be sensitive'.

The Defence Department also blocked the release of 34-year-old intelligence papers that would shed new light on the deaths of the Balibo Five journalists and potentially embarrass former Prime Minister Gough Whitlam. Defence Minister John Faulkner's department has withheld from public release the contents of Defence intelligence reports on the events surrounding Indonesia's 1975 invasion of the former Portuguese colony of East Timor.

In the same *Canberra Times* article, I was quoted as saying: 'Senator Faulkner ought to show his commitment to openness and accountability, rather than allow his officials to keep the cone of silence over the truth about Balibó.'

Also quoted was Professor Alan Dupont, of the University of Sydney's Centre for International Security Studies, who said, 'the intelligence reports should not be released, at least not for another 20 or 30 years, if ever.'

Eight years earlier, in 2001, in his *Quarterly Essay* 'Appeasing Jakarta', John Birmingham had said:

> Appeasement of Jakarta did not work because the problem of East Timor was permanent and insoluble. It was assumed before the invasion in 1975 that the East Timorese would accept incorporation. When they resisted, involving Jakarta in a long and brutal counter-insurgency campaign, genuine power realists should have foreseen the ultimately futile and self-destructive endgame that would play itself out there. And some did. But other more significant Australian policy makers, many of whom prided themselves on the 'hard-headed realism' of their analysis and

approach, deluded themselves. They chose to ignore dissonant information and analysis from within their own bureaucracy, preferring instead the consolations of wishful thinking. Foremost among their numbers are Gough Whitlam and Richard Woolcott.[1]

I appeal to Prime Minister Rudd to use his position to heal the weeping sore that will forever blight Australian relations with Indonesia. As long as the truth about Balibó is concealed, we will never trust each other. By ignoring human rights, the heads of our two great countries ensure that the wounds won't heal. Reconciliation never works without justice, and justice is not about vengeance, it's about accountability. I can drop dead tomorrow and Balibó will not go away. Please, Mr Rudd, prove to us that our relationship with Indonesia is healthy by taking action and bringing the remains of my husband home.

On 28 January 2010, I met with the Australian police who were investigating bringing the perpetrators of 'the deaths' to Australia for trial. All Victorian family members present remarked as they sat down at the large boardroom table that this was the first time in thirty-five years that any Australian organisation including all government bodies had chosen to consult us.

I was very disappointed to learn that Sergeant Stephen Cato who had been my direct contact because he was shouldering the brunt of the investigation was to be taken off the case.

My notes about that historic meeting may be instructive: After admitting that the investigators knew little about the historical background to the situation [at the time of the alleged

---

[1] John Birmingham, *Appeasing Jakarta*, op. cit.

murders] the families were asked not to talk to the media as it may compromise their investigation.

John Milkins politely suggested this instruction might compromise our freedom of speech. To my questions I received these replies:

1. The Australian Federal Police are dealing with section 7 of the Geneva Convention which allows them to investigate an unlawful killing. They are not engaged in an investigation of an offence of murder.
2. They won't reveal who they are investigating and refused to say if they have spoken with Richard Woolcott, former Australian Ambassador to Indonesia.
3. The process will take another five to six months at least.
4. They won't be publishing any form of report.
5. They will hand their findings to the Director of Public Prosecutions (DPP).
6. They have no inquisitorial powers and cannot cross examine.
7. They don't have access to classified or declassified material.
8. The DPP does not have to answer to government and will decide whether to demand extradition.

After the meeting, I wrote to Sergeant Stephen Cato for confirmation of these meeting notes – he replied that he had forwarded my letter, but at the time of writing I have not received a response.

At one point during the meeting someone observed that I was looking pensive. I could not say what was on my mind because it had nothing to do with the present proceedings.

* * *

If I had any success at all over the years of campaigning for the truth, it was because I did not make ambitious plans, for if your plans don't succeed you feel you have failed. I remember how guilty I felt when I was unable to achieve something I thought was important for East Timor, and everything for East Timor was not only important but also desperately urgent. It takes discipline not to bang on when you realise how little you have done in a day – I had to learn to forgive myself and try again tomorrow.

I'm resourceful (I still make my own clothes) and I'm good at turning a minus into a plus – when my car was stolen I was initially shocked and upset, but before my friends arrived to commiserate, I had realised that the thief might have done me a favour – as a result I walk or use public transport and I am amazed at how much more money I have in my purse.

I am still writing – my next book is set in Portuguese Timor in World War II. I got to know some of the 2/2nd and 2/4th Independent Company commandos very well, and the story of their campaign makes a cracking good tale.

I have one or two reasonable ambitions regarding Timor, and I get an occasional little thrill over something that works out. For example, when Xanana and Kirsty's first little boy was born I gave him two of Mem Fox's books signed by the author. Last year Mem Fox was invited to visit the first lady of Timor Leste and her family, and some of her prize-winning books are now translated into *Tetuñ*.

I am asked why I don't publish articles about Timor today. I decided ten years ago that it would be egotistical to tell Timorese what I think they should be doing – they know what is needed and I don't want to be their nanny. Their path to good governance is almost as difficult as ours; we don't have a perfect democracy and we have been at it for one-hell-of-a-lot longer than they have.

My son read law and practises in Perth. He is a barrister and solicitor. Greg would be as proud of him as I am. Evan has two gorgeous daughters and a beautiful, wonderful wife. In fact he has a wonderful life.

As related in this volume, much of my life has seemed to me to be unreal. I think this acts as a protection from unbelievable events. I am often asked how I stay sane after all that has happened. As Constantin Stanislavski says in *An Actor Prepares* (1936):

> In a circle of light [on the stage], in the midst of darkness, you have the sensation of being entirely alone ... it is what we call solitude in public ... During a performance, before an audience of thousands, you can always enclose yourself in this circle, like a snail in its shell ... You can carry it with you wherever you go.

On 25 May 2009 I was interviewed for the ABC *7.30 Report*. In relation to justice for the Balibo Five, Matt Peacock asked wasn't it time to move on?

'On to where?' I replied, tartly. The question deserved a far better answer; Matt was after all only doing his job in being the devil's advocate. I have resorted to that device many times. I mumbled something about justice and the fact that Australia has an extradition treaty with Indonesia. There was so much more to say, but from experience, knowing that most of the interview would end up on the cutting room floor in favour of 'grabs' I felt defeated. Besides, the question implied that I have no life beyond Balibó and gives my detractors reason to dismiss me as a widow seeking vengeance when after all my years of dedication to the truth I have been well and truly vindicated.

Peacock then asked what did I think the government should have done? I could have spoken at length, of course, but I settled for stating the simple truth. If each Australian government had done nothing at all it would have been better.

I was then asked if anyone cared about something that had happened so long ago. Again, I could have spoken volumes, but I settled for the short, definitive reply: 'Murder is murder no matter how much time elapses.'

On the way home I slumped dejectedly in the back of a taxi, pondering the impossibility of doing justice to the Balibo Five in any interview. The taxi driver broke the silence.

'Excuse me, please,' he said, 'have you seen this film about *Balibo?*'

'Do you know about Balibó?'

His reply thrilled me: 'Of course,' he said. My back straightened immediately and my optimistic nature grew roses that covered the thorns. His name was Yassin Ibrahim. He had come to Australia from Somalia in 1985 at the age of thirteen.

'So, did you learn about Balibó at school in Australia?'

'No!' he declared emphatically. 'We know it in my country.' When I showed surprise he turned and stared at me. 'Everyone knows,' he said. 'You'd have to be stupid not to.'

SELECT BIBLIOGRAPHY

I do not claim this list to be exhaustive; it is a small but vital collection of required reading for serious students regarding the undeclared war against East Timor. Some witnesses are not named in *The Circle of Silence* because of official restrictions and in a number of cases Timorese and Indonesians are not named for their own safety.

Ball, Desmond and McDonald, Hamish, *Death in Balibo, Lies in Canberra*, Allen & Unwin, Sydney, 2000.

Birmingham, John, 'Appeasing Jakarta', *Quarterly Essay*, Issue 2, 2001.

Budiardjo, Carmel and Liem, Soei Liong, *The War Against East Timor*, Zed Books, London 1984. (Including secret Indonesian counter-insurgency documents)

Burchill, Scott, 'The Jakarta Lobby – Mea Culpa', *Age*, 4 March 1999, http://www.scottburchill.net/Jakarta.html

Burchill, Scott, *Tainted Jakarta Lobby Left Stranded by History*, 2 May 2002, http://www.etan.org/et2002b/may/19-25/20taint.htm

'Cafe Timor Packages Refers to Tutut's Cartel's Brand Name', *Washington Post*, 29 July 1998.

Carey, Peter and Bentley, G. Carter (eds), *East Timor at the Crossroads: The Forging of a Nation*, Casell, London, 1995. (A record of papers given at the first conference to be held at St Anthony's College, Oxford, 8 December 1990 and the American University in Washington DC on 25–26 April 1991. Of particular interest is the paper on the illegality of Australian government claims to the oil in the Timor Gap, page 73, by Roger S. Clark, Distinguished Professor of Law, Rutgers University, NJ, USA.)

Conway, Judith (ed.), *Step by Step: Women of East Timor, Stories of Resistance and Survival*, Charles Darwin University Press, Darwin, 2010.

Cronau, Peter, *The Last Reporter: The True Story of Roger East and the Invasion of East Timor*, ABC Books–HarperCollins, Sydney, forthcoming 2010.

Elson, Robert, *Suharto: A Political Biography*, Cambridge University Press, Oakleigh, Victoria, 2001.

Fernandes, Clinton, *Reluctant Saviour: Australia, Indonesia and the Independence of East Timor*, Scribe, Melbourne, 2004.

Forman, Shepard, 'Testimony to Subcommittee on International Organisations of the Committee on International Relations of the House of Representatives', 28 June 1977.

Gunn, Geoffrey C., *Complicity in Genocide Report to the East Timor 'Truth Commission' on International Actors*, Geoffrey C. Gunn, 2006. (Otherwise known as 'Chega')

Jolliffe, Jill, *Balibo*, Scribe, Melbourne, 2009. (Originally published as *Cover-up: The Inside Story of the Balibo Five,* 2001)

King, Amanda, *Shadow Over East Timor*, documentary, SBS Television, 1987. (One of the first ground-breaking documentaries on East Timor; available from Amanda King, email: cavadini@tpg.com.au)

Kohen, Arnold and Taylor, John, *An Act of Genocide: Indonesia's Invasion of East Timor,* Tapol, London, 1979.

Martinkus, John, *A Dirty Little War*, Random House, Sydney, 2001.

Nairn, Alan, 'The Talk of the Town: Notes and Comment', *The New Yorker*, 9 December 1991, p. 41. (About the 12 November 1991 massacre by Indonesian troops in Dili)

Nairn, Alan, 'Testimony to the US State Committee on Foreign Relations', 17 February 1992, http://bsd.mojones.com/east timor/evidence/nairn.html. (Describing 'having witnessed deliberate mass murder at Santa Cruz')

Nordland, Rod, 'Hunger: Under Indonesia, Timor Remains a Land of Misery', *Philadelphia Inquirer*, 28 May 1982.

Pilger, John, *Death of a Nation: The Timor Conspiracy*, documentary, 1994, see http://www.johnpilger.net.au.

Pilger, John, *Distant Voices*, Vintage, London, 1992. (See pp. 233–94 for his visit to Timor)

Robinson, Geoffrey, *'If You Leave Us Here We Will Die': How Genocide was Stopped in East Timor*, Princeton University Press, Princeton, 2009.

Scrine, Gil, *Buried Alive,* documentary, Gil Scrine Films, 1989. (Available from www.gilscrinefilms.com.au)

'Suharto and Sons: Crony Capitalism, Suharto Style', *Washington Post*, 25 January 1998.

Tapol, *West Papua: The Obliteration of a People*, Tapol, London, 1983.

Turner, Michele, *Telling East Timor: Personal Testimonies, 1942–1992*, New South Wales University Press, Sydney, 1992.